KB210588

Bible, See the Big Picture!

By Reverend Paul In-Sik Kim

Bible, See the Big Picture!

Paperback: ISBN 979-11-92254-15-9
First paperback edition February 2024.

Translated by Ezra Choe
Designed by Sarah Park
Published by HayoungIn
a division of TwelveMountains Inc.
3, Daesin-ro, Buk-gu, Pohang-si, Gyeongsangbuk-do, Republic of Korea
https://blog.naver.com/navhayoungin
https://www.instagram.com/hayoungin7

Bible,

See the Big Picture!

Paul In-Sik Kim

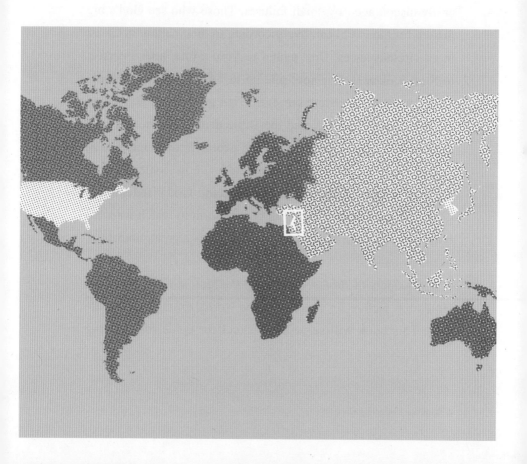

Dr. Sang Meyng Lee, president of the Presbyterian Theological
Seminary in America (PTSA)

The one who carries life's big picture in his or her heart is not
easily discouraged by small failures. Those who see God's big
picture for the world can live according to their calling in Christ
in all circumstances. Dots gather to form a line, lines intersect
to form a plane, and planes pile up to form a beautiful, three-
dimensional shape before our eyes. That goes for Bible reading
as well. Only when we read the Bible deeply and holistically,
for it has recorded many themes and genres throughout its long
history, we can comprehensively view its entire context. When
we read the entire Bible and begin seeing God's redemptive
history in three-dimensional big picture form to which we were
blind before, we will exclaim, "Eureka!" It is a great moment of
deep resonance.

The readers of *Bible, See the Big Picture!* will be able to see
God's big picture for redeeming the world, exactly as the title
says. This book will serve as an excellent guide for studying

the Bible for those readers who want to understand how the nation of Israel's restoration and salvation are related to God's redemptive work for mankind. It contains seven chapters in a Q & A format that is neither flashy nor complicated in delivering the important content for the readers. Through the simple and clear organization and content of the Bible's big picture, the readers will be able to see God's will, which is the ultimate hope of the world, and the development process of His Kingdom. God's redemptive history that flows through the entire Bible will at first be dimly revealed as if looking into a bronze mirror but will gradually grow clearer in the readers' eyes as if seeing face to face. I pray that all readers of this book, which gathers the small pictures scattered in the Bible one by one to assemble the big picture, will experience God's magna gratia (great grace).

Reverend Hee-Min Park, president of New Life Mission Foundation
and chairman of Kingdom Inter-Missions Network (KIMNET)

I sincerely congratulate the publication of Reverend Paul In-Sik Kim's third book entitled *Bible, See the Big Picture!* Reverend Paul In-Sik Kim graduated from Korea University in South Korea, earned a M.Div. at the Presbyterian University and Theological Seminary, and then immigrated to the United States to earn another master's degree and a Ph.D. in Missiology at Fuller Theological Seminary. Even after his retirement, he showed his passion for learning by earning an additional Ph.D. at the Presbyterian University and Theological Seminary in America, and he remains a scholarly minister engaging in lifelong study and research. After coming to the United States, Reverend Paul In-Sik Kim planted West Hills Presbyterian Church and served as an exemplary senior pastor to his retirement several years ago, and, during his pastoral ministry, he devoted himself to the growth and development of the Korean Presbyterian Church Abroad (KPCA) denomination by serving in many capacities, including moderator of KPCA and board chairman of the Presbyterian University and Theological Seminary in America. Reverend Paul In-Sik Kim has carried a special interest in God's redemptive history through the nation of Israel for a long time and has researched, lectured, and published books on this subject.

As we believers know well, the Bible was written by dozens of authors over thousands of years. Nevertheless, the Bible was written by the inspiration of the Holy Spirit, and thus a unity runs through the whole. The Old and New Testaments' main subject is Jesus Christ. Jesus Christ's First Advent, birth, suffering and death on the cross, resurrection, ascension, and Second Advent form the Bible's central vein. In this respect, within the context of God's election of the people of Israel as His, God sending Christ as a descendant of Abraham to redeem the world, God's vision and strategy for mankind's salvation through the people of Israel, and God's restoration of the nation of Israel, *Bible, See the Big Picture!* illuminates and interprets the Bible to show the big picture, giving believers new and correct insights and perspectives for reading, understanding, and interpreting the Bible. I wholeheartedly recommend this book, which will surely help many people become more interested in studying the Bible to understand and live out God's profound Word.

Reverend Choon-Min Kang, senior pastor of New Life Vision Church in Los Angeles

The author is a great pastor and a scholar who seeks deep truths. He is a leader of a holy movement. He is highly respected in the United States. The book he authored here reveals the big picture of the entire Bible. It is not easy to draw out the big picture. This is because to reveal the big picture, one needs to carefully comprehend the whole Bible. To fully comprehend the Bible, the author has been researching for a long time. And he has been teaching his research discoveries. He has acquired deep understanding. Only the one who has acquired deep understanding can help others understand as well. Only the one who has seen first can help others see. In this way, the author is a pioneer. The author illuminates the entire Bible from the perspective of Jesus Christ, Israel, and Jerusalem. The Garden of Eden, which was lost due to the first Adam's sin, is restored through the obedience of the Last Adam, Who is Jesus. The Bible's story is a drama of restoration and a drama of redemption. The One who leads this drama is Jesus Christ. Jesus fulfills the history of redemption with God the Father and God the Holy Spirit. Jesus, the Lord of creation, fulfills the work of re-creation through redemption. Jesus is the key to opening the Bible. The author reveals the drama of redemption contained in the Old and the New Testaments through Jesus. He also explains God's providence toward Israel described in Romans 9-11 through the big picture.

As Arthur Pink said, the Bible is not only a book to be read reverently but also a mine of spiritual wealth to be dug up. Only those who diligently dig up the treasure hidden in the Bible can obtain even more. The author has devoted himself to digging up the hidden treasures in the Bible for a long time. This book is the fruit of the author's dedication. Thus, this book is a treasure. The eschatology shown in this book is filled with hope. For Christians, it is a joyful eschatology. It is the eschatology of reigning with Christ. I highly recommend this book to anyone who desires to see God's big picture through the Bible. And I highly recommend this book to anyone who desires to understand the drama of redemption broadly and deeply.

Dr. Ky-Chun So, professor of New Testament at Presbyterian University and Theological Seminary

This book, the third one that Dr. Paul In-Sik Kim has devoted his heart and soul to write, is interesting because it systematically organizes the contents that many Christians have been curious about in a question-and-answer format like a catechism with concise answers, supporting Bible verses, and various pictures and diagrams. Through this book, Dr. Kim covers creationism to eschatology, Israel and the church, Jerusalem to the New Jerusalem, God's vision and His Kingdom, the contrasts between replacement theology and restoration theology, and the nation of Israel and God's people, and, in so doing, he draws out God's big picture for His people and continuously reveals God's redemptive history. If God's providential will was revealed in the Old Testament, then the New Testament reveals the fulfillment of God's Kingdom through Jesus Christ, the church in the age of the Holy Spirit testifies about the good news of salvation to people all over the world, and, in the end, through Jesus' Second Advent and the Final Judgment, God's will to save mankind will be completed. I strongly recommend this very clearly structured book to not only ministers and seminarians but also all who are interested in world history centered on the ancient Mediterranean region and are praying for Israel's restoration by God in the midst of the fierce struggles with the powerful states surrounding them, while longing for their salvation in Christ.

Reverend Jin Suk Park, senior pastor of The Joyful Church in Pohang,

South Korea, and professor at Youngnam Theological

University and Seminary (YTUS) and Presbyterian Theological

Seminary in America (PTSA)

Bible, See the Big Picture! is a recently published book that looks at the entire Bible from a high-level eagle's point of view in terms of the flow and development process of the protagonist Jesus' New Creation History. This book will help readers Biblically understand eschatological issues of interest that they had not dared to investigate in detail through the Bible, worldwide calamities such as the well-known COVID-19 pandemic, and changes in international dynamics centered on Israel. Although the gospel of Jesus Christ was first preached to the Gentiles through Israel, even now, 2,000 years later, anti-Semitism and replacement theology, which states that Israel has already been replaced by the church, are still rampant in theological thoughts and sentiments in Christendom. While the people of Israel, who were first entrusted with God's Word and called to be a priestly nation, received harsh trials under God's mysterious providence, the full number of Gentiles were being saved, and, as prophesied in Romans 11:25, when that number fills up, more and more Jews will be saved.

Looking back over the past decade, we see this occurring at an accelerated pace. Observing what is currently occurring in Israel through the Bible's prophetic big picture will be very helpful in understanding the timetable of God's redemptive history. It will also focus our attention on God's priorities. To fulfill the mission of this age well, understanding Israel in Christology will increasingly become an important issue for the global church as well as the Korean church. I believe that this book will serve as a tremendously useful guide for many saints and leaders of the church in these times.

Dr. Peter Im, director of the Ph.D. program in Intercultural Studies at the Presbyterian Theological Seminary in America

The psalmist sings, "Pray for the peace of Jerusalem: May they prosper who love you" (Ps. 122:6). Jerusalem was built by God Himself (Ps. 147:2). It is the place to meet the LORD. It is the city of peace and the holy city. It is the center of Israel and the center of history and faith. Based on Isaiah 2, Prof. Walter Kaiser describes Jerusalem as the center of peace. Jerusalem is the center of the Messiah's teaching and peace for all nations. Jerusalem is the city where all nations gather, where all nations are taught, where all nations experience peace, and where all nations are invited.

Professor Paul In-Sik Kim loves the Bible and Israel. He

invites us to Jerusalem. He sees God's big picture in the Bible. He focuses on three keywords: Jesus Christ Who is the one person chosen by God, Israel which is the one nation chosen by God, and Jerusalem (Zion) which is the one city chosen by God. He pays close attention to the fact that the most important events of the Bible are fulfilled and completed centering on Jerusalem. Indeed, God has placed Jerusalem at the center of the earth geographically. He made it the spiritual center of the world. Today's world media focus on Jerusalem. Jerusalem was where the Son of God had to die for the salvation and restoration of mankind. It is where Jesus Christ will return. Jerusalem is being restored. Israel has been re-established. The capital of God's Kingdom is being restored. Paul In-Sik Kim has devoted his life to researching, teaching, and shepherding with a focus on Jerusalem as revealed in the Bible and has served as a missionary in the movement to restore Israel. This book, *Bible, See the Big Picture!*, is an invitation, calling us once again to Jerusalem. Those who love Jerusalem will prosper!

Reveverd. Jung Myung Song, co-chairman of the Holy City Movement
in America and former president of World Mission University

Professor Paul In-Sik Kim has published his third book *Bible, See the Big Picture!* It's a joyful and celebratory occasion. He is a pastor who diligently served to proclaim God's work of salvation in church ministry, a professor who nurtured theology students from the seminary pulpit, and an experienced spiritual intellectual who has been active in a variety of ways for the movement for Jerusalem's restoration and the movement for the reunification of North and South Korea, through the Word, which is the cornerstone of the big picture drawn by God.

He helps the reader understand the Bible easily by focusing on three keywords, which are Jesus Christ, Israel, and Jerusalem, and by simply asking readers questions then presenting clear answers. Through this book, readers will be able wait with a proper understanding of Israel and Jerusalem, which is the center of the world media's attention, in terms of their Biblical background, and Jesus' Second Advent. The questions he asks can be understood as steppingstones to cross step-by-step to comprehend God's vision, plan, and strategy through the big picture God drew in the Bible. Through this book, readers will surely gain the strength and courage to comprehend the deep inner meaning of the big picture God drew in the Bible and to face the various issues encountered in life. I am convinced that this book will open eyes to bring the Scriptures closer, bring understanding of God's redemption plan and His deep strategy that will unfold in the future, and be a great challenge and grace for all of us who are living through these difficult times, so I strongly urge everyone to read this book.

Dr. Damien Sohn, professor at Midwest University

The prophet Isaiah, who saw a vision of the New Jerusalem, proclaimed, "In the last days the mountain of the LORD's temple will be established as chief among the mountains; it will be raised above the hills, and all nations will stream to it. Many peoples will come and say, 'Come, let us go up to the mountain of the LORD, to the house of the God of Jacob. He will teach us his ways, so that we may walk in his paths.' The law will go out from Zion, the word of the LORD from Jerusalem" (Isa. 2:2-3). Recognized by others as a student of Professor Walter Kaiser, Professor Paul In-Sik Kim has already published several books through the non-profit Kingdom World Mission that he founded, has hosted several seminars domestically and abroad, and is an established expert on Israel. Professor Kim's core motivation for speaking about Israel is the vision of the New Jerusalem described in Isaiah 2:2-3. His vision of the New Jerusalem is through three keywords. In other words, through Jesus Christ Who is the one man God has chosen, Israel which is the one nation God has chosen, and Jerusalem which is the one city God has chosen, we can arrive at the New Jerusalem.

Professor Kim's recent book *Bible, See the Big Picture!* cordially invites readers to the very vision of the New Jerusalem. This book covers seven important topics. They are God's vision, God's strategy, God's city, the apple of God's eye (God's pupil), God's time, and God's Kingdom. Professor Kim asks simple and clear questions about the seven important topics to the reader and presents clear answers to each question for the reader. As the questions are asked, and the answers are received, the vision of the New Jerusalem will finally appear clearly before the reader.

I recommend this book to faithful laypeople who desire to grasp the pulse of the Bible before re-reading the whole Bible. This book will provide the big picture for both novice ministers taking their first steps into church ministry and veteran preachers looking for an evangelical message. In particular, this book is essential without question for rookie missionaries who are waiting with eager hearts to be dispatched into spiritual battlefields to which they have been assigned as well as for senior missionaries who are planning for their next term as they wait to be re-dispatched and desire to grasp the pulse of the mission. This is because this book clearly shows the big picture of the Bible and missions as well as clearly showing the vision of the New Jerusalem.

Reverend Hyung Suk Rim, former senior pastor of Pyungchon Church
and former moderator of The General Assembly of the
Presbyterian Church of Korea

As a close, longtime friend and colleague of Reverend Paul In-Sik Kim, I know very well that his whole life and ministry is truly God's wonderful and amazing guidance.

In 1977, as a frustrated political science student, he joined the Presbyterian Theological Seminary, and God poured upon him the abundant grace of the Holy Spirit and gave him a fervent passion for saving souls. During my 20 years of ministry to immigrants in L.A., I witnessed Reverend Kim starting West Hills Presbyterian Church and ministering with all his strength in Christ. His ministry was unique from the beginning. At West Hills Presbyterian Church's inaugural service, I served in the order of prayer and witnessed the church commence with a commitment to support missions in India. Since then, West Hills Presbyterian Church grew rapidly as a fervently praying church and as a church committed to world missions, and Reverend Kim himself was a pastor who prayed for 3 hours daily. When we young fellow pastors used to meet often, Reverend Kim would doze off occasionally during conversations. This was because he was so devoted to prayer and ministry that he often lacked sleep.

I believe Reverend Kim is a pastor like Apostle Paul. Saul, who was a thorough scholar of the law, dramatically changed after meeting the Lord, receiving more grace than anyone else and devoting himself to missionary work more passionately than anyone else. Furthermore, Apostle Paul, who mastered the Scriptures, led the church with remarkable theological knowledge of God's dispensation.

Now, as a leader of the Korean churches in the United States who served as the moderator of the Korean Presbyterian Church Abroad (KPCA), Reverend Kim is dedicating the end of his ministry to Israel's restoration and preparation for the Lord's return. Although he already earned a doctorate in Missiology, he completed another Ph.D. to organize theological understandings with clarity, and, in so doing, he authored three books on this subject, and, when I witness him passionately ministering to awaken pastors and laypeople, all the saints, I once again admire and applaud his remarkable passion.

Most Christians believe that the Jews will return to the Lord and be saved before the Lord returns, as Apostle Paul taught in Romans 9-11. This book provides a detailed explanation of how this will unfold. Organized in a question-and-answer format, this book is easy to understand, and all discussions about Israel's restoration are laid out in a concise, readily accessible manner. I recommend this book as a very informative, beneficial read for pastors and laity who want to systematically understand eschatology.

The Bible is a book written over a long period of time of about 1,600 years by more than 40 authors, who lived in different times and different places, with diverse backgrounds and social statuses. For this reason, the various situations and events were recorded from the diverse perspectives of the writers. Thus, readers of the Bible today often have difficulty comprehending the big picture of the Bible.

Since the Bible is God's Word recorded by people who were inspired by the Holy Spirit (2 Pet. 1:21), although there appears to be differences, all the words are in harmony. Everything in the Bible is ultimately about one subject: Jesus Christ. Pastor Paul In-Sik Kim's recently written book *Bible, See the Big Picture!* shows readers the big picture of the Bible, which is salvation through Jesus Christ through God's plan for Israel which forms the main stem of the Bible. In God's great plan of salvation, the importance of Israel, which is the setting of Jesus' coming to this world and completing His work of salvation, cannot be overemphasized. I hope that, through this book, many readers will discover Jesus Christ, Who is the subject of all the contents of the Bible, and receive help in their spiritual growth and broader understanding of God's Word.

Reverend Jaehoon Lee, senior pastor of Onnuri Community Church

Some may think that the slightly different lenses through which people view the Bible are God's permission for a certain degree of freedom in that regard, but, if we read the Bible without God's covenant which acts as the wheel of Biblical history, we would be missing the essence and committing the fatal mistake of losing sight of Jesus Christ and the vision of God's Kingdom. If we keep following the big picture of the Bible which is structured as the history of God's covenants, we can see that the role of the nation of Israel is clearly revealed and understand God's purpose and vision in choosing Israel. The question "How can we see Israel?" risks leading to a political answer, but the question "What is Israel's position in Biblical history?" gives us the benefit of clearly seeing Jesus Christ and God's Kingdom through God's covenants given to Israel. Reverend Paul In-Sik Kim, who has been serving in missions focused ministry, has been devoted to overseas missions for a longtime including to Israel. He not only did missions work but also established a Biblical mission theology and led many pastors and saints to the mission of God's Kingdom. This book explains very well how the Bible is indeed the book of God's mission. His precious outcry that replacement theology should be changed to restoration theology is sufficient to clear away many of the misunderstandings and warped prejudices surrounding Israel and guide people to look at Israel through the theology of God's Kingdom and serve in missions. I pray that this book will become a channel that leads many to God's precious Kingdom and highly recommend it.

Reverend Jae Gwang Lee, former moderator of the Korean
Presbyterian Church Abroad (KPCA)

A few years ago, I attended an Israel seminar for pastors hosted by Reverend Paul In-Sik Kim. Until then, I had a prejudiced notion that Israel suffered historically because they were the perpetrators of Jesus Christ's death on the cross. However, while participating in the seminar, I realized that Israel could be a victim, and I was able to sympathize with their pain, suffering, and experiences of injustice. When seeing Israel from that perspective, I was able to vividly see the historical scene of salvation's door being opened.

Following Reverend Kim's books *God's Master Plan* and *The Restoration of Israel and the End Time*, his third book *Bible, See the Big Picture!* is being published. This book is structured in a question-and-answer format on seven topics, so that the readers can easily understand the contents. Through his research, the author leads readers to study the Bible in depth and breadth like observing a forest through a telescope and observing a tree under a microscope. Following this process through this book, readers will easily understand God's vision, plan, intention, and method as they see God's big picture. Readers will grow in the knowledge of God. Therefore, I highly recommend this book to those who want to see the forest and tree of the Bible by following Dr. Paul In-Sik Kim's insights.

Reverend Sharon Lee, senior pastor of International Calvary Church
and president of Christian World Mission for Israel (CWMI)

The disciples asked Jesus, "When is the time for Israel's restoration?" Jesus answered that the time and season was not for them to know and commanded them to be His witnesses to the ends of the earth when the Holy Spirit comes upon them (Acts 1:6-8). Thus, churches were established in all nations during the past 2,000 years, and the saints diligently went out to the ends of the earth to preach the gospel. It was the season when branches of the cultivated olive tree were broken off, and branches of the wild olive tree were grafted in (Rom. 11:17). Now, Jerusalem is being restored, and the times of the Gentiles are being fulfilled (Luke 21:24). It is the time for the broken original branches to be re-grafted in (Rom. 11:25-26). Now is the time for God to pour out His mercy upon Israel and peel off the veils from the eyes of the Jewish people to unblind them. This is an exciting season of God's kairos when the scattered Jews gather in their ancient land, receive Jesus as their Messiah, and form the one new man with the Gentiles in the Name of Jesus.

Yes, now is the time for Israel's restoration. It is the time for Gentiles to comfort, show mercy, and bless Israel, who were broken off for us, so that they believe in Jesus and become one with us. The one new man vision is the core vision of God's Kingdom. By fulfilling this vision, the big picture of God's Kingdom will be completed, and Jesus will return to establish the completed Kingdom of God on earth. If Gentile churches have the same dream for the restoration of God's Kingdom, Gentiles should reconcile with the Jews and bless them so that they believe in Jesus and are restored spiritually, physically, and nationally.

This book *Bible, See the Big Picture!* authored by Reverend Paul In-Sik Kim, who is the forerunner in ministry for Israel's restoration, is an outstanding apologetic book that uses the question-and-answer format to clearly and orderly summarize the relationship between Israel and the Gentiles that has been questioned for so long within Christendom and the core truths about the one new man vision. This book is worthy of recommendation for it will help the laity and theologians who want to understand the Biblical relationship between Israel and the church. I thank the Holy Spirit Who has been present to guide this book to publication, and I joyfully recommend it in the Name of the Lord. Maranatha!

Dr. Jin Sup Kim, former president of International Israel Forum, former president of Baekseok Theological Seminary, and former vice president of Baekseok University

I sincerely congratulate the publication of Dr. Paul In-Sik Kim's timely book *Bible, See the Big Picture!* which follows his previous books in Korean, 하나님의 마스터플랜(*God's Master Plan*) and 이스라엘 회복과 종말(*Israel's Restoration and the End Times*), to present three keywords(Lord Jesus, Israel, and Jerusalem) and seven subjects(God's vision, God's strategy, God's city, the apple of God's eye, God's people, God's time, and God's Kingdom) in a question-and-answer format.

Until recently, there has been a flood of books published globally with titles along the lines of how to read and understand the entire Old and New Testaments, the Bible's meta-narrative, the big picture, and the grand story, but a book with a specific theological framework on God's redemptive work through Israel is a rarity that is hard to find, so I greatly anticipate the fresh impact this book will bring and welcome it.

70% of Korean Protestants are Presbyterians, so much so that "Korea is a Presbyterian Republic" is a circulating slogan. However, the Korean church's fixation with theological anti-Semitism, due to the replacement theological interpretation of covenant theology coupled with the Millennial Kingdom, plainly reveals our ignorance of the Bible and our egoistic obstinacy. In the Bible, which consists of 31,102 verses in total, the word "Israel" (nation and territory) is found 2,063 times, the word "Jew" (ethnic group) is found 275 times, the word "Hebrew" (language) is found 43 times, which all add up to 2,381 times as a whole. This means that the words "Israel," "Jew," "Hebrew" appear in every 13 verses in the Bible, but aren't we either ignoring or replacing these terms with the church? Even though the Bible records that "He came to that which was his own, but his own did not receive him" (Jn. 1:11) and "...This same Jesus, who has been taken from you into heaven, will come back in the same way you have seen him go into heaven" (Acts 1:11), we prevalently misunderstand the site of Jesus' First and Second Advents and are often out of touch with the main point of the Bible while reading it. We should once again properly read the Bible by clearly recognizing the Abrahamic Covenant's dual structure, "through (Gal. 3:8, 14, 28-29; the particularities of being a Jew) you (Abraham, David, Jesus Christ; Matt. 1:1)," "all peoples on the earth will be blessed" (Gen. 12:3; Isa. 19:23-25; Rev. 7:4, 9-10; the universal goal for all mankind) as God's big picture presented in the Bible's introduction (creation of the universe and man; Gen. 1-2), main body (mankind's fall and God's redemption; Gen. 3 to Rev. 20), and conclusion (the perfection of the universe and mankind; Rev. 21-22).

We should ask why the 7.5. million Korean Diaspora (the largest in the world) is scattered in 180 countries and centered around the church, why 28,000 Korean missionaries (2nd in the world) have been sent to more than 169 countries, why more than 7 million Jews are scattered in 108 countries outside Israel, and why Koreans are called the "second Jews" and expected to be the Gentile nation (Isa. 41:25, 55:5, 59:19; Rom. 10:19-20 quoting Deut. 32:21 and Isa. 65:1-2) who will save the Jews, and we should seriously contemplate our God-given vision and mission for these times.

The quiet outcry of Dr. Paul In-Sik Kim's book *Bible, See the Big Picture!* and the work of Kingdom World Mission, established in the context of his lifelong Korean immigrant ministry in the United States to embrace the globe, are vanguards for accelerating (speudō; 2 Pet. 3:12) our Lord Jesus' return as He unites the Jews once described as pigs and the Gentiles once described as dogs (2 Pet. 2:22; Eph. 2:14-15, 18) into the one new man (Eph. 2:15; Gal. 3:28) in accordance with God's eschatological promise that "Israel has experienced a hardening in part until the full number of the Gentiles has come in" and "so all Israel will be saved" (Rom. 11:25-26). By all means, I sincerely bless this endeavor of sowing seeds that please the Spirit to bear abundant fruits and reap the joy of eternal life from the Spirit (Gal. 6:8). Maranatha (Rev. 22:20)!

Asher Intrater, president of Tikkun Global

I had the opportunity to read the manuscript of Pastor Paul In-Sik Kim's book, *Bible, See the Big Picture!* For many years

I have encouraged people to study the Bible as one continuous theme, from Genesis to Revelation. Of course, there are many authors in many generations, however the inspiration of the Spirit of God gives a consistent worldview, with a logical plan from beginning to end.

This is exactly how Pastor Kim has explained the entire Scriptural vision. It starts with paradise lost and ends with paradise regained. Pastor Kim has done a remarkable job of summarizing very complex topics in a very pointed way. His ability to make concise conclusions is inspiring. Reading his manuscript makes the theological discussions quite clear.

The book shows a deep knowledge both of the Scriptures themselves and also the academic literature backing the interpretations. I believe the book will be very helpful for the readers. I recommend the book and commend Pastor Kim for writing it.

Eitan Shishkoff, pastor emeritus of the Tents of Mercy Congregation, founder of the Fields of Wheat National Youth Ministry, and author of *What About Us: The End-Time Calling of Gentiles in Israel's Revival*

Remarkable! Refreshing! Few Christian theologians have grasped the place of Israel and the Jewish people in God's plan with Dr. Paul In-Sik Kim's clarity. I am encouraged by his insights into the unfolding of spiritual history as he follows the covenants through which the Lord is redeeming mankind and preparing us for His reign over all the earth. I applaud the author's integration of the Old and New Testaments as a key to grasping the true meaning of Scripture. *Bible, See the Big Picture!* uses an "out of the box" question and answer method that anticipates the reader's toughest questions and is much easier to follow than the typical "theological tome."

As a Messianic Jew, I confess that I turned immediately to his treatment of "Replacement Theology," the long held erroneous idea that the Church replaces Israel. This error has led to devastating anti-Semitism and pushed the Jewish people away from our own Messiah. The author, systematically using Scripture itself, presents a clear and compelling case against this teaching. At the same time he rightly recognizes that Jew and Gentile are one in Yeshua (Jesus). But beyond exposing the lie of Israel's rejection, my brother helps us rejoice in the drama of Israel's restoration after nearly 2000 years of exile. We have returned to the land originally promised by eternal covenant to Abraham 4000 years ago! And now, increasing numbers of Jewish people are coming to faith in our true King, Messiah Jesus. Here is a phenomenal sentence, a treasure in a volume of treasures: "The restoration of the land of Israel is the most practical and concrete evidence that God is faithful and keeps His covenants." I and my family became a part of this phenomenon over 30 years ago. How marvelous that this

Korean scholar and lover of God recognizes the miracle we are a part of. On page after page, Pastor Kim draws us together, healing the breach that has wrongly separated the Church and Israel. I highly recommend this book. It is a breakthrough, like the sound of a shofar, signaling a new era of biblical understanding just when we need it to prepare the way for the return of our Redeemer and His everlasting Kingdom.

When we read and meditate on the Bible, we can garner new insights from a single verse or word. However, it is vital to comprehend the Author's intent throughout the entire flow of the text. Is it possible to understand a sender's intent by reading only a part of a letter? When we gaze at a tree immediately before us on a mountain, we are not viewing the entire forest. We cannot understand the whole forest by observing a singular tree. Will an architect finish building a home if he does not have the completed image of the house in his mind? We should not commit the blunder of being obsessed with a small portion and thus missing the whole. When we first believe, we are deeply touched by seeing even one aspect, but gradually as the eyes of our hearts are opened to the vast whole, we behold God's majestic and enthralling wisdom and power.

The author of *Draw a Big Picture*, Og Pyo Jun, wrote that seeing a "big picture" means understanding a certain problem or situation wholly, while life's big picture cannot be immediately seen in the present. However, God's big picture is already recorded in the Bible. The Bible reveals in precise details the final city perfected for God's children, the eternal home, which constitutes the ultimate big picture.

To see God's big picture in the Bible, we must grasp three keywords that God chose for mankind's salvation. Jesus Christ, the one God chose, appears in the Bible more than 1,800 times. From beginning to end, the Bible is a story about Jesus Christ. This epic story's two axes are the First and Second Advents of Jesus. Israel, the nation God chose, is mentioned in the Bible more than 2,300 times. Jesus Christ first came through the nation of Israel for mankind's salvation and will come again in connection with Israel. Jerusalem (Zion), the city God chose, appears in the Bible about 1,000 times. The most important events in the Bible are accomplished and fulfilled with Jerusalem at the core.

Centered on the three keywords are seven significant subjects that emanate throughout the Bible. These are: God's vision, God's strategy, God's city, God's pupil (the apple of God's eye), God's people, God's time, and God's Kingdom.

This book utilizes the Q&A (question and answer) format to research each subject in depth through the study of the whole Bible to seek to see God's big picture.

When we see God's big picture and understand God's vision, plan, intent, and method, we experience a stronger assurance of faith in Christ through the power of the Holy Spirit, and we grow to distribute spiritual food to the saints in due season. My prayer is for all of us to experience the deeper grace of understanding God's heart and the joy of participating in God's work in this era.

For readers interested in theology, I further discuss "Replacement Theology and Restoration Theology" in the Appendix. I recommend reading it. Because God is sovereign over history, accurate interpretation of the Bible does not ignore historical facts. The assertion that the church has replaced Israel does not align with the historical facts known today and the currents of these times. If we have held onto a theology in which Israel was missing until Israel became reborn, and if we have held onto a theology in which Jerusalem was missing until Jerusalem became restored to Israel, now is the time for us to adopt a theology that is predicated on the realities of Israel and Jerusalem.

Some readers may have different views regarding God's history of salvation in Christ that proceeded through Israel and its orientation toward Jerusalem. Even for such readers, this book can become a good reference.

I am grateful to President Sang Meyng Lee, Dr. Peter Im, and Dr. Damien Sohn for their encouragement and guidance. I am also grateful to the pastors who took the time during their busy schedules to pen words of recommendation for this book and to the coworkers, members, and especially the intercessory prayer team of West Hills Presbyterian Church who encouraged and prayed for me constantly. I am also grateful for the predecessors of faith who were awakened to the words before me and enlightened me. Lastly, I express my thanks to my wife who shares her insight with me, prays for me, and helps me, and to my two daughters, Gloria and Victoria, who encourage, love, and pray for me all the time, and I give all the glory to God, Him alone.

August 2021, from West Hills, California
Paul In-Sik Kim
Pastor Emeritus, West Hills Presbyterian Church
President, Kingdom World Mission

Since the publication of the first edition of this book in Korean, I have been leading seminars on its content around the globe. Many of the missionaries and pastors in attendance testified that they were able to see the core of the Bible and God's big picture and were grateful for the transformation of their perspective. One missionary confessed, "Thank you for opening our eyes to see, opening our ears to hear, and opening our hearts to understand." With the enthusiastic responses of attendees, their recommendations, and their prayers, the seminar continues. Last year alone, 10 seminars were held in Israel, Korea, Mongolia, Brazil, and the United States. During the first half of this year, I delivered lectures in Israel twice and also in Korea, Bulgaria, and the United States to pastors and missionaries. Additional seminars have been scheduled for the second half of this year and the first half of next year as well. This book has been translated into Mongolian, and translations into Spanish and Chinese are in progress. Everywhere I went, I met people asking for an English translation. Missionary Ezra Choe translated the Korean edition into English with great diligence, and my daughter Gloria Jin Kim carefully edited the English edition, refining each Q&A set with her native English and adding English footnotes. The Scriptures quoted in the English edition are from the 1984 New International Version (NIV) of the Bible. For clarity, the King James Version (KJV) and the New King James Version (NKJV) are at times utilized as well and are marked as such. The English edition is now being released into the world. It is an answer to intercessory prayer and only by God's grace. I am grateful to the book publisher, Hayoungin, and everyone who helped along the way. Soli Deo gloria (Only to God the glory)!

January 2024, from West Hills, California
Paul In-Sik Kim
Pastor Emeritus, West Hills Presbyterian Church
President, Kingdom World Mission

Table of Contents

Chapter 1

God's Vision

Introduction

God's first vision is His final vision. However, the Bible reveals a more comprehensive final vision than the first. God's vision is for God's people to live together in the place where God reigns and to enjoy His presence. The Bible's denouement focuses on the holy city of New Jerusalem, which is God's master plan. Those who know this denouement can carry in their hearts a glorious and splendid vision of the future and overcome the world without fear

Question 1 **How should we interpret the Bible?**

If we do not interpret the Bible rightly, God's intent through the Bible cannot be conveyed to us accurately. To know God's intent, we need basic principles for proper Biblical interpretation. The basic methods for Biblical interpretation in Reformed Theology include literal, grammatical, and historical interpretations. However, adhering only to strict literalism should be rejected.

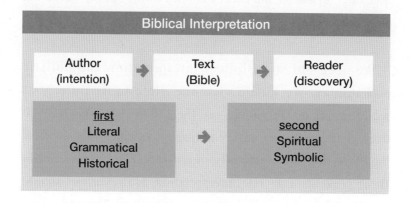

We should believe that the Bible is the trustworthy and reliable Word of God. Those who read the Bible should first accept and believe the literal meaning of the Word before seeking its spiritual interpretation and meaning. If we do not receive the Word of God literally, all accuracy is lost. We can always derive spiritual lessons from the Word of God but should not make the Word of God into something only spiritual or into an allegory. There are some verses that call for symbolic and spiritual interpretation. However, to overlook real facts due to excessive spiritual interpretation can result in a huge and terrible fallacy.

2 Cor. 1:20   For no matter how many promises God has made, they are "Yes" in Christ. And so through him the "Amen" is spoken by us to the glory of God.

Matt. 24:35   Heaven and earth will pass away, but my words will never pass away.

We need holistic Biblical interpretation and holistic eschatology. We should view the Bible in its entirety as we interpret it. We should see the forest first and then the trees. The Bible should be interpreted by the Bible. Correct theology that systematically organizes all the truths in the Bible prevents a deviate interpretation. However, we should humbly acknowledge the limitation of theology. This is because theology can limit the Word of God. The reason why the Word must take precedence over theology is because theology comes out of the Word. The two most important axes of the Bible are the Messiah's First and Second Advents. The Bible spoke in advance about Christ's First Advent more than 360 times. The Bible is speaking in advance about Christ's Second Advent as well more than 1,560 times and concludes with "Amen. Come,

Lord Jesus" (Rev. 22:20-21).

Question 2 What are the four major themes of the Bible?

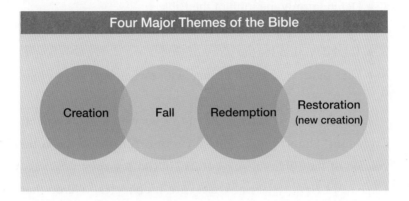

Biblical interpretation requires a single framework that binds the details together. Before considering the details, we need to draw the big picture. The Bible focuses on the fulfillment of God's purpose for mankind, which is the advent of the everlasting Kingdom of God (the New Heaven and New Earth, and the New Jerusalem). In this respect, the Bible can be considered eschatological from the very beginning. The Bible's scope ranges from creation in the beginning to the new creation that can be described as creation's renewal through redemption.

Question 3 What are the characteristics of Reformed Theology?

- Assert the truthfulness and infallibility of the Bible
- Defend firmly the truth of the Bible
- Acknowledge the absolute sovereignty of God
- Total devotion for the glory of God
- Lack of seriousness in dealing with eschatology

According to J. Barton Payne, who was a professor at Covenant Theological Seminary, one fourth of the total volume of the Bible (27%: 6,641/23,210 Old Testament verses and 1,711/7,914 New Testament verses) are prophecies.[1] Given that God's prophecies as written in the Bible have testified and are testifying to realities within the space and time of this world, they must be treated seriously.

Question 4 Why is the beginning and the end of the Bible important?

The Bible has a beginning and an end. It commences with Genesis 1 to 2 and concludes with Revelation 21 to 22. It starts with the Garden of Eden and finishes with the New Jerusalem. If we understand the beginning well, we can comprehend the conclusion well, and vice versa. The Bible is a story of restoration. If we know the completion to come, there is no need to fear. This is because God's final vision becomes my final vision and, therefore, is my final goal.

Question 5 Who is God?

Mark 1:10-11 10 As Jesus was coming up out of the water, he saw heaven being torn open and the Spirit descending on him like a dove. 11 And a voice came from heaven: "You are my Son, whom I love; with you I am well pleased."

Phil. 2:6   Who, being in very nature God, did not consider equality with God something to be grasped,

John 14:9   Jesus answered: "Don't you know me, Philip, even after I have been among you such a long time? Anyone who has seen me has seen the Father. How can you say, 'Show us the Father'?

Rom. 8:11   And if the Spirit of him who raised Jesus from the dead is living in you, he who raised Christ from the dead will also give life to your mortal bodies through his Spirit, who lives in you.

The Trinity is the most unique attribute of God. The Trinity means that God is not one person, and that instead the three clearly distinguished Persons – the Father, the Son, and the

Holy Spirit – are one God. The mutually distinguished Father, Son, and Holy Spirit are one God, and so, if any of the three is missing, that cannot be the one true God. The Father, the Son, and the Holy Spirit existed by themselves before the beginning of time. Each Person is perfect and equal with the others, and none of the three Persons come from the others nor belong to the others.

Among God's fundamental attributes that make God Who He is, the first is holiness. God, Who is holy, is the God of righteousness. Since the God of righteousness cannot overlook sin, a sinner cannot stand before Him. The only way to satisfy God's righteousness is to have Jesus, the Son of God Who is sinless, offered up as a sacrifice. To satisfy His righteousness, the loving God came to this earth in the form of His Son, clothed

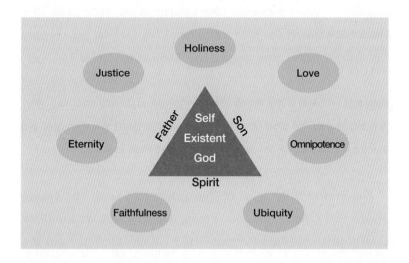

in a man's body, and accomplished atonement for all mankind. Therefore, God requires holiness from all the saints who have been saved (1 Pet. 1:16). The saints must seek to give and receive abundant love within the boundaries of righteousness and holiness. Love that goes beyond these boundaries becomes self-indulgence and inflicts harm and disorder upon the church and society.

Question 6 What are the image and the likeness of God?

Gen. 1:26-27 26 Then God said, "Let us make man in our image, in our likeness, and let them rule over the fish of the sea and the birds of the air, over the livestock, over all the earth, and over all the creatures that move along the ground. 27 So God created man in his own image, in the image of God he created him; male and female he created them."

The Hebrew word for image (tselem, צֶלֶם) means having a close resemblance. Intelligence, emotion, will, conscience, morality, freedom, fellowship, righteousness, holiness, and so forth are characteristics of God that He has shared with mankind. This indicates that mankind carries the role of representing God with his or her whole personal being or personality. Personality can only be activated within the context of relationships. Bearing the image of God is an essential element of human existence.

That mankind was created in God's likeness (demuth, דְּמוּת) means that human beings are spiritual beings and can have fellowship with God, Who is Spirit. Since the first man and woman were initially good and without sin, Adam and Eve must have morally resembled God at the beginning.

Col. 1:15   He is the image of the invisible God, the firstborn over all creation.

Jesus is the visible manifestation of the invisible God. Therefore, if one sees Jesus, one has seen God Himself (John 14:8-9). Jesus said, "I and the Father are one" (John 10:30). Jesus is the complete image (eikón, εἰκών) of God. Just as a mirror reflects the reality in front of it, the eikón perfectly reflects God and is God, while mankind imperfectly reflects and represents God.

Herman Bavinck, an orthodox Reformed, Dutch theologian, stated that, according to the Bible, "The whole being, therefore, and not something in man but man himself, is the image of God." [2] A human being's whole being is the image of God.

Question 7 What are the constituents of man?

1 Thess. 5:23 May God himself, the God of peace, sanctify you through and through. May your whole spirit, soul and body be kept blameless at the coming of our Lord Jesus Christ.

Ontologically, human beings, created in the image of God, are beings consisting of two substances: the soul and the body (bipartite). We are spiritual beings having physical bodies. Functionally, however, human beings can be described as beings consisting of the spirit, the soul, and the body (tripartite). The body is conscious of the world through sensory organs (touching, seeing, hearing, smelling, tasting, sensing pressure, sensing temperature, sensing pain, etc.), the soul is conscious of the self, and the spirit is conscious of God. All of us are each born with a spirit that is dead, and, therefore, we cannot be conscious of God by our own nature. Only when we hear God's Word and receive Jesus as our Lord and Savior, our dead spirits come alive, and by being born again, we become conscious of God and can call Him Father.

Question 8 What is the blessing and calling given to mankind at the time of creation?

Gen. 1:28   God blessed them and said to them, "Be fruitful and increase in number; fill the earth and subdue it. Rule over the fish of the sea and the birds of the air and over every living creature that moves on the ground."

Adam and Eve's calling was to fill the earth with images of God. Thus, the authoritative agency and stewardship of mankind, created in the image of God, was to expand all over the world, and, through the spread of God's glory to the ends of the earth, mankind was to subdue and rule the earth.

Question 9 What was the task given to man in the Garden of Eden?

Gen. 2:15   The LORD God took the man and put him in the Garden of Eden to work it and take care of it.

In God's commandment to "work" and "take care" of the Garden of Eden, the two Hebrew verbs ʿāḇaḏ (עָבַד, meaning to serve, work, rule) and shamar (שָׁמַר, meaning to keep, observe, protect, watch), are also found side-by-side only in verses describing the duties of the Levites in the Holy Tabernacle (Num. 3:7-8, 8:26, 18:5). We can infer that, in the Garden of Eden, Adam had the priestly position to meet and serve God. The earth was created to be God's dwelling place. This is because God intended to live with His people there.

Question 10 Considering the task given to man, what kind of a being is man?

God's command to "work" the Garden of Eden connotes that

Adam was given the responsibility to rule, serve, and work at the same time. God's command to "take care" of the Garden encompasses not only forbidding Adam from eating the fruit of the tree of the knowledge of good and evil but also calling him to guard Eden from Satan's attacks. As such, Adam was created to be a kingly priest. (Reference: Question 9)

Question 11 What is the tree of the knowledge of good and evil?

Gen. 2:16-17 16 And the LORD God commanded the man, "You are free to eat from any tree in the garden; 17 but you must not eat from the tree of the knowledge of good and evil, for when you eat of it you will certainly die."

The tree of the knowledge of good and evil distinguishes the Creator from His creatures. God, Who is the God of love and blessing, gives mankind free will (choice) (Gen. 2:16). However, as creatures, mankind, through obedience to the Word, can love the Creator and sustain their life. The tree of the knowledge of good and evil was given to test mankind's obedience, and, at the same time, forbidding its fruit was God's first law for mankind to protect them from Satan's temptations. Eventually, by eating the forbidden fruit, mankind learns that obeying God is good, and disobeying Him is evil. Disobedience is sin, because it is done not according to faith (Rom. 14:23), and because sin is lawlessness (1 John 3:4). Disobedience (sin) made mankind imperfect, and, accordingly, the earth also became imperfect. And mankind had to handle the fruit of disobedience.

Question 12 Why is Eden considered a holy place?

Gen. 3:8   Then the man and his wife heard the sound of the LORD God as he was walking in the garden in the cool of the day, and they hid from the LORD God among the trees of the garden.

The words "walking" in Genesis 3:8, "walk" in Leviticus 26:12, and "moving" in 2 Samuel 7:6 use the same Hebrew word, הָלַךְ(halak). The Garden of Eden was God's holy place, where He walked. God did the same in the Holy Tabernacle that was built later.

The Garden of Eden was the first sanctuary that ever existed on earth. The Garden of Eden was in the east on a mountain. In the Garden, there were rivers, trees, jewels, and precious metals, cherubim, the presence of God, and the responsibilities given to mankind. Eden's nature was that of a holy place. If we view the entire created world as a cosmic holy temple, the Garden of Eden may correspond to the first Holy of Holies. The Holy Tabernacle and Holy Temple built later are small replicas of the cosmic temple of God: His created world.

Question 13 Adam was a kingly priest (Gen. 1:28, 2:15). What is the identity of believers in the present and future?

1 Pet. 2:9   But you are a chosen people, a royal priesthood...

Rev. 5:10   You have made them to be a kingdom (kings, KJV) and priests to serve our God, and they will reign on the earth."

Rev. 20:6   Blessed and holy are those who have part in the first resurrection. The second death has no power over them, but they will be priests of God and of Christ and will reign with him for a thousand years.

Rev. 22:5   There will be no more night. They will not need the light of a lamp or the light of the sun, for the Lord God will give them light. And they will reign for ever and ever.

The identity of those who become God's children by believing in Jesus is a kingly priest. Believers live in this identity in the present, will enjoy it in earnest in the Millennial Kingdom, and will enjoy it fully and forever in the New Heaven and New Earth, and the New Jerusalem.

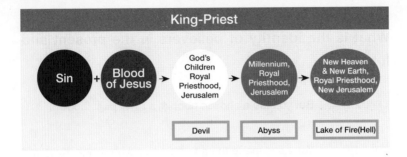

Question 14 Where is God's dwelling place?

The Garden of Eden was God's first dwelling place (Gen. 3:8). Later, God built the Holy Tabernacle through Moses as His dwelling place, and then God dwelt in the immovable Holy Temple He built through Solomon. After Jesus' death on the cross and His resurrection, God dwells within believers through His promised Holy Spirit (1 Cor. 6:19). Ultimately, God will dwell fully in the Millennial Kingdom and then in the New Jerusalem as His perfect and eternal dwelling place.

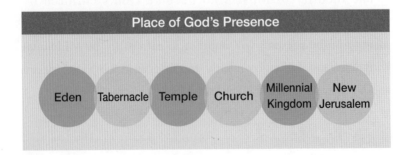

God's vision is for His people to live in a place where He reigns and to enjoy His presence. In Genesis 1 to 2, the Garden of Eden was God's dwelling place. And God gave Adam and Eve the mission to expand the territory of their residence and to fill the earth with mankind.

The Garden of Eden was God's dwelling place. The place where God dwells is a place of worship. The expansion of Eden is the expansion of worship. Worshiping God fuels the mission received in Eden. The calling is for those who have the image of God to reveal His presence in worship and, as they reveal His glory, to advance the mission of filling the earth (Gen. 1:28). In fact, worshiping God is the goal of the mission given in Eden, and this mission is to fill the temple, where people will worship God and reveal His glory to the ends of the earth, with people created in His image, and so, fill the world. John Stephen Piper, a representative Calvinist, Baptist pastor, and writer from the U.S. preached, "Worship is the fuel and the goal of missions."[3]

Question 15 Can we deduce the location of the Garden of Eden?

Gen. 2:11-14   11 The name of the first is the Pishon; it winds through the entire land of Havilah, where there is gold. 12 (The gold of that land is good; aromatic resin and onyx are also there.) 13 The name of the second river is the Gihon; it winds through the entire land of Cush.

14 The name of the third river is the Tigris (Hiddekel, KJV); it runs along the east side of Asshur. And the fourth river is the Euphrates.

The "entire land of Havilah" may refer to the whole Arabian Peninsula.[4]

The Pishon River ran through the Arabian Peninsula, and the Gihon River ran through Ethiopia. The Hiddekel River is the Tigris River in modern days, appearing with the Euphrates River on the map.

Ezek. 38:12   ...the people...living at the center of the land."

Here, the land (erets, אֶרֶץ) refers to the earth. This means that Israel is the center of the earth.

Gen. 1:9   And God said, "Let the water under the sky be gathered to one place, and let dry ground appear." And it was so.

Geologists accept as orthodox the theory that the earth originally consisted of one continent, which was later divided into several pieces. One vast continent gradually split to form several continents. This is the theory of plate tectonics combined with the theory of continental drift that is academically dominant today. Biologists also support the theory of continental drift. This theory is substantiated by the discovery of the same kinds of unique fossilized animals and plants in continents that are geographically distant from each other by several thousand to several ten thousand kilometers. The Bible records in Genesis 7 that there was a catastrophic diastrophism during the Great Flood and in Genesis 10 that the earth was divided during Peleg's time.

The Bible says a river flowed from the Garden of Eden (Gen. 2:10). In *The Bible, Genesis & Geology*, Gaines R. Johnson, an Independent Bible Doctrine Teacher, states, "More specifically, those waters could have originated in or near Jerusalem in present-day Israel, or even up welled from a massive spring under the sea of Tiberius..."[5]

Gen. 2:6   **but streams came up from the earth and watered the whole surface of the ground –**

Since there was no rain yet (Gen. 2:5), the mist (vapor) that came up from the earth watered the surface of the ground and formed rivers (Gen. 2:10). In other words, rivers were formed by the eruption of groundwaters. The name of the Gihon River, one of the first four rivers, means eruption.

Lawrence E. Stager, who was a professor in the Archeology Department of Harvard University, proved that Jerusalem is the most plausible location of the Garden of Eden by noting that Gihon is the name of the only spring in Jerusalem and the only place by that name in the Middle East.[6]

Gaines R. Johnson, an Independent Bible Doctrine Teacher, concludes that "Although the modern-day geology and topography of the Middle-East does not readily reveal the exact location of the Garden of Eden and the four rivers source, guidance by faith from the Holy Bible and a forensic study of the region's geology and topography reveals the matter. The available data appears to suggest that present-day Israel was the central location of the Garden of Eden."[7]

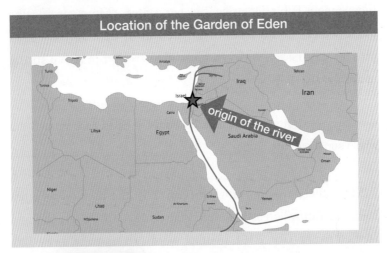

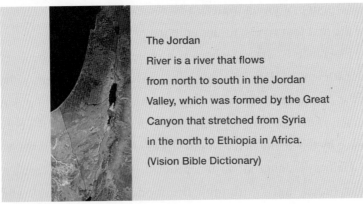

The Jordan River is a river that flows from north to south in the Jordan Valley, which was formed by the Great Canyon that stretched from Syria in the north to Ethiopia in Africa. (Vision Bible Dictionary)

Dr. Myung Hyun Kim of the Institute of Biblical Science states in his lecture on the Garden of Eden and the 4 rivers that it is plausible that the location of the Garden of Eden was indeed Jerusalem.[8]

Rev. Lee Mun Bum says that if we combine the origins of the four rivers, we can get the location of the Garden of Eden.[9] If we pull together the water origins in Europe, Asia, and Africa into one place while considering the drastic topographical change that happened during Noah's Flood, the location of the Garden of Eden turns out to be in the vicinity of Jerusalem.[10]

Ezek. 31:8-9   8 The cedars in the garden of God could not rival it, nor could the pine trees equal its boughs, nor could the plane trees compare with its branches – no tree in the garden of God could match its beauty. 9 I made it beautiful with abundant branches, the envy of all the trees of Eden in the garden of God.

Here, the garden of God symbolizes the land of Israel. The cedars in the garden of God symbolize Israel's people, leaders, or kings. In verse 9, the garden of God is called Eden. This implies that the land of Israel was Eden.

Dr. Young Ihl Chang, former president of the Presbyterian University and Theological Seminary and an expert on the Old Testament, states that God chose the land of Canaan to be the center of the earth and the heart of world history, and chose Jerusalem to be the center of that land, the headquarter of Israel's history, and the cosmic capital city where our Lord Jesus Christ will be given all authority under heaven and earth and be enthroned as the King.[11] In this location, God fulfilled the Scriptures, which is the Word of truth, to save all mankind and will complete His mission.[12] In the last days, with Jesus' return as the King of kings, God's redemptive history will be complete, and the New Heaven and the New Earth will begin.[13]

Inside the Church of the Holy Sepulcher at Golgotha in Jerusalem, there is a marker stone called the navel of the earth. This means it is the center of the world. The land of Israel is at the center of the earth, Jerusalem is at the center of the land of Israel, and the Holy Temple is at the center of Jerusalem. Jerusalem is at the center of the Garden of Eden as well as the Promised Land. God placed Jerusalem at the center of the earth geographically and made it the spiritual center of the world. The Lord will return to Jerusalem and dwell in it (Zech. 8:3).

Question 16 Who is the offspring of the woman?

Gen. 3:15   And I will put enmity between you and the woman, and between your offspring and hers; he will crush his head, and you will strike his heel.

Gal. 4:4   But when the time had fully come, God sent his Son, born of a woman, born under law,

God promised to send Christ, the offspring of the woman, to redeem man and all of creation from sin and the resultant curse. All humans are the offspring of man, but only Christ, the Son of God, is conceived by the Holy Spirit and born of the Virgin Mary. Approximately 4,000 years after man's fall, when the time had fully come, Christ came as promised, shed his blood on the cross and died, and was resurrected on the third day.

Question 17 What is Millennialism?

Rev. 20:1-6   1 And I saw an angel coming down out of heaven, having the key to the Abyss and holding in his hand a great chain. 2 He seized the dragon, that ancient serpent, who is the devil, or Satan, and bound him for a thousand years. 3 He threw him into the Abyss, and locked and sealed it over him, to keep him from deceiving the nations anymore until the thousand years were ended. After that, he must be set free for a short time. 4 I saw thrones on which were seated those who had been given authority to judge. And I saw the souls of those who had been beheaded because of their testimony for Jesus and because of the word of God. They had not worshiped the beast or his image and had not received his mark on their foreheads or their hands. They came to life and reigned with Christ a thousand years. 5 (The rest of the dead did not come to life until the thousand years were ended.) This is the first resurrection. 6 Blessed and holy are those who have part in the first resurrection. The second death has no power over them, but they will be priests of God and of Christ and will reign with him for a thousand years.

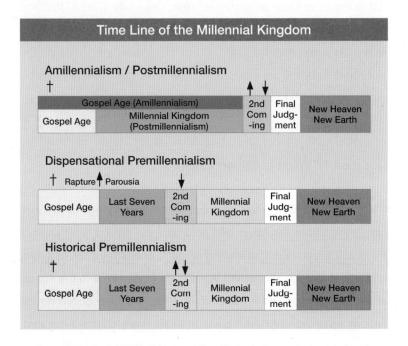

Time Line of the Millennial Kingdom

Amillennialism / Postmillennialism

Gospel Age	Gospel Age (Amillennialism) / Millennial Kingdom (Postmillennialism)	2nd Com -ing	Final Judg- ment	New Heaven New Earth

Dispensational Premillennialism

✝ Rapture Parousia

Gospel Age	Last Seven Years	2nd Com -ing	Millennial Kingdom	Final Judg- ment	New Heaven New Earth

Historical Premillennialism

Gospel Age	Last Seven Years	2nd Com -ing	Millennial Kingdom	Final Judg- ment	New Heaven New Earth

Amillennialism/Postmillennialism: There is no distinction between the advent to the air (Rapture) and the advent to the earth. After a thousand years, Christ comes again. At the time of the Second Advent, both the believers and the unbelievers resurrect. There is no distinction between the church and Israel. The church is the new Israel. In amillennialism, the Millennial Kingdom (the Kingdom of God) exists in the present generation, and the period of a thousand years is not a literal thousand years but a symbolic period. In postmillennialism, the Millennial Kingdom refers to the golden age of the gospel.

Dispensational Premillennialism: The thousand years is understood as a literal thousand years. The Second Advent is divided into the advent to the air (Rapture) and the advent to the earth. The advent to the earth occurs after the seven years of tribulation, and the church is raptured before the seven years of tribulation at the time of the advent to the air. The church is distinguished from Israel, and God has a plan for each.

Historical Premillennialism: The thousand years is understood as a literal thousand years. The advent to the air (Rapture) and the advent to the earth occur consecutively. Christ Himself comes to the earth to reign. During the thousand years of Jesus' reign, Satan is bound and imprisoned in the abyss. After the thousand years end, Satan is released for a while, attempts a final attack, is defeated, and cast into the lake of fire (hell) forever.

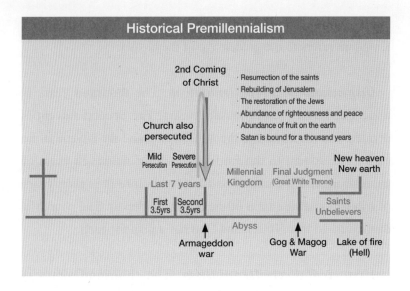

Historical Premillennialism

2nd Coming
of Christ

· Resurrection of the saints
· Rebuilding of Jerusalem
· The restoration of the Jews
· Abundance of righteousness and peace
· Abundance of fruit on the earth
· Satan is bound for a thousand years

Church also
persecuted

New heaven
New earth

Mild   Severe
Persecution Persecution

Millennial   Final Judgment
Kingdom   (Great White Throne)

Last 7 years

First   Second
3.5yrs   3.5yrs

Saints
Unbelievers

Abyss

Armageddon
war

Gog & Magog
War

Lake of fire
(Hell)

Question 18 Who will reign with Christ in the Millennial Kingdom?

Rev. 20:4   I saw thrones on which were seated those who had been given authority to judge. And I saw the souls of those who had been beheaded because of their testimony for Jesus and because of the word of God. They had not worshiped the beast or his image and had not received its mark on their foreheads or their hands. They came to life and reigned with Christ a thousand years.

Those who receive the authority to judge, who were beheaded, and who did not worship the beast nor his image and did not receive the beast's mark will reign with Christ in the Millennial Kingdom.

2 Tim. 2:12　if we endure, **we will also** reign **with him. If we disown him, he will also disown us;**

Those who endure to the end will reign.

Matt. 19:28　**Jesus said to them, "I tell you the truth, at the renewal of all things, when the Son of Man sits on his glorious throne,** you who have followed me will also sit on twelve thrones, judging the twelve tribes of Israel**.**

Those who leave behind the self out of love for Jesus and follow His teachings and His life will reign.

Dan. 7:22　**until the Ancient of Days came and pronounced judgment in favor of the saints of the Most High, and the time came when** they possessed the kingdom**.**

Although the saints of the Most High will experience persecution, they will be freed from it at last, will gain the victory and the kingdom that the Son of Man has obtained, and will reign with Him.

Rev. 5:9-10   9 And they sang a new song: "You are worthy to take the scroll and to open its seals, because you were slain, and with your blood you purchased men for God from every tribe and language and people and nation. 10 You have made them to be a kingdom and priests to serve our God, and they will reign on the earth."

Those who have been redeemed by the blood of Jesus and offered to God will reign. Mankind was created to reign over the world (Gen. 1:28) but fell due to disobedience. Through Christ, the lost blessing and calling to reign on the earth will be restored to mankind. Mankind will return to the position that was foreordained from the very beginning. It is to reign in the Millennial (Messianic) Kingdom together with the Almighty Lord. The happiness, joy, and the glory of participating in that Kingdom will indeed be wonderful.

Question 19 Who are those being ruled in the Millennial Kingdom?

Ps. 2:6-11   6 "I have installed my King on Zion, my holy hill." 7 I will proclaim the decree of the Lord: He said to me, "You are my Son; today I have become your Father. 8 Ask of me, and I will make the nations your inheritance, the ends of the earth your possession. 9 You will rule them with an iron scepter; you will dash them to pieces like pottery." 10 Therefore, you kings, be wise; be warned, you rulers of the earth. 11 Serve the LORD with fear and rejoice with trembling.

Rev. 20:7-10   7 When the thousand years are over, Satan will be released from his prison 8 and will go out to deceive the nations in the four corners of the earth – Gog and Magog – to gather them for battle. In number they are like the sand on the seashore. 9 They marched across the breadth of the earth and surrounded the camp of God's people, the city he loves. But fire came down from heaven and devoured them. 10 And the devil, who deceived them, was thrown into the lake of burning sulfur, where the beast and the false prophet had been thrown. They will be tormented day and night for ever and ever.

Isa. 65:20   "Never again will there be in it an infant who lives but a few days, or an old man who does not live out his years; he who dies at a hundred will be thought a mere youth; he who fails to reach a hundred will be considered accursed.

Psalm 2 is describing the ultimate reign of the Messiah Jesus Christ over all nations. Gog, the king who rules Magog, a land far in the north (Ezek. 38:1), is the adversary of God's chosen people, Israel. Since Ezekiel's prophecy, these names represent people throughout the earth who oppose God and His people. They are not the resurrected saints. This is because they will surround the camp of the saints for attack. That fire will come down from heaven and devour them indicates that they will die. The saints, having been resurrected, are glorious spiritual beings who cannot die. Those who are ruled in the Millennial Kingdom will be the survivors of the Seventh Bowl Judgment and the final War of Armageddon.

Question 20 What will life in the Millennial Kingdom be like?

Isa. 35:5-6   5 Then will the eyes of the blind be opened and the ears of the deaf unstopped. 6 Then will the lame leap like a deer, and the mute tongue shout for joy. Water will gush forth in the wilderness and streams in the desert.

Luke 24:39   Look at my hands and my feet. It is I myself! Touch me and see; a ghost does not have flesh and bones, as you see I have."

Isa. 11:8-9   8 The infant will play near the hole of the cobra, and the young child put his hand into the viper's nest. 9 They will neither harm nor destroy on all my holy mountain, for the earth will be full of the knowledge of the LORD as the waters cover the sea.

Rom. 8:19-21   19 The creation waits in eager expectation for the sons of God to be revealed. 20 For the creation was subjected to frustration, not by its own choice, but by the will of the one who subjected it, in hope 21 that the creation itself will be liberated from its bondage to decay and brought into the glorious freedom of the children of God.

The Millennial Kingdom is the kingdom that Christ Himself reigns over. Although Christ has been ruling the whole world providentially from the beginning of time, His direct ruling practically starts in the Millennial Kingdom. Christ and the saints will rule the Millennial Kingdom together. It is a kingdom full of the knowledge of the LORD, a kingdom of peace and justice, a kingdom of prosperity where the curse has been removed, and a kingdom of glory without any diseases.

Question 21 Where will God's people live forever?

Rev. 21:1-2   1 Then I saw a new heaven and a new earth, for the first heaven and the first earth had passed away, and there was no longer any sea. 2 I saw the Holy City, the new Jerusalem, coming down out of heaven from God, prepared as a bride beautifully dressed for her husband.

The place where God's people will eventually dwell is not a spiritual world without substance but rather a concrete and tangible place. The New Heaven and New Earth is a world restored from the old one, both physical and spiritual in nature at the same time. It is a world both natural and supernatural. Therefore, we should not disregard or overlook the physical aspect of this future paradise. The vision of God is to be with "Godly offspring" (אֱלֹהִים זֶרַע, zera' Elohim, Mal. 2:15) forever and reign in the New Heaven and the New Earth and in the New Jerusalem. Therefore, God's children should know how precious the earth that God created is. The fact that Jesus Christ came to this earth and shed His precious blood shows how important the earth is. Since the earth is the dwelling place of all God's children who are redeemed by the blood of Jesus, and, since it is the land of calling and ministry, the earth is important and precious to God. Since the New Heaven and New Earth and the New Jerusalem will be the cosmic center of the completed Kingdom of God where the throne of God will be present, they are even more significant.

Question 22 What is the relationship between the final vision of God and world missions?

World missions is the process of fulfilling God's vision, commencing from Genesis 1 and ending at Revelation 21 to 22 when the New Heaven and New Earth becomes the dwelling place of the LORD God Almighty. This image of the whole world being filled with the presence of God and the children of God who have been saved is the accomplishment of the original intent that God had in the Garden of Eden.

Question 23 Will the New Heaven and New Earth be a completely new creation, or will it be a new world that is obtained by renewing the old world?

2 Pet. 3:10-13   10 But the day of the Lord will come like a thief. The heavens will disappear with a roar; the elements will be destroyed by fire, and the earth and everything in it will be laid bare. 11 Since everything will be destroyed in this way, what kind of people ought you to be? You ought to live holy and godly lives 12 as you look forward to the day of God and speed its coming. That day will bring about the destruction of the heavens by fire, and the elements will melt in the heat. 13 But in keeping with his promise we are looking forward to a new heaven and a new earth, the home of righteousness.

Rev. 21:1   Then I saw a new heaven and a new earth, for the first heaven and the first earth had passed away, and there was no longer any sea.

Isa. 65:17   "Behold, I will create new heavens and a new earth. The former things will not be remembered, nor will they come to mind.

The Greek for the word "new" in "a new heaven and a new earth" is not neos (νέος) which means new in time or origin. Instead, it is kainos (καινός) in Greek and is chadash (חָדָשׁ) in Hebrew which mean new in features or attributes. Thus, the word "new" means newness, not in the spacetime dimension but rather in the qualitative dimension (Isa. 65:17). The old world with sin, suffering, and rebellion completely perishes, and a new world of righteousness is established where God dwells with His people. The New Heaven and New Earth is made from the old world, not by burning it away completely but instead by radically renewing and restoring it while preserving continuity.

Rev. 21:1   ...the first heaven and the first earth had passed away...

The Greek for "passed away" in Revelation 21:1, parerchomai (παρέρχομαι), does not mean abrogation or extinction but rather a change or transformation of a place or kind into another.

Question 24 **Using the table below, explain how heaven and earth changed and will change.**

Stage 1	Heaven and Earth (Creation)	Past
Stage 2	Before Noah's Flood	Past
Stage 3	After Noah's Flood	Present
Stage 4	Millennial Kingdom	Future
Stage 5	New Heaven and Earth	Future

Question 25 What is the New Jerusalem like?

Rev. 21:11   It shone with the glory of God, and its brilliance was like that of a very precious jewel, like a jasper, clear as crystal.

Rev. 21:12   It had a great, high wall with twelve gates, and with twelve angels at the gates. On the gates were written the names of the twelve tribes of Israel.

Rev. 21:14   The wall of the city had twelve foundations, and on them were the names of the twelve apostles of the Lamb.

Rev. 21:16   The city was laid out like a square, as long as it was wide. He measured the city with the rod and found it to be 12,000 stadia in length, and as wide and high as it is long.

The holy city New Jerusalem that comes down from heaven from God shines a light that is as pure and beautiful as a very precious jewel. The city has a high wall with twelve gates upon which the names of the twelve tribes of Israel are written and is guarded by an angel at each gate. The wall of the city has twelve foundations upon which the names of the twelve apostles of the Lamb are inscribed. The New Jerusalem shows that the saints of the Old Testament and the saints of the New Testament are united into one community of God's church. The walls are built of jasper, and the city is made of pure gold, looking like a clear crystal. With the foundations of the walls made of all kinds of jewels, the New Jerusalem looks beautiful, clean, precious, and glorious. It is a New Jerusalem prepared by the God of beauty. It is the glory that all saved saints will enjoy forever while wearing glorious, resurrected bodies in the glorious paradise. The New Jerusalem has the dimensions of an identical length, width, and height of 12,000 stadia each. One stadia is the circumference of an outdoor stadium, which is about 200 meters. A single side of the New Jerusalem is calculated to be about 2,400 kilometers (1,500 miles) long.

Question 26 What is absent in the New Jerusalem?

Rev. 21:22   I did not see a temple in the city, because the Lord God Almighty and the Lamb are its temple.

Rev. 21:23   The city does not need the sun or the moon to shine on it, for the glory of God gives it light, and the Lamb is its lamp.

Rev. 22:5   There will be no more night. They will not need the light of a lamp or the light of the sun, for the Lord God will give them light. And they will reign for ever and ever.

Rev. 21:4   He will wipe every tear from their eyes. There will be no more death or mourning or crying or pain, for the old order of things has passed away."

Rev. 22:3   No longer will there be any curse. The throne of God and of the Lamb will be in the city, and his servants will serve him.

Rev. 20:10   And the devil, who deceived them, was thrown into the lake of burning sulfur, where the beast and the false prophet had been thrown. They will be tormented day and night for ever and ever.

Since God and the Lamb, Jesus, Themselves become the temple, there is no need for any other temple in the New Jerusalem. The reason why the light of the sun or moon is no longer needed is that God Who is Light Himself shines bright with His glory, and Jesus Christ is the Lamp. There is no death, tear, mourning, sickness, curse, or the devil. Since Satan who sneaked into the Garden of Eden is absent, the saints, having spiritual bodies, can live forever without being exposed to any temptation, test, or deception from him.

Question 27 What kind of life will the saints live in the New Jerusalem?

Rev. 22:1-2   1 Then the angel showed me the river of the water of life, as clear as crystal, flowing from the throne of God and of the Lamb 2 down the middle of the great street of the city. On each side of the river stood the tree of life, bearing twelve crops of fruit, yielding its fruit every month. And the leaves of the tree are for the healing of the nations.

Rev. 22:4   They will see his face, and his name will be on their foreheads.

Rev. 21:24   The nations will walk by its light, and the kings of the earth will bring their splendor into it.

Rev. 21:26   The glory and honor of the nations will be brought into it.

In the New Jerusalem, all God's people can live forever with God and enjoy fellowship with Him, walking with Him under the tree of life planted on the sides of the river of the water of life and talking with Him face to face. This was the ultimate purpose for which God had created the universe, the earth, and mankind in the midst of it.

After the fall of Adam and Eve, they could not eat from the tree of life anymore since angels were blocking their access to it. However, the tree of life will be revealed once again in the New Jerusalem on the New Earth. Anyone who dwells in the New Earth can freely access the tree of life. The leaves of the tree of life will heal all the nations, which will not stand against each other but instead live harmoniously together.

The fact that kings still exist indicates that nations are still functional. Being in the New Earth, all nations and kings will surrender themselves to the Lord, the greatest King of kings. People of the nations will enter the New Jerusalem with their own splendor and honor. The nations will glorify God and make contributions to the New Jerusalem with diverse cultures developed from their respective talents and gifts.

The New Jerusalem is the place where God dwells with us forever. It is a place of complete healing. It is a place full of God's grace and blessing.

Question 28 What is the vision of God expressed as "from Eden to the New Eden?"

The Bible begins with a picture of God and His people walking together in the Garden of Eden and ends with a vision of God and His people meeting face to face in the New Heaven and the New Earth, and the New Jerusalem. In Genesis 1 to 2, Adam walked with God intimately. In Revelation 21 to 22, God once again walks with His people in the Garden, meeting with them face to face.

Chapter 22 of Revelation describes what the restored Garden of Eden will look like. There will be a river of living water flowing out from the throne of God, which will water the tree of life planted alongside the river, growing exuberantly and bearing twelve crops of fruit, yielding its fruit every month, and thereby, everyone in God's Kingdom will enjoy eternal life (Rev. 22:1-2).

All that God intended for in Genesis 1 to 2 is perfectly restored in Revelation 21 to 22, the last two chapters of the Bible, by eliminating all curses that resulted from sin.

Chapter 2 of Genesis describes Adam as having the authority to rule over all in the Garden of Eden and on the earth, but Chapter 22 of Revelation describes the saints, having resurrected bodies, ruling over the entire universe. The completed Kingdom of God fulfills the perfect, ideal world dreamed by perfect human beings where everything is full and joyful.

In short, it is like restoring all that has been lost in the Garden of Eden. But the New Heaven and the New Earth does not mean only restoring what has been lost in the Garden of Eden but also means a better world where even the possibility of any kind of fall, like the one in the Garden of Eden, has been totally, preemptively removed, because there will be no more Satan who brings sin, temptation, and curses. The New Heaven and the New Earth is where all of God's children who are redeemed will enjoy indescribably full lives together with God forever without any chance of sin, temptation, and curses.

	Eden (Gen. 1-3)	New Eden (Gen. 20-22)
1	first heaven and earth (Gen. 1-2)	New Heaven and New Earth (Rev. 21:1-2)
2	the tree of life and the four rivers (Gen. 2:9-14)	the tree of life and the river of the water of life (Rev. 22:1-2)

3	Adam and Eve (Gen. 2:15-25)	Lamb's Bride (Rev. 21:9)
4	Satan's victory (Gen. 3:1-7)	Satan's destruction (Rev. 20:10)
5	God is in the Garden (Gen. 3:8)	God is with the saints (Rev. 22:3)
6	rule the earth (Gen. 1:28)	rule the entire universe (Rev. 22:5)
7	fleeing the face of God (Gen. 3:8)	seeing the face of God (Gen. 3:8)
8	fear of God (Gen. 3:10)	intimacy with God (Gen. 3:10)
9	Curse is declared (Gen. 3:14-19)	Curse is removed (Rev. 22:3)
10	First Gospel Promises Given (Gen. 3:15).	The Final Fulfillment of the Promise of the Gospel (Rev.21:1-2:5)
11	death begins (Gen. 3:22)	death has been removed (Rev. 21:4)
12	Expelled from the Garden of Eden (Gen. 3:24)	Life in the New Jerusalem (Rev. 21:26-27)
13	Angels block the way to the Garden of Eden (Gen. 3:24)	Angels welcomes entry into paradise (Rev. 21:9, 12)
14	Satan's intention (Gen. 3:1)	Satan will be cast into the eternal lake of fire (Rev. 20:10)

Question 29 What does "to bring unity to all things in heaven and on earth" mean?

Eph. 1:10 to be put into effect when the times will have reached their fulfillment – to bring all things in heaven and on earth together under one head, even Christ.

God's Kingdom is where physical things on earth and

spiritual things become mutually harmonized. If dying and going to heaven is all there is, there is no need for resurrection. The promise of resurrected bodies presupposes the restoration of the earth. If we miss the revelation of the physical aspect of the Garden of Eden, we are missing the glory of the Creator Jesus in Genesis 1 to 2. The New Heaven and the New Earth, which is also the New Eden, is a world both physical and spiritual, both natural and supernatural, which is a world perfect, beautiful, and full, where heaven and earth are united. God will run the entire universe together with His children with the New Jerusalem at its center.

Conclusion

God's vision is to dwell in the New Heaven and the New Earth and the New Jerusalem with His people and to reign together. The New Jerusalem is the ultimate destination for us who will be resurrected and our eternal dwelling place. The New Heaven and the New Earth is not just a spiritual realm without physical realities nor substance but instead a concrete, realistic place where the people of God will actually dwell. While looking forward to the beauty and glory of the New Jerusalem, which is God's final vision, let us overcome the world with a burning heart, with peace, and with boldness, and fulfill the calling.

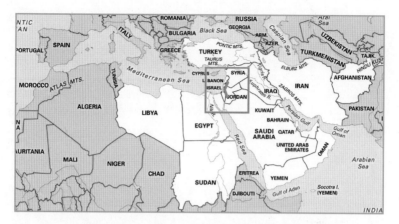

The picture above is a current day map. The earth will be totally renewed, and the center of the renewed earth will still be Jerusalem. The square drawn in the picture is to roughly give the sense of how big the New Jerusalem will be.

Chapter 2

God's Strategy

Introduction

God's strategy to achieve His master plan is His covenants. God's covenants are closely connected to the basic elements of faith and are an important framework for interpreting the Bible. The covenants of God reveal His purpose and plan for us. The Bible is the record of how God fulfilled His covenants, and all the covenants remaining to be fulfilled will surely be fulfilled. Human history testifies to how God has fulfilled His covenants and promises. Let us understand God's covenants properly, know His purpose and plan well, and look with conviction toward the future, moving forward in hope.

Question 1 Why does God speak in advance?

Amos 3:7   Surely the Sovereign LORD does nothing without revealing his plan to his servants the prophets.

Only the Bible earnestly proclaims prophecies that are fulfilled and will be fulfilled. This is because only the Bible is God's Word. All other religions are false and cannot tell true prophecies. Prophecy reveals how God is leading history. In many cases, prophecies tend to move forward over the waves of history, shedding its light only at their peaks. Therefore, it is hard to understand the whole from only observing its parts. The only, complete explanation of a prophecy is revealed to us after its fulfillment.

Question 2 What is a covenant?

A covenant (berith, בְּרִית / diathéké, διαθήκη) is a solemn promise that must be kept and deeply connects God and His people. God makes covenants with His own people, and, through new promises, He provides His grace to His people. The foundation of God's promises is His covenant, and God's faithfulness surely fulfills His covenant. Those who understand God's covenant can look at the future clearly, and thus fulfill the calling and obtain victory.

Question 3 With whom did God make covenants?

Acts 3:25   And you are heirs of the prophets and of the covenant God made with your fathers. He said to Abraham, 'Through your offspring all peoples on earth will be blessed.'

Eph. 2:12   remember that at that time you were separate from Christ, excluded from citizenship in Israel and foreigners to the covenants of the promise, without hope and without God in the world.

God made a covenant with Abraham. Israel is the offspring carrying on the genealogical line of the Abrahamic covenant. God never made a covenant with Gentile nations. However, those Gentiles who believe Jesus Christ become descendants of Abraham in Christ and heirs to the inheritance. All tribes on earth are thus blessed through the Seed of Abraham.

Question 4 How can we believe that God will surely fulfill His covenant?

Ps. 89:34   I will not violate my covenant or alter what my lips have uttered.

Isa. 46:10   I make known the end from the beginning, from ancient times, what is still to come. I say: My purpose will stand, and I will do all that I please.

God's covenant is God's promise and His plan. God is faithful
and almighty. Therefore, God is sure to fulfill His promise and
plan and achieve His goal.

Question 5 What blessing and calling did God give Adam in the Garden of Eden?

Gen. 1:28   God blessed them and said to them, "Be fruitful and
increase in number; fill the earth and subdue it. Rule over the fish of
the sea and the birds of the air and over every living creature that
moves on the ground."

Gen. 2:15   The LORD God took the man and put him in the Garden
of Eden to work it and take care of it.

Adam, who was created in God's image, received God's
blessing to conquer the land and rule over all other moving
creatures. Conquering the land encompasses possessing the
land and, at the same time, meeting needs by utilizing resources
from the land to give glory to God. The blessing to rule over
all living creatures implies that Adam was given a vice-regency
or stewardship to manage all that God created. Adam had to
cultivate and protect the Garden of Eden. Before the Fall, labor

was pleasant, not painful.

Question 6 What is Adam's Covenant given in the Garden of Eden?

Gen. 2:16-17   16 And the LORD God commanded the man, "You are free to eat from any tree in the garden; 17 but you must not eat from the tree of the knowledge of good and evil, for when you eat from it you will surely die."

Hosea 6:7   Like Adam, they have broken the covenant – they were unfaithful to me there.

Adam's Covenant was the first covenant God ever made with mankind. When seeing the tree of the knowledge of good and evil, mankind had to remember that there is a Creator, while he or she is only a created being. Mankind's vice-regency was conditioned upon faithfully obeying God's commandment of the forbidden fruit. However, Adam and Eve fell by abusing the limited free will granted to mankind, and, as a result, was driven out of the Garden of Eden.

Question 7 What was the cause of Adam and Eve's Fall?

Gen. 3:1   Now the serpent was more crafty than any of the wild animals the LORD God had made. He said to the woman, "Did God really say, 'You must not eat from any tree in the garden'?"

Satan who appeared in the form of a serpent was the source of temptation. Satan was the one who had been expelled for opposing and rebelling against God. To corrupt man, the crown of God's creation, Satan controlled the crafty serpent to tempt Eve. For this reason, the Bible calls Satan "the ancient serpent" (Rev. 12:9, 20:2). By deception the serpent made Eve doubt God's command and fall into temptation (Gen. 3:4-5). The forbidden fruit, when viewed with unfaithful eyes, looked good for food, pleasing to the eye, and desirable for gaining wisdom (Gen. 3:6). The lack of faith begot disobedience, and the result of disobedience was sin, curse, and death.

Question 8 How does Satan tempt us today?

1John 2:15-16 15 Do not love the world or anything in the world. If anyone loves the world, the love of the Father is not in him. 16 For everything in the world – the cravings of sinful man, the lust of his eyes and the boasting of what he has and does – comes not from the Father but from the world.

Even today, Satan tempts us through the lust of the flesh. This refers to the wrongful desires generated by our corrupt bodies. He tempts us through the lust of our eyes. This refers to the wrongful desires generated by seeing with our eyes. He also tempts us through our pride of life. While living in this world, we can have the wrong desire to lift ourselves up and show off. The vanity that is generated then is the pride of life. The Devil tempts mankind by using these three channels. He tries to tempt humans to commit sin and to make them his servants.

Question 9 What was the consequence of Adam and Eve's Fall?

Gen. 3:10　　He answered, "I heard you in the garden, and I was afraid because I was naked; so I hid."

Gen. 3:18-19　18 It will produce thorns and thistles for you, and you will eat the plants of the field. 19 By the sweat of your brow you will eat your food until you return to the ground, since from it you were taken; for dust you are and to dust you will return."

Gen. 3:16　　To the woman he said, "I will greatly increase your pains in childbearing; with pain you will give birth to children. Your desire will be for your husband, and he will rule over you."

Through the breaking of Adam's Covenant, the relationships among God, mankind, and creatures were broken (Gen. 3:7; 3:10). Man must live a laborious life on the cursed earth (Gen. 3:17). Man can only survive by working perspiringly among thorns and thistles, and death came. (Gen. 3:18-19). Pain in childbearing and desire for her husband is the woman's lot (Gen. 3:16). Mankind lost their standing and was evicted from the Garden of Eden.

Question 10 Can we know exactly when Adam and Eve's Fall occurred?

1 Kings 6:1   In the four hundred and eightieth year after the Israelites came out of Egypt, in the fourth year of Solomon's reign over Israel, in the month of Ziv, the second month, he began to build the temple of the LORD.

Adam and Eve were created as immortal beings in God's image. Therefore, originally, Adam and Eve were beings whose ages did not need to be calculated, but, after the Fall, they entered the temporal world. Solomon was enthroned as a king in 970 B.C. and started building the Temple in 966 B.C. That year was the 480th year after the Exodus, so the year of the Exodus is about 1,446 B.C. Jacob arrived in Egypt at the age of 130 (Gen. 47:9), and the children of Israel dwelled in Egypt for 430 years (Exod. 12:40). Therefore, Jacob was born in 2,006 B.C., and Abraham was born in 2,166 B.C. Based on the genealogy in Genesis 5 to 11, Adam's Fall occurred about 4,114 B.C. (Gen. 5:32, 7:11, 11:10). For reference, Noah begot Shem after the age of 500 (Gen. 5:32). Shem reached 100 years of age two years after the Flood, which is the year 602 B.C. (Gen. 11:10). Therefore, Noah begot Shem at the age of 502.

Temple construction	B.C. 966	Name	Age	Period	Name	Age	Period
		Adam	130	130	Shem	100	1,658
Exodus	480	Seth	105	235	Arphaxad	35	1,693
Exodus	BC 1,446	Enosh	90	325	Shelah	30	1,723
Abram	100	Cainan	70	395	Eber	34	1,757
Isaac	60	Mahalalel	65	460	Peleg	30	1,787
Jacob Immigration	130	Jared	162	622	Reu	32	1,819
		Enoch	65	687	Serug	30	1,849
Life in Egypt	430	Methuselah	187	874	Nahor	29	1,878
Abram born	B.C. 2,166	Lamech	182	1,056	Terah	70	1,948
		Noah	502	1,658	Abram		4,114

Question 11 What is the Seed of the Woman Covenant (Messiah Covenant)?

Gen. 3:15   And I will put enmity between you and the woman, and between your offspring and hers; he will crush your head, and you will strike his heel."

To redeem fallen mankind doomed to destruction, God made the covenant to send the Seed of the woman (the Messiah) to destroy the serpent (Satan). As the first direct prophecy about Jesus Christ, this is known as the protoevangelium. By this, God's great redemptive plan began.

Gal. 4:4-5   4 But when the time had fully come, God sent his Son, born of a woman, born under law, 5 to redeem those under law, that we might receive the full rights of sons.

About 4,000 years later, Jesus came and fulfilled this covenant by His victory on the cross (Col. 2:15). God's history of redemption is the process of fulfilling His covenants, and at the center of it is the Messiah.

Question 12 Why did Noah's Flood occur?

Gen. 6:5-7   5 The LORD saw how great man's wickedness on the earth had become, and that every inclination of the thoughts of his heart was only evil all the time. 6 The LORD was grieved that he had made man on the earth, and his heart was filled with pain. 7 So the LORD said, "I will wipe mankind, whom I have created, from the face of the earth – men and animals, and creatures that move along the ground, and birds of the air – for I am grieved that I have made them."

God, Who seeks Godly offspring (Mal. 2:15), judged the world full of sin with a great deluge for 40 days and nights. Noah, a righteous man in his generation, received God's grace, built the ark in obedience to Him, and safely evacuated his family and animals whose seeds must be preserved.

Question 13 Why did God establish Noah's Covenant, and for whom was it given?

Gen. 9:11   I establish my covenant with you: Never again will all life be cut off by the waters of a flood; never again will there be a flood to destroy the earth."

Gen. 9:16   Whenever the rainbow appears in the clouds, I will see it and remember the everlasting covenant between God and all living creatures of every kind on the earth."

After judging the world full of sin with water, God gave the same blessing as in Genesis 1:28, "Be fruitful and increase in number and fill the earth," to Noah's family who survived the great flood (Gen. 9:1). Then God gave the covenant of preservation (Rainbow Covenant) that there will never be a flood to destroy the whole earth again. Through Noah's declared blessing, "Blessed be the LORD, the God of Shem!" (Gen. 9:26), Jesus would later come through the line of Shem. For this reason, all God's revelations were given through the tribe of Shem (the Hebrews, the Jews). The genealogy of Shem leads to

Abraham.

Question 14 What kinds of offspring appear from the three sons of Noah?

Gen. 10:1   This is the account of Shem, Ham and Japheth, Noah's sons, who themselves had sons after the flood.

Gen. 10:32   These are the clans of Noah's sons, according to their lines of descent, within their nations. From these the nations spread out over the earth after the flood.

Genesis 10 lists 70 tribes that descended from Noah's offspring, which are the 14 tribes of Japheth, the 30 tribes of Ham, and the 26 tribes of Shem. These original 70 tribes scattered all over the world now form more than 260 nations and 24,000 tribes.

Question 15 Who is Nimrod?

Gen. 10:8-9   8 Cush was the father of Nimrod, who became a mighty warrior on the earth. 9 He was a mighty hunter before the LORD; that is why it is said, "Like Nimrod, a mighty hunter before the LORD."

Nimrod was a tyrant with strong belligerence, who built a great empire for the first time in history. He was the founder of the ancient Babylonian Empire and the one who constructed the city of Nineveh. Nimrod started a new system of religion. He hunted those who refused to accept his divinity and absolute authority as a tyrant and who instead worshiped the Creator God. He fully controlled all the people on the earth with his own religious system. He was the one who planned and instigated the construction of the Tower of Babel in defiance of God. Also, he was the type of antichrist who will appear at the end of history.

Question 16 Why was it wrong to build the Tower of Babel?

Gen. 11:3-4   3 They said to each other, "Come, let's make bricks and bake them thoroughly." They used brick instead of stone, and tar for mortar. 4 Then they said, "Come, let us build ourselves a city, with a tower that reaches to the heavens, so that we may make a name for ourselves and not be scattered over the face of the whole earth."

Gen. 11:7-8   7 Come, let us go down and confuse their language so they will not understand each other." 8 So the LORD scattered them from there over all the earth, and they stopped building the city.

To build a city with a tower was an act of rebellion against God because it was constructing a temple for idols. By confusing their language, God scattered mankind all over the face of the earth. Those who were scattered all over the earth formed their own communities and developed their Babylonian culture. However, God planned to call Abram, who was living in the Babylonian culture, out of it and make from him God's people to save the world.

Question 17 What did God promise through the Abrahamic Covenant?

Gen. 12:1-3   1 The LORD had said to Abram, "Leave your country, your people and your father's household and go to the land I will show you. 2 "I will make you into a great nation, and I will bless you; I will make your name great, and you will be a blessing. 3 I will bless those who bless you, and whoever curses you I will curse; and all peoples on earth will be blessed through you."

Gen. 17:7   I will establish my covenant as an everlasting covenant between me and you and your descendants after you for the generations to come, to be your God and the God of your descendants after you.

The three elements of the Abrahamic Covenant are the offspring, the land, and the blessing. As a result of the Abrahamic Covenant, all tribes on the earth will receive God's blessing. This covenant constitutes the very foundation and the backbone of God's history of world redemption. The blessing in this covenant was to be realized by establishing the nation of Israel through Abraham, bringing them into the land of Canaan, settling them down as a nation in the land, and then calling them into the role of a priestly nation to bring all other nations to God. The covenant also includes God's promised blessing to bless those who bless Israel and to curse those who curse Israel. The Abrahamic Covenant is an everlasting and unconditional covenant unilaterally made by God and thus will surely be fulfilled by His unchanging faithfulness.

Question 18 Is Ishmael included in the line of the Abrahamic Covenant?

Gen. 26:3-4   3 Stay in this land for a while, and I will be with you and will bless you. For to you and your descendants I will give all these lands and will confirm the oath I swore to your father Abraham. 4 I will make your descendants as numerous as the stars in the sky and will give them all these lands, and through your offspring all nations on earth will be blessed,

Gen. 28:13-14   13 There above it stood the LORD, and he said: "I am the LORD, the God of your father Abraham and the God of Isaac. I will give you and your descendants the land on which you are lying.

14 Your descendants will be like the dust of the earth, and you will spread out to the west and to the east, to the north and to the south. All peoples on earth will be blessed through you and your offspring.

God reveals Himself as the God of Abraham, Isaac, and Jacob. Being the son of Abraham, Ishmael received blessing as well (Gen. 16:10), but he was excluded from the line of the Abrahamic Covenant. The line of the Abrahamic Covenant continued through Isaac, Jacob, and Jacob's twelve sons and continues through the twelve tribes of Israel.

Question 19 What evidence is there that Israel is a blessing to all mankind?

Rom. 3:1-2   1 What advantage, then, is there in being a Jew, or what value is there in circumcision? 2 Much in every way! First of all, they have been entrusted with the very words of God.

John 4:22   You Samaritans worship what you do not know; we worship what we do know, for salvation is from the Jews.

Rom. 9:4-5   4 the people of Israel. Theirs is the adoption as sons; theirs the divine glory, the covenants, the receiving of the law, the temple worship and the promises. 5 Theirs are the patriarchs, and from them is traced the human ancestry of Christ, who is God over all, forever praised! Amen.

God called the people of Israel "my firstborn son" (Exod. 4:22).
By dwelling among them, God made Israel excel as a glorious
people. To bestow the history of world redemption, God gave
Israel covenants and promises. Israel was granted precious laws
that no other nation in the world had ever had. They received
the privilege of serving God with worship not made by man but
by God's commandment. All the heroes of the faith were their
ancestors, and, by coming as a Jew, Christ became the greatest
blessing to all mankind.

In fact, the Jews contributed countless inventions, are 25% of
the winners of the Nobel Prize, are 20% of the faculties at the
top universities in the U.S., are one third of the millionaires in
the U.S., are 40% of the richest 40 people in the U.S., and are
40% of the partners in leading law firms in New York City and
Washington D.C. They are living as leaders in society.

Question 20 When was the Covenant of the Land of Israel (Canaan) given in concrete form, and when was it fulfilled?

Gen. 15:13-17   13 Then the LORD said to him, "Know for certain that
your descendants will be strangers in a country not their own, and
they will be enslaved and mistreated four hundred years. 14 But I will

punish the nation they serve as slaves, and afterward they will come out with great possessions. 15 You, however, will go to your fathers in peace and be buried at a good old age. 16 In the fourth generation your descendants will come back here, for the sin of the Amorites has not yet reached its full measure." 17 When the sun had set and darkness had fallen, a smoking firepot with a blazing torch appeared and passed between the pieces.

Gen. 15:18-21   18 On that day the LORD made a covenant with Abram and said, "To your descendants I give this land, from the river of Egypt to the great river, the Euphrates – 19 the land of the Kenites, Kenizzites, Kadmonites, 20 Hittites, Perizzites, Rephaites, 21 Amorites, Canaanites, Girgashites and Jebusites."

To seal a covenant in the ancient Middle East, the parties walked between the split pieces of dead animals they killed. Such a covenant was to be followed at the risk of one's own life. Utilizing this ancient custom of the time, God made a firm covenant with Abraham by passing between the dead animals by Himself, alone. In Genesis 16, Abraham begot Ishmael in 2,080 B.C. at the age of 86. Since Israel came out of Egypt about 1,446 B.C. and entered the land of Canaan about 1,406 B.C., God spoke about the entrance into Canaan accurately about 674 years prior and fulfilled His promise when the time was full.

The land promised to Abraham and his descendants includes the whole area ranging from the river of Egypt in the south to the Sinai Peninsula and a broad area including Lebanon and Syria. The Gaza Strip and the West Bank today are also included in it. The Covenant of the Promised Land is an unconditional and everlasting covenant that God gave to Israel.

Question 21 Who is responsible for fulfilling the Covenant of the Land of Israel (Canaan)?

1 Chron. 16:16-18   16 the covenant he made with Abraham, the oath he swore to Isaac. 17 He confirmed it to Jacob as a decree, to Israel as an everlasting covenant: 18 "To you I will give the land of Canaan as the portion you will inherit."

Jer. 32:37   I will surely gather them from all the lands where I banish them in my furious anger and great wrath; I will bring them back to this place and let them live in safety.

Jer. 32:41   I will rejoice in doing them good and will assuredly plant them in this land with all my heart and soul.

God will return the people of Israel to the Promised Land from all the nations and let them live there safely. Since the Covenant of the Land of Israel (Canaan) is an everlasting covenant, God will plant Israel in this land and guard them so that they will never be uprooted from it again (Amos 9:15).

Presently, we are witnessing the fulfillment of this covenant in our generation. However, the unfortunate reality is that there are still so many Christians who do not agree with the fact that God is now recovering His sovereignty over the land, even though they claim that they believe the Bible is the truthful and infallible Word of God and fully agree that Adam's descendants become saved from sin.

Question 22 What is the Mosaic Covenant (Mt. Sinai Covenant), and how is it different from the Abrahamic Covenant?

Exod. 19:5-6   5 Now if you obey me fully and keep my covenant, then out of all nations you will be my treasured possession. Although the whole earth is mine, 6 you will be for me a kingdom of priests and a holy nation.' These are the words you are to speak to the Israelites."

The Mosaic Covenant was a covenant made with blood between God and the nation of Israel at Mt. Sinai. Through the rite of the covenant, the LORD God became the God of Israel, and Israel became God's covenantal people. To become a kingdom of priests means that Israel was called to become a nation that helps people draw closer to God and enjoy the truth, love, justice, grace, protection, and blessings of God. God attached the condition: "if you obey me fully and keep my covenant." The law given to Israel shows what that condition entails. God gave Moses the law to govern the relationship of the children of Israel to their God in terms of their ethical life (Exod. 19-20), social life (Exod. 21-23), and religious life (Exod. 24-31). If they obeyed, they would receive blessings, but, if they disobeyed, they would receive punishments. Although the Abrahamic Covenant was an unconditional, unilateral covenant, the Mosaic Covenant was a conditional covenant.

Question 23 What is the essence of the Mosaic Covenant?

Jer. 11:4   the terms I commanded your forefathers when I brought them out of Egypt, out of the iron-smelting furnace.' I said, 'Obey me and do everything I command you, and you will be my people, and I will be your God.

The essence of the Mosaic Covenant is that God would do His own work as Israel's God, and Israel should live as the people of God. This is the biggest grace and blessing given to Israel after the Exodus. The essence and goal of the Mosaic Covenant is that God is taking the people of Israel to be His own people (Jer. 31:33; Ezek. 36:28).

Question 24 What is the content of the Davidic Covenant?

2 Sam. 7:12-13 12 When your days are over and you rest with your fathers, I will raise up your offspring to succeed you, who will come from your own body, and I will establish his kingdom. 13 He is the one who will build a house for my Name, and I will establish the throne of his kingdom forever.

2 Sam. 7:16   Your house and your kingdom will endure forever before me; your throne will be established forever.'"

Matt. 1:1   A record of the genealogy of Jesus Christ the son of David, the son of Abraham:

God gave a covenant to David through His prophet Nathan. The content of the Davidic Covenant is that God will let Israel escape all its enemies and rest, that He will establish the throne of David forever through an offspring that comes from David, and that He will have the offspring build a house for the name of the LORD.

Since Jesus, the Son of God and the offspring of David, will fulfill the covenant, the Davidic Covenant is an unconditional covenant. By that, Jesus will establish His Kingdom, receive the throne of King David, and reign forever.

Question 25 Four hundred years after David's death, how does Ezekiel prophesy that David will become a king?

Ezek. 37:25   They will live in the land I gave to my servant Jacob, the land where your fathers lived. They and their children and their children's children will live there forever, and David my servant will be their prince forever.

The true King David in substance is Jesus Christ, Who will achieve the eschatological fulfillment.

Luke 1:32-33   32 He will be great and will be called the Son of the Most High. The Lord God will give him the throne of his father David, 33 and he will reign over the house of Jacob forever; his kingdom will never end."

John 19:19   Pilate had a notice prepared and fastened to the cross. It read: JESUS OF NAZARETH, THE KING OF THE JEWS.

Rev. 19:16   On his robe and on his thigh he has this name written: KING OF KINGS AND LORD OF LORDS.

About 2,000 years after God gave the promise to Abraham and about 1,000 years after God gave the promise to David, God fulfilled His covenants through Jesus Christ. The Davidic Covenant will ultimately be fulfilled in the Messianic Kingdom

(Millennial Kingdom) that the Messiah, who will return as the King of kings, will establish in the future.

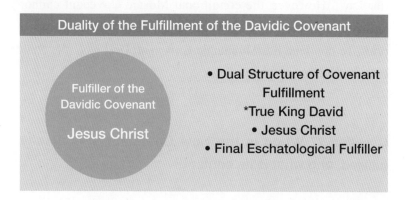

Question 26 What is the New Covenant given by God?

Jer. 31:31-32   31 "The time is coming," declares the LORD, "when I will make a new covenant with the house of Israel and with the house of Judah. 32 It will not be like the covenant I made with their forefathers when I took them by the hand to lead them out of Egypt, because they broke my covenant, though I was a husband to them," declares the LORD.

Gal. 3:17   What I mean is this: The law, introduced 430 years later, does not set aside the covenant previously established by God and thus do away with the promise.

The New Covenant contrasts with the Old Covenant, the Mosaic Covenant. Israel failed to keep the Mosaic Covenant (the Law). However, the conditional Mosaic Covenant cannot nullify the unconditional Abrahamic Covenant given 430 years prior. To continue the Abrahamic Covenant, God gave the New Covenant to the people of Israel.

Question 27 When is the New Covenant specifically fulfilled, and what is its content?

Jer. 31:33 "This is the covenant I will make with the house of Israel after that time," declares the LORD. "I will put my law in their minds and write it on their hearts. I will be their God, and they will be my people.

Ezek. 36:26-28 26 I will give you a new heart and put a new spirit in you; I will remove from you your heart of stone and give you a heart of flesh. 27 And I will put my Spirit in you and move you to follow my decrees and be careful to keep my laws. 28 You will live in the land I gave your forefathers; you will be my people, and I will be your God.

The internalization of the Law (Torah), promised in the New Covenant, is effectuated by the blood of Jesus shed on the cross (Luke 22:20) and realized through the descent of the Holy Spirit. The Law and the Old Covenant cause people to recognize and acknowledge their sinfulness, but the New Covenant creates righteousness in them. Fulfilling the Law is enabled by the power of the Holy Spirit and is the fruit of a life that follows the Holy Spirit.

Jer. 31:34   No longer will a man teach his neighbor, or a man his brother, saying, 'Know the LORD,' because they will all know me, from the least of them to the greatest," declares the LORD. "For I will forgive their wickedness and will remember their sins no more."

The New Covenant's fulfillment is when the full numbers of the Gentiles are reached and so all Israel is saved (Rom. 11:25-27). The fullness of the New Covenant will be experienced in the Messianic Kingdom (Millennial Kingdom) where everyone, from the least to the greatest, will know God.

Question 28 How are the Gentiles related to the New Covenant?

Luke 22:20   In the same way, after the supper he took the cup, saying, "This cup is the new covenant in my blood, which is poured out for you.

1 Cor. 11:25   In the same way, after supper he took the cup, saying, "This cup is the new covenant in my blood; do this, whenever you

drink it, in remembrance of me."

Gal. 3:13-14   13 **Christ** redeemed us **from** the curse of the law **by becoming a curse for us, for it is written: "Cursed is everyone who is hung on a tree."** 14 **He redeemed us in order that** the blessing given to Abraham **might come to** the Gentiles **through Christ Jesus, so that by faith we might receive** the promise of the Spirit.

Gal. 3:29   **If you belong to Christ, then you are** Abraham's seed, **and heirs according to the promise.**

2 Cor. 3:6   **He has made us competent as** ministers of a new covenant – **not of the letter but of the Spirit; for the letter kills, but the Spirit gives life.**

Acts 10:44-45   44 **While Peter was still speaking these words, the Holy Spirit came on all who heard the message.** 45 **The circumcised believers who had come with Peter were astonished that the gift of** the Holy Spirit had been poured out even on Gentiles.

The New Covenant was originally promised to Israel (Jer. 31:31). However, Gentiles were grafted into Israel by faith in Christ (Rom. 11). As spiritual descendants of Abraham, Gentiles receive the blessings of the New Covenant and are used as servants of the New Covenant. (Gal. 3:13-14; 2 Cor. 3:6). This truth was demonstrated by the salvation of Cornelius' household in the Book of Acts and confirmed by the outpouring of the Holy Spirit upon the Gentiles.

Question 30 Why is Ezekiel 16 called the Jerusalem chapter?

In Ezekiel 16, God and Jerusalem's relationship is portrayed as a husband and wife's relationship. Jerusalem is accused of being an abominable harlot who abandoned her tremendously gracious husband out of her own greed and lust. As its title, "Jerusalem as an Adulterous Wife," indicates, Ezekiel 16 is Jerusalem's chapter. The three sections of the chapter are: Jerusalem's past and present (Ezek. 16:1-22); the harlotry of Jerusalem and its consequence (Ezek. 16:23-43); and sin and God's grace (Ezek. 16:44-63).

Question 31 What is the Jerusalem Covenant?

Ezek. 16:59-60 59 " 'This is what the Sovereign LORD says: I will deal with you as you deserve, because you have despised my oath by breaking the covenant. 60 Yet I will remember the covenant I made with you in the days of your youth, and I will establish an everlasting covenant with you.

Ezek. 16:62-63   62 So I will establish my covenant with you, and you will know that I am the LORD. 63 Then, when I make atonement for you for all you have done, you will remember and be ashamed and never again open your mouth because of your humiliation, declares the Sovereign LORD.' "

The covenant Israel broke is the Mosaic Covenant, the covenant God made with Israel at its youth is the Abrahamic Covenant, and the everlasting covenant is the New Covenant. However, since Ezekiel 16 is Jerusalem's chapter, it is not logical to assume that the covenant in the conclusion is the New Covenant. If it was truly the New Covenant, it would not make Israel ashamed and never again open its mouth (Ezek. 16:63). When the Jerusalem Covenant is fulfilled, there will be an amazing and great occurrence that causes Israel to be speechless.

Isa. 24:23   The moon will be abashed, the sun ashamed; for the LORD Almighty will reign on Mount Zion and in Jerusalem, and before its elders, gloriously.

When God reigns in Jerusalem, even the sun will be ashamed by that amazing occurrence. Jerusalem, a detestable city deserving destruction due to its countless sins, will be forgiven, and the tremendous blessing of God's reign there will astonish His people to speechlessness. The Jerusalem Covenant is an everlasting covenant that God will reestablish after Israel's eschatological repentance, reawakening, and salvation (Ezek. 16:59-60). From the Abrahamic Covenant to the Jerusalem Covenant, all God's covenants will be integrated and fulfilled in the Messianic Kingdom with Jerusalem at its center. This is the covenant that will be fully realized in the Messianic Kingdom where Jerusalem is the capital, in the New Heaven and New Earth, and in the New Jerusalem (Isa. 65:17-18). When this covenant is fulfilled, Jerusalem will be recreated into the city of God and the city of joy where God dwells with His own people forever.

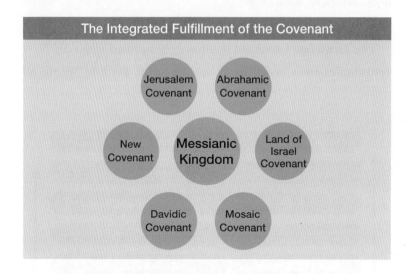

The Integrated Fulfillment of the Covenant

Jerusalem Covenant

Abrahamic Covenant

New Covenant

Messianic Kingdom

Land of Israel Covenant

Davidic Covenant

Mosaic Covenant

Question 32 When is the Jerusalem Covenant ultimately completed?

Rev. 21:1-2   1 Then I saw a new heaven and a new earth, for the first heaven and the first earth had passed away, and there was no longer any sea. 2 I saw the Holy City, the new Jerusalem, coming down out of heaven from God, prepared as a bride beautifully dressed for her husband.

Eph. 1:10   to be put into effect when the times will have reached their fulfillment – to bring all things in heaven and on earth together under one head, even Christ.

The Jerusalem Covenant is ultimately fulfilled when the New Jerusalem comes down from heaven to the earth to "bring all

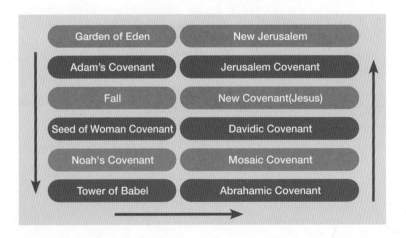

things in heaven and on earth together" in Christ (Eph. 1:10).

Conclusion

God's strategy to achieve His vision is to first give His covenants and then accomplish His vision through fulfilling them. Satan's strategy is to make people ignorant of God's covenants and to hamper the covenants' fulfillment. In the future, we will witness the integrated fulfillment of all the covenants – the Abrahamic Covenant, the Land of Israel (Canaan) Covenant, the Mosaic (Mt. Sinai) Covenant, the Davidic. Covenant, the New Covenant, and the Jerusalem Covenant – in the Messianic (Millennial) Kingdom. The Jerusalem Covenant will be fulfilled by the descent of the New Jerusalem from heaven to the earth. Let us understand God's covenants, and, as we look clearly forward to the beautiful and glorious future, let us fulfill our calling and win the victory with passionate hearts.

Chapter 3

God's City

Introduction

Jerusalem, as the place of the most serious conflict and controversy today, receives the unceasing focus of the world's mass media communications. It is the place where the Son of God had to die for the redemption and restoration of mankind, and where He will return. The reestablishment of the modern state of Israel is also a part of the process of restoring Jerusalem. Only with the restoration of its capital can God's Kingdom be truly restored. God has placed Jerusalem geographically at the center of the earth (Omphalos) and made it the spiritual center of the world. Let us understand God's will and heart for Jerusalem and set our faith afire.

Question 1 Where is the place of the most serious conflict and controversy in international politics?

Zech. 12:2   "I am going to make Jerusalem a cup that sends all the surrounding peoples reeling. ...

Due to an excessive obsession with destroying Israel, nations will become psychologically inflamed and reckless, lose sound judgment, and stumble. Many nations in the Middle East are already drunk with hostility against Israel. Biblical prophecy is being fulfilled.

- UN: Israel's decision of Jerusalem as its capital cannot be accepted.
- Pope: Jerusalem should be internationalized as the holy place for all three major religions (Judaism, Christianity, Islam).
- Obama: The border should return to what it was before the Six-Day War.
- Islamic nations: Israel has no right to exist.
- Islamic Jihad: Israel's destruction is the goal (Hamas/Hezbollah/Boko Haram/IS).
- Palestine: All the land of ancient Jerusalem should be the capital of the Palestinian state.
- Secular Humanism: Israel is an illegitimate nation, which bullies the weak as a conqueror.

- Trump: Based on effective control and historical grounds, Jerusalem is Israel's capital. Pronounced that he will move the U.S. Embassy to Jerusalem and did.

All the powers that oppose God will attack Jerusalem. People seem to have forgotten that throughout history Jerusalem was largely unimportant to the Arab and Muslim world. Jerusalem has never been a capital of any Arab nation. Only after the Jewish people began to return to Israel did a charlatan-like zeal for Jerusalem spread across the Muslim world. Although Jerusalem had been under the jurisdiction of the Ottoman Empire (1517-1917) for 400 years, they left it in total desolation during that time.

Question 2 Who are the Palestinians?

Gen. 10:14   Pathrusites, Casluhites (from whom the Philistines came) and Caphtorites.

The Philistines came from the Casluhites, the offspring of Mizraim who was one of Ham's sons (Gen. 10:6, 10:13-14). In A.D. 135, the Roman Emperor Hadrian changed the name of the land of Israel (Matt. 2:20) to Palestine (the Latin for Philistines) to quell Simon Bar Kokhba's independence movement and cut off the root of the Jewish nation. The Palestinians today are not the descendants of the Philistines but are Arabs. Historically, there was never an independent Arab nation that ever existed in the region. When the Jewish people were in exile, the Arabs immigrated to the land. The Middle East issue has gone beyond territorial disputes and turned into a religious war.

Question 3 Was the establishment of the modern state of Israel legitimate?

Years	Historical Events
1864	Jews are the majority in Jerusalem according to official documents
1897	Zionist Parliament held in Basel, Switzerland, led by Theodor Herzl
1917	Balfour Declaration promises to establish the Jewish state
1920	San Remo Accords promise to create the Jewish residential state (Israel's Magna Carta)
1922	League of Nations delegates authority to build the Jewish state to Britain
1924	Anglo-American treaty in which the U.S. consents to the administration
1939	6 million Jews murdered during the Holocaust in 1939-1945
1947	Passed the U.N. Partition Plan (33 in favor, 10 abstaining, 13 against)
1948	Israel's independence followed by the 1st Middle East War (May 1948-March 1949)
1967	Six-Day War (June 5-10) and the Restoration of Jerusalem

Nov 29, 1947

UN partition
plan passed

For 33
Against 13
Abstention 10

Declaration of Israel's Independence (May 14, 1948)

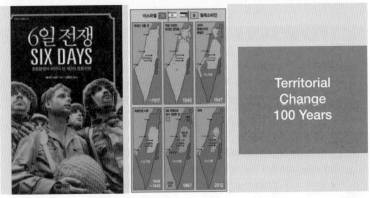

Territorial Change 100 Years

Although the establishment of the modern state of Israel was legitimate under international law, the surrounding nations and Palestinian organizations never acknowledged Israel since Israel's independence in 1948 to this day and have been attacking Israel with war and acts of terror.

After the establishment of the modern state of Israel, over 700,000 Arabs, who fled during Israel's War of Independence, never returned. A similar number of Jews were evicted from Arab nations where they had been living for thousands of years. The Arab nations have been neglecting those Arab refugees for over 70 years. In contrast, Israel accepted all Jewish refugees and granted citizenship to those Arabs who did not evacuate. No other nation is so surrounded by enemies, regularly threatened by terrorism, and constantly suffering from national security threats as Israel. The Jewish people have the right to have their own country as well. However, today, anti-Semitism has evolved to urge the destruction of Israel through various means such as boycotting all Israeli products, withdrawing all investments from Israeli companies, and sanctioning people or organizations related to Israel. This is called the BDS (Boycott, Divestment and Sanctions) movement.

Question 4 What does the Bible say about Jerusalem?

Jerusalem (יְרוּשָׁלַיִם, Yerushalayim, a dual form referring to Jerusalem in Heaven and Earth) means the foundation of peace and is also known by various other names including the holy mountain, Zion, the city of Zion, the city of God, Salem, alien city, Jebus, and Ariel. The word "Jerusalem" appears in the Bible 766 times (628 times in the Old Testament, 138 times in the New Testament), and, if the word "Zion" is counted as well, it appears about 1,000 times. In contrast, the word "Jerusalem" is never mentioned in the Koran, not even once.

Question 5 Is Jerusalem the city of God's greatest interest?

Gen. 14:18   **Then** Melchizedek king of Salem **brought out bread and wine. He was priest of God Most High,**

Heb. 7:1-2   1 **This** Melchizedek was king of Salem **and** priest of God Most High. **He met Abraham returning from the defeat of the kings and blessed him,** 2 **and Abraham gave him a tenth of everything. First, his name means** "king of righteousness"; **then also,** "king of Salem" **means** "king of peace."

Heb. 7:3   **Without father or mother, without genealogy, without beginning of days or end of life, like the Son of God he remains a priest forever.**

Isa. 9:6-7   6 **For to us a child is born, to us a son is given, and the government will be on his shoulders. And he will be called Wonderful Counselor, Mighty God, Everlasting Father,** Prince of Peace. 7 **Of the increase of his government and peace there will be no end. He will** reign **on** David's throne **and** over his kingdom, **establishing and upholding it with** justice and righteousness **from that time on and forever.** The zeal of the LORD **Almighty will accomplish this.**

Salem (Jerusalem's name in its earliest days) is where Melchizedek ruled as king. In Genesis 14, Jerusalem was already revealed as the city of God's greatest interest to Abraham. Melchizedek was king of Salem as well as a priest (king-priest). In this respect, later revelations in the Bible view him as a type of Christ (Ps. 110:4; Heb. 7:17, 7:21).

Question 6 When did God reveal that Jerusalem is the land that He Himself prepared?

Gen. 22:14   So Abraham called that place The LORD Will Provide. And to this day it is said, "On the mountain of the LORD it will be provided."

Jehovah Jireh means "the LORD will provide." After Abraham built an altar on Mt. Moriah, he called that place Jehovah Jireh. This is because God prepared a ram as the substitute for Isaac. Nevertheless, the deeper significance is that this place is the very land that God Himself prepared for the Messiah's substitutive death, His resurrection, the Holy Spirit's descent, and the Second Advent; it is the capital of the Messianic Kingdom and the center of the whole universe.

Question 7 What does it mean that God chose Jerusalem to put His Name there?

Deut. 16:11   And rejoice before the LORD your God at the place he will choose as a dwelling for his Name – you, your sons and daughters, your menservants and maidservants, the Levites in your towns, and the aliens, the fatherless and the widows living among you. (See also: Deut. 12:5, 12:11, 12:21, 14:23-24, 16:2, 16:6, 26:2)

Deut. 12:14   Offer them only at the place the LORD will choose in one of your tribes, and there observe everything I command you.

2 Kings 21:7   ... "In this temple and in Jerusalem, which I have chosen out of all the tribes of Israel, I will put my Name forever.

In the Bible, the statement that God chose a place to put His Name appears 37 times. Where God places His Name is where God dwells. A name is the very existence of its bearer. Thus, where God has chosen to place His Name is where He has chosen for His Name to dwell. It is where God dwells and receives worship. From our viewpoint, it refers to a place of worship where God is present. Therefore, the place God has chosen to put His Name is the very place chosen for us to worship and serve God. For the sake of the holy Name of Israel's God, Yahweh, the Temple in Jerusalem was built (2 Chron. 6:7, 6:9-10, 6:20, 6:24, 6:33-34, 6:38).

Question 8 Where did God receive David's offering and respond by fire?

1 Chron. 21:25-26   25 So David paid Araunah six hundred shekels of gold for the site. 26 David built an altar to the LORD there and sacrificed burnt offerings and fellowship offerings. He called on the LORD, and the LORD answered him with fire from heaven on the altar of burnt offering.

David paid six hundred shekels in gold for the entire site of Mt. Moriah, including the threshing floor. He declined Araunah's offer of the free use of the threshing floor. He demonstrated his repentance and devotion to God by rightfully paying the price needed for the sacrifice. As a sign of His acceptance of David's offering, God sent down fire. David's actions provide an answer to today's international conflict over the ownership of the Temple Mount in Jerusalem.

Question 9 Why was the Holy Temple constructed at Mt. Moriah?

2 Chron. 3:1   Then Solomon began to build the temple of the LORD in Jerusalem on Mount Moriah, where the LORD had appeared to his father David. It was on the threshing floor of Araunah the Jebusite, the place provided by David. (See also: 2 Sam. 24:18)

Mount Moriah is where Abraham, in obedience to God, was going to sacrifice his only son Isaac whom he had at the age of 100. It is the place where God acknowledged Abraham's faith and the place where Abraham met God (Gen. 22). In addition, to stop God's fearful disaster upon Israel, King David built an altar on Araunah's threshing floor and sacrificed burnt offerings to God, thereby receiving God's answer and meeting Him there.

Question 10 Where is God's eternal dwelling place?

Ps. 132:13-14   13 For the LORD has chosen Zion, he has desired it for his dwelling: 14 "This is my resting place for ever and ever; here I will sit enthroned, for I have desired it –

1 Chron. 23:25   For David had said, "Since the LORD, the God of Israel, has granted rest to his people and has come to dwell in Jerusalem forever,

God chose Zion (Jerusalem) as His eternal dwelling place. As a result, the Israelites had the unique place of worship and, unlike the Canaanites, were able to preserve a pure faith for Jehovah. This one and only place of worship united the 12 tribes of Israel into a national community of one faith. This place will become the Messianic Kingdom's capital and the center of the whole universe.

Question 11 Where are God's eyes and heart always present?

1 Kings 9:3   The LORD said to him: "I have heard the prayer and plea you have made before me; I have consecrated this temple, which you have built, by putting my Name there forever. My eyes and my heart will always be there.

During the dedication prayer, Solomon asked God to keep His eyes upon the Jerusalem Temple day and night (1 Kings 8:29). God answered that not only His eyes but also His heart will always be at the Jerusalem Temple.

Question 12 What is the significance of where Jesus the Son of God died?

Luke 13:33   In any case, I must keep going today and tomorrow and the next day – for surely no prophet can die outside Jerusalem!

In Luke 13:33, Jesus stated that He would soon fulfill His calling for mankind's redemption through His death and resurrection in Jerusalem. This means that, in the same place where many prophets were murdered with much bloodshed, Jesus Himself would now die as well on the cross. The Son of

God Jesus came to the world to die specifically in Jerusalem. The deeper significance is that where Adam ate the fruit of the forbidden tree, and the curse came, is where Jesus was crucified upon a tree to bear the curse.

Question 13 To where will the Son of God Jesus return?

Acts 1:11 "Men of Galilee," they said, "why do you stand here looking into the sky? This same Jesus, who has been taken from you into heaven, will come back in the same way you have seen him go into heaven."

Zech. 14:4 On that day his feet will stand on the Mount of Olives, east of Jerusalem, and the Mount of Olives will be split in two from east to west, forming a great valley, with half of the mountain moving north and half moving south.

Jerusalem was where Jesus was sent to fulfill His mission. There, He debated with teachers of the law, cleansed the Temple, taught, and gave the greatest commandment (Matt. 22:37-40). It is where He spoke about the signs of His return (Matt. 24:14, 23:37-39). It is where Jesus was judged and killed to complete and fulfill His sacrifice. Jerusalem is where Jesus resurrected and ascended into heaven. It is where the Holy Spirit came, where the church was born, and, most of all, where the Lord will return (Zech. 14:4). All the important events in God's history of redemption have occurred and will occur in Jerusalem.

Question 14 Where is the center of the world (Omphalos)?

Jerusalem is the center of God's interest and plan. Not only spiritually but also physically, Jerusalem is located at the center of the world. According to the theory of continental drift, which is academically dominant today, all the continents on earth were originally a single piece of land.

Ezek. 38:12   …the people…living at the center of the land."

Here, "the land" means the earth (אֶרֶץ, erets). Israel is at the center of the earth, and Jerusalem is at the center of Israel. The Garden of Eden was likely at the center of the round earth. The place where mankind fell and was subjected to death by eating from the tree of the knowledge of good and evil at the center of the Garden was likely the center of the earth (Jerusalem). Where mankind fell, Jesus was crucified on a tree to atone for their sins. And there, He lived again and became the Tree of Life (Bread of Life). Whoever eats from this Tree of Life (Bread of Life) will receive eternal life (John 6:51). God chose one place (Jerusalem), one nation (Israel), and one man (Jesus). To reject this is, ultimately, to deny God's authority.

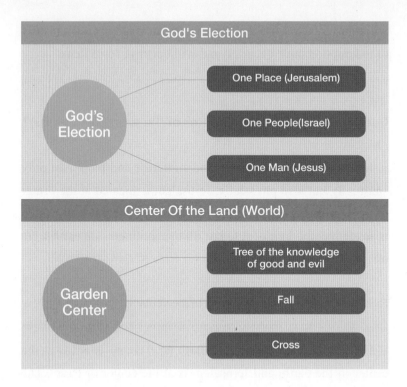

God's Election

God's Election
- One Place (Jerusalem)
- One People(Israel)
- One Man (Jesus)

Center Of the Land (World)

Garden Center
- Tree of the knowledge of good and evil
- Fall
- Cross

Question 15 **Historically, what is the strongest evidence that God is indeed fulfilling His promises?**

Amos 3:7 Surely the Sovereign LORD does nothing without revealing his plan to his servants the prophets.

Isa. 66:8 Who has ever heard of such a thing? Who has ever seen such things? Can a country be born in a day or a nation be brought forth in a moment? Yet no sooner is Zion in labor than she gives birth to her children.

Luke 21:24   They will fall by the sword and will be taken as prisoners to all the nations. Jerusalem will be trampled on by the Gentiles until the times of the Gentiles are fulfilled.

For about 1,900 years, the Israelites, who were scattered all over the world, suffered from discrimination, persecutions, forced exiles, and massacres. Israel, a nation once as dead as dry bones, survived and miraculously gained independence on May 14, 1948. In 1967, through the Six-Day War, Israel experienced God's miracles and recaptured Jerusalem. The restoration of Jerusalem is a sign that the times of the Gentiles are fulfilled. This is humanly inexplicable and can only be explained as the Almighty God's fulfillment of His promises. Having experienced God's prophecies being fulfilled through the reestablishment of Israel and the restoration of Jerusalem, we look forward to the assured completion of those prophecies yet to be fulfilled.

Question 16 What is the basis for the assertion that the Third Temple in Jerusalem is unnecessary?

1 Cor. 3:16   Don't you know that you yourselves are God's temple

and that God's Spirit lives in you?

Heb. 10:12   But when this priest had offered for all time one sacrifice for sins, he sat down at the right hand of God.

Heb. 10:18   And where these have been forgiven, there is no longer any sacrifice for sin.

Eph. 2:21-22   21 In him the whole building is joined together and rises to become a holy temple in the Lord. 22 And in him you too are being built together to become a dwelling in which God lives by his Spirit.

The Book of Hebrews states that the tabernacle, temple, sacrifices, and feasts in the Old Testament are all finished. Because the blood of Jesus atoned for all sins in the world once and for all, there is no need for sacrifices nor feasts anymore. Jesus' death and resurrection replaced the old covenant. Jesus and His people have become the true temple. Instead of any building or any one place, Jesus Himself is the temple and is omnipresent. Because Jesus said that "a time is coming when you will worship the Father neither on this mountain nor in Jerusalem" (John 4:21) and "worship the Father in spirit and truth" (John 4:23), some assert that the Third Temple is unnecessary. However, this view does not consider all related Scriptures (See Question 17).

Question 17 What is the basis for the assertion that the Third Temple in Jerusalem is necessary?

Dan. 9:27   He will confirm a covenant with many for one 'seven.' In the middle of the 'seven' he will put an end to sacrifice and offering. And on a wing [of the temple] he will set up an abomination that causes desolation, until the end that is decreed is poured out on him."

Matt. 24:15   "So when you see standing in the holy place 'the abomination that causes desolation,' spoken of through the prophet Daniel – let the reader understand –

2 Thess. 2:3-4   3 Don't let anyone deceive you in any way, for that day will not come until the rebellion occurs and the man of lawlessness is revealed, the man doomed to destruction. 4 He will oppose and will exalt himself over everything that is called God or is worshiped, so that he sets himself up in God's temple, proclaiming himself to be God.

Lev. 23:4   " 'These are the LORD's appointed feasts, the sacred assemblies you are to proclaim at their appointed times:

Daniel 9:27, which Jesus Himself quoted, states that the antichrist will make a peace treaty, forbid sacrifice and offering, and erect an idol of himself in the Jerusalem temple. According to 2 Thessalonians 2:3-4 as well, the antichrist will sit in God's temple, declaring himself to be God. This requires the Third Temple in Jerusalem to be built prior. Furthermore, in Leviticus 23:4, the "sacred assemblies" can be understood as the rehearsal for Jesus' redeeming work. Jesus died and resurrected during the spring feasts, and Jesus' second coming will align with the fall feasts. For those who have the faith to keep the fall feasts as a rehearsal for the Second Advent, the Third Temple is deeply vital.

Today, plans to construct the Jerusalem Temple are in progress, and the surrounding situations are changing favorably. The Sanhedrin organized a committee for establishing the temple and finished manufacturing all items for use in the temple including the Menorah. The blueprint has been made, and they are waiting for the days when construction can commence. They have been searching for the bloodline of the tribe of Levites through DNA Testing to find those who will perform the temple duties and are educating those who have been found.

Question 18 How will the future largest battle in Jerusalem proceed and end?

Zech. 14:1-2   1 A day of the LORD is coming when your plunder will be divided among you. 2 I will gather all the nations to Jerusalem to fight against it; the city will be captured, the houses ransacked, and the women raped. Half of the city will go into exile, but the rest of the people will not be taken from the city.

Zech. 14:4   On that day his feet will stand on the Mount of Olives, east of Jerusalem, and the Mount of Olives will be split in two from east to west, forming a great valley, with half of the mountain moving north and half moving south.

Rev. 19:11   I saw heaven standing open and there before me was a white horse, whose rider is called Faithful and True. With justice he judges and makes war.

Rev. 19:16   On his robe and on his thigh he has this name written: KING OF KINGS AND LORD OF LORDS.

Zech. 12:10   "And I will pour out on the house of David and the inhabitants of Jerusalem a spirit of grace and supplication. They will look on me, the one they have pierced, and they will mourn for him as one mourns for an only child, and grieve bitterly for him as one grieves for a firstborn son.

Rom. 11:26   And so all Israel will be saved, as it is written: "The deliverer will come from Zion; he will turn godlessness away from Jacob.

Jerusalem will become the stage for mankind's final catastrophic battle. The Bible foretells that in the last days there will be the Armageddon War in which all nations on earth, instigated by Satan, will attack Jerusalem. At that time, the Messiah will return to Jerusalem and save Israel from the crisis of national despair (Zech. 12-14; Rev. 19:11-21). Israel's national repentance and spiritual awakening will follow, and "all Israel will be saved." (Rom. 11:26). The nations that opposed Israel will be judged by Christ.

Question 19 Where will the Messianic Kingdom's capital city be located?

1 Kings 11:36   I will give one tribe to his son so that David my servant may always have a lamp before me in Jerusalem, the city where I chose to put my Name.

Matt. 5:35   or by the earth, for it is his footstool; or by Jerusalem, for it is the city of the Great King.

Ps. 147:2   The LORD builds up Jerusalem; he gathers the exiles of Israel.

Zech. 14:9   The LORD will be king over the whole earth. On that day there will be one LORD, and his name the only name.

Isa. 24:23   The moon will be abashed, the sun ashamed; for the LORD Almighty will reign on Mount Zion and in Jerusalem, and before its elders, gloriously.

The Messianic Kingdom's capital city is Jerusalem, which the Messiah Himself, the King of kings, called "the city of the Great King."

Question 20 Where is the center of worship in the Messianic Kingdom?

Zech. 14:16   Then the survivors from all the nations that have attacked Jerusalem will go up year after year to worship the King, the LORD Almighty, and to celebrate the Feast of Tabernacles.

Isa. 2:2-3   2 In the last days the mountain of the LORD's temple will be established as chief among the mountains; it will be raised above the hills, and all nations will stream to it. 3 Many peoples will come and say, "Come, let us go up to the mountain of the LORD, to the house of the God of Jacob. He will teach us his ways, so that we may walk in his paths." The law will go out from Zion, the word of the LORD from Jerusalem.

The remnant will come to Jerusalem every year to celebrate the Feast of Tabernacles, which is the feast to give thanks for the harvest and their new, everlasting life. The Messianic Kingdom will be ruled by the Word of God coming out of Jerusalem.

Isaiah saw the highest and most concrete vision of God's Kingdom being established all over the world and Jerusalem becoming its capital. The King of the Jews, the Messiah, will restore David's kingdom and will place His own throne in Jerusalem, which will become the center of the earth (Isa. 9:6-7, 2:1-3). The Son of David, the Messiah, will reign over not only the kingdom of the Jews but also the whole world with His justice and peace (Isa. 2:3-4, 11:1-7; Zech. 14:9). As a result of God's Kingdom being established in Israel, the Gentiles will come to honor and worship the King of Israel, the God of Israel (Isa. 52:8-9, 11:10).

Question 21 What will the Church, the Bride of Christ, be like in the Messianic Kingdom?

Rev. 20:6   Blessed and holy are those who have part in the first resurrection. The second death has no power over them, but they will be priests of God and of Christ and will reign with him for a thousand years.

2 Tim. 2:12   if we endure, we will also reign with him...

Israel is at the very center of the world, but, because they were thoroughly isolated, they were able to purely preserve the revelations they received from God. The Jewish believers who had been waiting for the Messiah dispersed and spread the Gospel. For the Gentiles and Jews born again in Jesus, the cross breaks down the wall that separated them, and the two become "one new man" as brothers and sisters who call God their Father. Together, believing Gentiles and Jews will become the Bride of Christ, one church. When the Messiah establishes His Kingdom of peace and prosperity (Isa. 2:4; Joel 3:17-18), the church will reign with Him as His Bride.

Question 22 Where will Jerusalem be in the New Heaven and New Earth?

Rev. 21:1 Then I saw a new heaven and a new earth, for the first heaven and the first earth had passed away, and there was no longer any sea.

Isa. 65:17-18 17 "Behold, I will create new heavens and a new earth. The former things will not be remembered, nor will they come to mind. 18 But be glad and rejoice forever in what I will create, for I will create Jerusalem to be a delight and its people a joy.

The New Heaven and New Earth is not from burning away the old world but rather from thoroughly renewing it while preserving continuity. On the renewed earth, Jerusalem will still exist as the city of joy. And it will still be the center of the earth.

Question 23 To where will the Holy City, the New Jerusalem, come down?

Rev. 21:2   I saw the Holy City, the new Jerusalem, coming down out of heaven from God, prepared as a bride beautifully dressed for

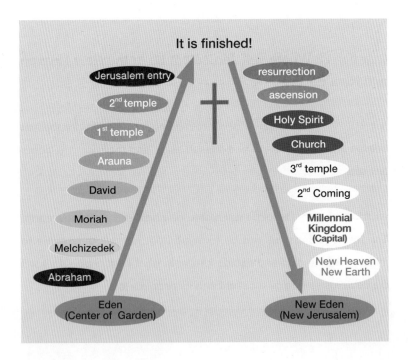

her husband.

Eph. 1:10   to be put into effect when the times will have reached their fulfillment – to bring all things in heaven and on earth together under one head, even Christ.

The Holy City, the New Jerusalem, which will look as pure and beautiful as a very precious jewel, will come down from God in heaven to the earthly Jerusalem to be unified with it and thereby complete the biggest picture in the Bible.

Conclusion

The LORD will return and establish a kingdom of peace and prosperity with Jerusalem as its capital (Isa. 2:4; Mic. 4:4-6; Joel 3:17-18; Zech. 14:14). And from Jerusalem, He will rule the whole world with His Word. God's people will enlighten and serve the world with the Lord. Just as God chose one man, Jesus, for the sake of salvation, He chose one place, Jerusalem. When we pray for the peace of Jerusalem and love Jerusalem, we are secure and prosper (Ps. 122:6), and, when we acknowledge God's sovereignty over Jerusalem, we can look forward with hope.

Chapter 4

God's Pupil
(Apple of God's Eye)

Introduction

God the Creator is the God of Abraham, Isaac, and Jacob, the God of Israel. God chose Israel as His firstborn, and He loves Israel as the apple (pupil) of His eye. To hate and persecute Israel is to hate God Who chose Israel as a channel of blessing for the world. Anti-Semitism has existed throughout Israel's history and is growing stronger every day. However, God, in accordance with His Word, never abandons Israel. Through numerous miraculous events, God has been restoring Israel and thereby revealing Himself as the faithful God Who keeps His covenants. We should understand God's will and heart to restore Israel and become not a stumbling stone but instead a stepping stone for the fulfillment of God's master plan.

Question 1 **What does God call Israel?**

Exod. 4:22   Then say to Pharaoh, 'This is what the LORD says: Israel is my firstborn son,

Zech. 2:8   For this is what the LORD Almighty says: "After he has honored me and has sent me against the nations that have plundered you – for whoever touches you touches the apple of his eye –

Gen. 12:3   I will bless those who bless you, and whoever curses you I will curse; and all peoples on earth will be blessed through you."

Exod. 19:6   you will be for me a kingdom of priests and a holy nation.' These are the words you are to speak to the Israelites."

Isa. 49:6   he says: "It is too small a thing for you to be my servant to restore the tribes of Jacob and bring back those of Israel I have kept. I will also make you a light for the Gentiles, that you may bring my salvation to the ends of the earth."

Jer. 3:14   "Return, faithless people," declares the LORD, "for I am your husband. I will choose you – one from a town and two from a clan – and bring you to Zion.

Mentioned more than 2,300 times in the Bible, Israel is cherished by God, and He calls Israel "My firstborn son."

A firstborn son has special privileges but also has weighty responsibilities. Just as we protect our eyes, God watches over and protects Israel as the apple of His eye (His Pupil). Israel has been called to become a light to the nations as well as a channel of God's blessing to all peoples on the earth. As a priestly nation, Israel was entrusted with God's words (Rom. 3:1-2) and was called to reveal God to the nations and to help them draw near to Him. A priestly nation serves as a mediator not for itself but for the relationships between God and the nations.

God calls Himself Israel's husband (Hosea 2:16, 2:19-20). Although Israel failed as God's beloved bride to keep the covenant due to disobedience, God as Israel's husband never forsakes her and restores the damaged relationship through the New Covenant (Jer. 31:31-33).

Question 2 What are the cause and consequences of the destruction of Jerusalem?

Matt. 23:37-38 37 "O Jerusalem, Jerusalem, you who kill the prophets and stone those sent to you, how often I have longed to gather your children together, as a hen gathers her chicks under her wings, but you were not willing. 38 Look, your house is left to you desolate.

Luke 21:22-24 22 For this is the time of punishment in fulfillment of all that has been written. 23 How dreadful it will be in those days for pregnant women and nursing mothers! There will be great distress in the land and wrath against this people. 24 They will fall by the sword and will be taken as prisoners to all the nations. Jerusalem will be trampled on by the Gentiles until the times of the Gentiles are fulfilled.

Jerusalem was destroyed because Israel, from its leaders to its lay people, was stained with evil acts. God sent many prophets to provide them warnings. However, they stubbornly did not listen. Thus, Jerusalem became the object of God's wrath.

Question 3 What was the cause of the Jewish people's suffering?

2 Chron. 7:19-20   19 "But if you turn away and forsake the decrees and commands I have given you and go off to serve other gods and worship them, 20 then I will uproot Israel from my land, which I have given them, and will reject this temple I have consecrated for my Name. I will make it a byword and an object of ridicule among all peoples.

Ezek. 39:23   And the nations will know that the people of Israel went into exile for their sin, because they were unfaithful to me. So I hid my face from them and handed them over to their enemies, and they all fell by the sword.

The Jewish people suffered due to their disobedience of God's commandments, their lack of faith in Him, and their betrayal against God through idolatries.

Deut. 29:3-4   3 With your own eyes you saw those great trials, those miraculous signs and great wonders. 4 But to this day the LORD has not given you a mind that understands or eyes that see or ears that hear.

God gave numerous great wonders and signs to the Israelites that He wanted them to understand. However, due to their hardened hearts, the Israelites neither saw nor heard nor understood God's will as revealed through those great wonders. However, the fundamental reason for the Israelites not seeing nor hearing nor understanding includes Almighty God not allowing them to do so. (Isa. 6:9-10; Matt. 13:11-17; Acts 28:23-28; Rom. 11:8).

Luke 21:24   They will fall by the sword and will be taken as prisoners to all the nations. Jerusalem will be trampled on by the Gentiles until the times of the Gentiles are fulfilled.

Rom. 11:25-26   25 I do not want you to be ignorant of this mystery, brothers, so that you may not be conceited: Israel has experienced a hardening in part until the full number of the Gentiles has come in. 26 And so all Israel will be saved, as it is written: "The deliverer will come from Zion; he will turn godlessness away from Jacob.

Since the salvation first promised to the Jews (Rom. 1:16) was rejected by them and was thus given to the Gentiles, "until the times of the Gentiles are fulfilled" refers to when the full number of saved Gentiles has been reached. Paul called this a mystery. God's mysterious plan is to redirect salvation to the Jews after "the full number of the Gentiles has come in" so that all Israel will be saved. For now, most Jews are in a spirit of stupor and are unable to recognize Who Jesus is. This can only be understood as God's providence. On the other hand, as discussed in answer to the next question, this is also due to Satan's strategy.

Question 4 What was Satan's strategy until God's Son Jesus' First Advent?

Exod. 1:22   Then Pharaoh gave this order to all his people: "Every boy that is born you must throw into the Nile, but let every girl live."

Esther 3:6   Yet having learned who Mordecai's people were, he scorned the idea of killing only Mordecai. Instead Haman looked for a way to destroy all Mordecai's people, the Jews, throughout the whole kingdom of Xerxes.

Matt. 2:16   When Herod realized that he had been outwitted by the Magi, he was furious, and he gave orders to kill all the boys in Bethlehem and its vicinity who were two years old and under, in accordance with the time he had learned from the Magi.

Due to God's promise that the Savior would be born as a Jew, Pharaoh and Haman tried to kill all the Jews, and Herod tried to kill all Jewish children under age two. These were Satan's attempts to obstruct the Savior's birth.

Question 5 Why are the Jews being persecuted continually and cruelly?

Rev. 20:2-3   2 He seized the dragon, that ancient serpent, who is the devil, or Satan, and bound him for a thousand years. 3 He threw him into the Abyss, and locked and sealed it over him, to keep him from deceiving the nations anymore until the thousand years were ended. After that, he must be set free for a short time.

Rev. 20:10   And the devil, who deceived them, was thrown into the lake of burning sulfur, where the beast and the false prophet had been thrown. They will be tormented day and night for ever and ever.

The Jews are envied for their identity as the chosen people, their exclusivity, and their excellence. Their monotheism and unique social and religious customs alienated them from the Gentiles, and, as a result, many nations hated them. They are also hated due to the erroneous belief that the Jews are permanently outside God's grace due to their sin of killing Jesus. However, the major culprit behind the terrible and persistent persecutions against the Jews is Satan because he knows that he will be imprisoned in the abyss and eventually cast into the lake of fire and sulfur forever when the Jewish Messiah Jesus returns.

Question 6 How does the Bible describe the sufferings that Israel would receive?

Deut. 28:64-67 64 Then the LORD will scatter you among all nations, from one end of the earth to the other. There you will worship other gods – gods of wood and stone, which neither you nor your fathers have known. 65 Among those nations you will find no repose, no resting place for the sole of your foot. 66 There the LORD will give you an anxious mind, eyes weary with longing, and a despairing heart. You will live in constant suspense, filled with dread both night and day, never sure of your life. 67 In the morning you will say, "If only it were evening!" and in the evening, "If only it were morning!" – because of the terror that will fill your hearts and the sights that your eyes will see.

God foretold that He would scatter the Israelites all over the world and that they would worship foreign idols made of wood and stone. Their eyes would become weary and their minds anxious. They would be afraid day and night and uncertain about their survival. Due to terror and fear, they would wish for time to pass faster. Even before the Israelites entered the Promised Land, God already spoke about their sufferings.

Question 7 What persecutions did the Diaspora Jews experience at the hands of the Gentile nations for the last two thousand years?

1) In A.D. 70, Jerusalem was conquered by Rome, and the Temple was burned to the ground. According to Josephus, 1.1 million Jewish pilgrims, who were keeping the Feast of the LORD in Jerusalem, were slaughtered by the Romans, and 97,000 Jews were taken into captivity.

2) During the final Jewish uprising led by Bar Kokhba in A.D. 132 to 135, about 580,000 Jews were killed, and, if those who died from starvation and disease are counted as well, more than a million Jews died. The survivors were sold into slavery across the Roman Empire, and Jerusalem was renamed Aelia Capitolina and reshaped into a Roman-styled city from which all Jews were barred.

3) In A.D. 313, Constantine officially approved Christianity,

abolishing all Jewish Feasts and Sabbaths, and replacing them with new Christian holidays, thereby laying down the foundation for cutting off all Jewish roots.

4) During the First Crusade (1096 to 1291), approximately 300,000 Jews lived in Jerusalem. Under the accusation of having killed Jesus, an estimated 299,000 Jews were murdered by the Crusaders. In one incident, Jews in Jerusalem were locked into a synagogue and burned to death, and those Jews who tried to escape were pushed back into the burning synagogue. About 1,000 Jewish survivors from Jerusalem were sold into slavery in Europe or sent to Egypt if ransom was paid.

5) The persecution of the Jews that started with the Crusades spread all over Europe. (In A.D. 1290, 16,000 Jews were forced out of England; in A.D. 1298, 10,000 Jews were killed over a period of 6 months in Austria, Bavaria, etc.)

6) In A.D. 1215, Pope Innocent III forced every Jews to wear a yellow star to distinguish them from Gentiles.

7) In A.D. 1348 to 1349, as the death toll during the Great Plague rose to around 25 to 35 million, drastically reducing the population of Europe, the Jews, a people who wash their hands well, were wrongly accused of poisoning wells and shamefully killed. In Strasburg, 900 Jews were burned alive.

8) During the Middle Ages in Europe, an Inquisition Court was in every city. Its purpose was to judge heresies, but it mainly targeted the Jews who were forced to convert to Christianity but secretly practiced Judaism. The most severe

inquisition was conducted in Spain. Many Jews were subjected to the confiscation of their property, forced baptism, terrorism, forced exile, etc. During the Spanish Inquisition (A.D. 1480), more than 300,000 Jews were executed by burning or similar methods.

9) The "Ghetto" was a separate street or area in a city to isolate the Jews. In the 14th to 15th centuries, the policy of forced segregation of the Jews was enforced across Europe.

10) In Russia and Eastern European countries, systematic persecutions, and attacks, called pogroms, reached a peak during the late 19th century to the early 20th century. In 1881, the Pogroms began in Russia due to the false accusation that Jews assassinated the Emperor. Despite many massacres perpetrated against the Jews in 167 villages in southern Russia, the police

stood by and allowed the pogroms. Due to the pogroms, about 1 million Jews fled into Western Europe, overwhelming the whole of Europe with poor, starving Jews. In addition, many Jews immigrated to America, seeking a new place of settlement.

11) From 1933 when Hitler was appointed chancellor of Germany to 1945 at the end of World War II, for 12 years and 4 months, 6 million Jews were murdered for the untenable policy of Aryanizing Europe. The Holocaust was perpetrated in three stages.

The first stage started in 1933 when Hitler, the son of a tax officer from Austria, seized power, and ended in 1939 when World War II began. The Nazis constantly persecuted the Jews as it supervised, interrupted, or attacked Jewish stores. Laws legalizing the persecution of the Jews, the Nuremberg Laws, were enacted. Consequently, 500,000 Jews living in Germany and 400,000 Jews living in Austria suffered damages.

The second stage was when Hitler swept through Europe (1939 to 1941) and built a number of concentration camps across Europe, including Dachau in Germany, Auschwitz in Poland, Treblinka in Poland, and more to massacre the Jews. All the Jews in Austria and Germany were moved by force to the Ghetto in Poland. The Nazis loaded the Jews into trains heading for the camps, lying to them that they will be given new residences in Eastern Europe, and, upon the Jews' arrivals at the camps, the Nazis sorted out the intellectuals and doctors, compelled the healthy into forced labor, and sent the weak directly to the gas chambers for slaughter.

The third stage began in 1941. During this period a great massacre called "the Final Solution" was perpetrated, killing 3 million Jews within a year in Poland alone. Prior to World War II, Poland was where most Jews were living in the world. During the third stage of the Holocaust from 1941 to 1945, 75% of the Jews in the Netherlands, and 90% of the Jews in the Three Baltic States were murdered. According to a document of the German secret police, the Gestapo, handed over to the War Criminal Tribunal in Nuremberg in October 1945, the number of Jews murdered during the Holocaust was approximately 6 million. Those Jewish victims include about 3 million adult men, about 2 million adult women, and more than 1,5 million children. They correspond to two thirds of the 9.5 million Jews who had been living in Europe at the time. Those 6 million Jews were murdered in the most inhumane, cruel method, and it is hard to find any suitable words to describe the tragedy. During the Holocaust, most churches and nations in the world stood by and even locked their doors to the Jewish refugees seeking to escape the Holocaust.

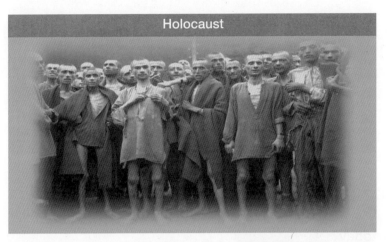

Holocaust

Corpses piled up on a truck

12) Today, a number of anti-Semitic events have been occurring globally in several regions in the world, including in France and in the United States.

Question 8 In what forms does anti-Semitism appear today?

Today, anti-Semitism wears diverse faces such as Humanistic anti-Semitism, Christian anti-Semitism, Muslim anti-Semitism, and Nazi anti-Semitism. Attacks on the Jewish people and Israel are underway in the U.N., the media, politics, the scientific world, and all other areas.

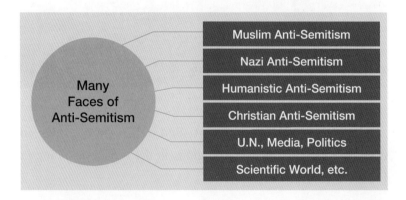

Question 9 What is Muslim anti-Semitism?

Muslims believe themselves to be the people of God who replaced the followers of Judaism and Christianity. The Prophet Mohamed promised that the whole world would serve Allah. Muslims argue that Jerusalem is Islam's third holy place and should be governed by them. Muslim fundamentalists believe that Israel should be wiped off the map and that all parts of Jerusalem should be under Muslim control. However, the Koran never mentions Jerusalem, not even once.

Question 10 What is the root of Christian anti-Semitism?

Christian anti-Semitism gave birth to Replacement Theology, which in turn strengthened Christian anti-Semitism. Replacement Theology argues that, although the early churches were established entirely by Jews, the covenant God made with Israel was revoked due to their disbelief. For that reason, Replacement Theology further states that the church acquired the qualification to replace Israel in receiving all the covenants. Replacement Theology considers the promise to restore Israel's land to instead mean the promise to bless the Christian church.

Some Gentiles, who express faith in a Jewish man Jesus Christ, condemn Israel as the nation that killed Jesus and raise their voice of anti-Semitism. They have been persecuting the

Jews through the Crusades, the Spanish Inquisition, and the Holocaust, which all took place in Christian nations. These persecutions alienated the Jews more and more from Jesus and the church. Within church history, many great men of God and outstanding theologians ironically took the lead in promoting anti-Semitism. Through their repetitive and erroneous anti-Semitic proclamations, the public was misled to believe and follow them. Anti-Semitism has been slaughtering the Jews with unimaginable cruelties and atrocities like the Holocaust. The next table summarizes the untenable arguments of Christian anti-Semites.

Arguments of Christian Anti-Semites	
Justin Martyr (100-165)	He stated that the covenant God made with the Jews is no longer valid and that the Gentiles replaced the Jews in God's redemption plan for mankind.
Ignatius (2nd c.)	He said that whoever celebrates a Jewish feast with the Jews or accepts its sign is an accomplice of those who killed the Lord and His disciples.
Tertullian (160-220)	As a renowned Christian writer who authored against the Jews, he accused the entire Jewish nation of killing Jesus.
Origen (185-253)	As an expert in philosophy and theology, he introduced the "allegorical" method of Bible interpretation, which was the hermeneutics of Greek philosophy, and he invented the concept of the church as the "true Israel of God" to replace the nation of Israel. He provided the grounds for anti-Semitism by applying verses about curses to Israel and verses about blessings to the church.
Eusebius (263-339)	As an ardent follower of Origen and the friend and counselor of Emperor Constantine, he influenced Constantine to enroot anti-Semitic ideas into Rome's national policies.

Constantine (274-337)	In A.D. 313, he officially approved Christianity. Believing that despising and discriminating against Jews is what Christians ought to do, he forced Jewish believers of Jesus to renounce all Jewish traditions such as circumcision, the Law, Feasts, rituals and customs.
Chrysostom (349-407)	He stated that hating the Jews is the duty of all Christians, that the Jews are possessed by demons and are like greedy pigs, and that God has always hated the Jews.
Jerome (345-420)	He said that the Jews do not have the ability to understand the Bible and that they should be severely persecuted until they confess true faith.
Augustine (354-430)	He stated that, although the Jews deserve to die, instead, they were destined to wander the earth under divine punishment as the witness to the victory of the church over the synagogue.
Luther (1483-1546)	In 1517, he began the Reformation in Germany. In 1543, he authored About the Jews and Their Lies, in which he urged the burning of synagogues, destruction of Jewish homes, confiscation of Jewish prayer books and Talmud, banning of rabbis' teachings, deprivation of travel rights for Jews, banning of usury, and imposition of forced labor upon Jews. Hitler inherited Luther's anti-Semitic arguments.

The Holocaust, which resulted in the deaths of 6 million Jews, reveals human cruelty. Even amid rampant anti-Semitism, God in His infinite love rebirthed Israel.

Question 11 What is anti-Semitism ultimately attacking?

Anti-Semitism is hatred against the Jews and against Israel, and ultimately it is tantamount to hating God. Anti-Semitism is an attack against God's character. The argument that God has rejected the Jewish people is against the very character and nature of God that He Himself has revealed. The loving, covenantal relationship between God and the Jewish people, Israel, is an everlasting one.

Question 12 Did God forsake Israel?

Jer. 31:35-37   35 This is what the LORD says, he who appoints the sun to shine by day, who decrees the moon and stars to shine by night, who stirs up the sea so that its waves roar – the LORD Almighty is his name: 36 "Only if these decrees vanish from my sight," declares the LORD, "will the descendants of Israel ever cease to be a nation before me." 37 This is what the LORD says: "Only if the heavens above can be measured and the foundations of the earth below be searched out will I reject all the descendants of Israel because of all they have done," declares the LORD.

Rom. 11:1   I ask then: Did God reject his people? By no means! I am an Israelite myself, a descendant of Abraham, from tho tribo of Benjamin.

Rom. 11:28-29 28 As far as the gospel is concerned, they are enemies on your account; but as far as election is concerned, they are loved on account of the patriarchs, 29 for God's gifts and his call are irrevocable.

If we still see the sun, moon, and the stars today, we know that Israel is still within God's plan. God has not forsaken His people, Israel. This is evident in the fact that there is still the remnant of Israel. The remnant (Isa. 10:21; Jer. 31:7; Ezek. 11:13; Joel 2:32) refers, first, to those who survived when the nation was destroyed, and, secondly, those believers who deeply trust God. Jesus' disciples and first believers were all Jewish and so was Paul. Although the Israelites appear to be God's enemy due to their rejection of the Gospel, as God's chosen people, they have been receiving God's special love as the descendants of Abraham, Isaac, and Jacob. God's love for Israel as His chosen people has not been abolished. It is why God is restoring them. Israel will experience national repentance in the future.

Question 13 How would it affect the church if God can forsake His everlasting covenant?

If God can abandon Israel despite His everlasting, unconditional covenant for them, He can also abandon the church. If the church believes that God can forsake the everlasting covenant that He made unilaterally and unconditionally, the church is directly destroying the foundation upon which it stands. Isn't the only hope for Christians the truth that God always and certainly keeps His promises? Christians who believe that God can forsake His everlasting covenant are thus digging their own graves.

Question 14 How should the church treat Israel and the Jewish people?

Matt. 25:40   "The King will reply, 'I tell you the truth, whatever you did for one of the least of these brothers of mine, you did for me.'

The phrase "one of the least of these brothers of mine" refers first to the Jewish people. To care for them is to love our Lord. God did not forsake Israel as He has said. The church must repent of the Replacement Theology it has adhered to for the last two thousand years and change it to Restoration Theology (Read the Appendix: Replacement Theology and Restoration Theology). We must understand the covenants God made with Israel. We must protect the Jews from all anti-Semitic attacks and stand by Israel. We must help Israel with acts of love.

Question 15 Who killed Jesus?

Matt. 27:25   All the people answered, "Let his blood be on us and on our children!"

John 10:18   No one takes it from me, but I lay it down of my own accord. I have authority to lay it down and authority to take it up again. This command I received from my Father."

Luke 23:34   Jesus said, "Father, forgive them, for they do not know what they are doing." And they divided up his clothes by casting lots.

Acts 4:27   Indeed Herod and Pontius Pilate met together with the Gentiles and the people of Israel in this city to conspire against your holy servant Jesus, whom you anointed.

Acts 2:23   This man was handed over to you by God's set purpose and foreknowledge; and you, with the help of wicked men, put him to death by nailing him to the cross.

Isa. 53:5   But he was pierced for our transgressions, he was crushed for our iniquities; the punishment that brought us peace was upon him, and by his wounds we are healed.

What likely happened at the time was that a few hundred Jews, stirred up by a few religious leaders, shouted out "Crucify Him" and "Let his blood be on us and on our children!" before Pilate. However, it was not because of their demand that Jesus was crucified. Jesus said that he was laying down His life of His own accord and prayed on the cross, "Father, forgive them, for they do not know what they are doing." In fact, those who nailed Jesus on the cross were Roman soldiers (the Gentiles). Furthermore, the truth is that it was our sins that crucified Jesus. At the cross, Jesus bore all our sins upon Himself for us.

"Israel's Restoration"

Question 16 **What is the basis for the restoration of Israel?**

Ps. 89:34   I will not violate my covenant or alter what my lips have uttered.

Ezek. 36:23   I will show the holiness of my great name, which has been profaned among the nations, the name you have profaned among them. Then the nations will know that I am the LORD, declares the Sovereign LORD, when I show myself holy through you before their eyes.

Jer. 31:10   "Hear the word of the LORD, O nations; proclaim it in distant coastlands: 'He who scattered Israel will gather them and will watch over his flock like a shepherd.'

Based on God's faithfulness in keeping His covenants and His omnipotence, He certainly restores Israel. For His holy Name, and for people of all nations to know the Holy One, God surely restores Israel as promised. The restoration of Israel is also a sign to the Gentiles to testify all over the world that God is gathering and protecting Israel.

Question 17 What is the significance of Israel's restoration in the Promised Land for us?

Gen. 17:8   The whole land of Canaan, where you are now an alien, I will give as an everlasting possession to you and your descendants after you; and I will be their God."

Ezek. 36:24   "For I will take you out of the nations; I will gather you from all the countries and bring you back into your own land.

Isa. 40:8   The grass withers and the flowers fall, but the word of our God stands forever."

The restoration of the land of Israel is the most practical and concrete evidence that God is faithful and keeps His covenants. Within God's covenants, God's promise regarding the land is the most important part to understand. Israel must possess the Promised Land. This is because there are Biblical prophecies involving Israel that must still be fulfilled in the Promised Land.

Question 18 From where do the Jewish people return to the Promised Land?

Isa. 43:5-6   5 Do not be afraid, for I am with you; I will bring your children from the east and gather you from the west. 6 I will say to the north, 'Give them up!' and to the south, 'Do not hold them back.' Bring my sons from afar and my daughters from the ends of the earth

Isa. 49:12   Surely these shall come from afar; Look! Those from the north and the west, And these from the land of Sinim (China)." (NKJV)

- East: Iraq, Syria, Iran, India, China, etc.
- West: Eastern Europe, Western Europe, British Commonwealth, North America, South America, etc.
- North: Various places in the former Soviet Union
- South: Yemen, Africa, etc.
- Afar/ends of the earth: Global return

Jer. 16:14-16   14 "However, the days are coming," declares the LORD, "when men will no longer say, 'As surely as the LORD lives, who brought the Israelites up out of Egypt,' 15 but they will say, 'As surely as the LORD lives, who brought the Israelites up out of the land of the north and out of all the countries where he had banished them.' For I will restore them to the land I gave their fathers. 16 "But now I will send for many fishermen," declares the LORD, "and they will catch them. After that I will send for many hunters, and they will hunt them down on every mountain and hill and from the crevices of the rocks.

The greatest event in Israel's history is the Exodus. Thus, the children of Israel vow to the living God of the Exodus. However, the Bible states that the children of Israel will instead vow to the living God who, more amazingly, brings them out of all the nations. God will lead the Israelites back to their land that God gave to their ancestors. For this purpose, God will first send many fishermen to them to deliver His Word. Those who do not obey His word or miss the chance to return will suffer great pain and bloodshed at the hands of persecutors, and thus they will either return to the land or be killed.

Question 19 What is the second most mentioned promise in the Old Testament, next to the most mentioned promise of the Messiah's First and Second Advents?

The promise to give Abraham and his descendants the land of Israel is revealed throughout the entire Bible. Aliyah (עֲלִיָּה), which literally means "to go up," is the return of the Jewish Diaspora to the land of the Jews, Eretz Israel. The Bible devotes about 700 verses to the Aliyah.

Question 20 What is the blessing that comes from the reestablishment of Israel and the restoration of Jerusalem?

Isa. 52:10   The LORD will lay bare his holy arm in the sight of all the nations, and all the ends of the earth will see the salvation of our God.

According to René Pache, "prophecy walks on the heights of history. It only projects its light on the peaks. The only full explanation of the prophecy will be given to us by its fulfillment."[14] Jesus' First Advent enabled us to understand many parts of the Bible and breathes life into many Bible verses. Israel's rebirth in 1948 and the restoration of Jerusalem in 1967 also enabled us to understand many Bible verses as they came to life. Rebirthing a nation and restoring Jerusalem after approximately 1,900 years of exile is humanly impossible. It must be one of the greatest miracles in history. Indeed, these events are the most powerful testimony that the Bible is the truth.

Question 21 Among God's promises and plans, what is the most practical and concrete one?

Gen. 12:7   The LORD appeared to Abram and said, "To your

offspring I will give this land." So he built an altar there to the LORD, who had appeared to him.

God's plans and promises are not always something vague or merely spiritual. He promised to give the practical, concrete, physical land of Canaan. Abraham called the land bridging Europe, Asia, and Africa, "Jehovah Jireh" (Gen. 22:14), and promised to prepare the land and give it to Abraham and his descendants. When the time became full, God placed Israel on the small, centrally located land connecting continents and nations.

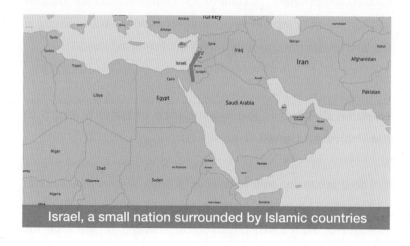

Israel, a small nation surrounded by Islamic countries

Question 22 Where is the Land Covenant that began in Genesis 12 further specified?

Gen. 15:18-21   18 On that day the LORD made a covenant with Abram and said, "To your descendants I give this land, from the river of Egypt to the great river, the Euphrates – 19 the land of the Kenites, Kenizzites, Kadmonites 20 Hittites, Perizzites, Rephaites, 21 Amorites, Canaanites, Girgashites and Jebusites."

God's spiritual blessing is an important factor, yet the concrete land that exists as the foothold to enjoy that blessing is even more important. In Genesis 15, God promised the location and scope of the land in detail, and revealed the tribes living in the land at that time, to fully reveal the Promised Land.

Question 23 What is the significance of Israel's return to the Promised Land?

There are many people who only hope for spiritual revival without the restoration of the Promised Land. When the land is restored, Israel will return to their Messiah, and then the Messiah will return to His nation, resulting in the restoration of God's Kingdom. Therefore, Israel's return to the Promised Land is important not only for Israel but also for all of us. Israel's return to the Promised Land is the prelude to the Messiah's return for the restoration of all things, which is God's ultimate purpose. The church today should help the restoration of Israel and thereby participate in God's work of restoring all things according to His promises and plan.

Question 24 When and how did the Jews' first return take place?

Josh. 1:4   Your territory will extend from the desert to Lebanon, and from the great river, the Euphrates – all the Hittite country – to the Great Sea on the west.

The Book of Joshua records Israel's first return to the Promised Land. God prepared the Israelites for more than 600 years for the first return to the land that He had revealed in Genesis 15:13-21, and He led Israel exactly as He said. For this precious return, God spoke of the land to Abraham even before Isaac was born. To fulfill the first return, Jacob, Abraham's grandson, had to go down to Egypt with his household to escape the famine. God formed the nation of Israel in Egypt, and, when the time came, He led them into the Promised Land through Moses and Joshua.

When and how did the Jews' second return take place?

Jer. 29:10   This is what the LORD says: "When seventy years are completed for Babylon, I will come to you and fulfill my gracious promise to bring you back to this place.

In the Promised Land, the Israelites worshiped pagan gods and fell into serious moral corruption. As a result, Israel was defeated by Assyria and Babylon, and exiled from the land. Around 722 B.C., the Assyrian army took the ten northern tribes of Israel as captives. Thereafter, in 586 B.C., Nebuchadnezzar of Babylon conquered the two southern tribes of Israel and exiled them from the land. Numerous Jews were taken to Babylon in captivity.

The Jewish people continued to despise and disobey God, but God never forgot His promise to them. Through the prophet Jeremiah, God promised the Jews' return. Jeremiah's prophecy and Daniel's prayers were answered. As recorded in the Book of Ezra, in 536 B.C., about 50,000 Jews left Babylon and returned to their homeland. After 20 years of internal conflict, in 516 B.C., they rebuilt the Second Temple in Jerusalem. In 459 B.C., Ezra, who was knowledgeable of Moses' law, returned to Jerusalem with the Jews who had been living in Babylon. Around 20 B.C., with the favor of Rome, Israel started to restore the Second Temple that had been rebuilt in 516 B.C. and finished the work in 26 A.D. However, the glory of the Second Temple, which was expanded by Herod, did not last long. In 70 A.D., Jerusalem fell by Rome and the Temple was burned, and, according to Josephus, 1.1 million Jewish pilgrims who were keeping the Feast in Jerusalem were slaughtered by the Romans, and 97,000 Jews were taken into captivity.

Question 26 When and how will the Jews' third return take place?

Isa. 66:7-8   7 "Before she goes into labor, she gives birth; before the pains come upon her, she delivers a son. 8 Who has ever heard of such a thing? Who has ever seen such things? Can a country be born in a day or a nation be brought forth in a moment? Yet no sooner is Zion in labor than she gives birth to her children.

There is a record of some Jews, who had been living in Babylon, returning to the land of Israel between 200 to 500 A.D., and, in the 10th to 11th centuries, a small number of Jews, who had been living in the Persian Empire, returned to Jerusalem and settled down to the west of the Kidron valley. From the 13th to the 19th century, an increasing number of Jews living in Europe returned to the land of Israel to escape religious persecution. In 1210, 300 rabbis and their descendants returned to the land of Israel, but most of them were killed by the Crusaders in 1229 and the Muslims in 1291.

Some of the Jews, who were expelled from Britain (1290), France (1391), Austria (1421), Spain (1492), and Portugal (1498), returned to their homeland. However, they were driven from their land by the Gentiles and Christians. The land of Israel was ruled by the Romans, then by the Byzantines, then by the Muslims, then by the Crusaders, and then by the Mamluks. From Mamluk rule to that of the Ottoman Empire and then to British rule, Israel seemed permanently cut off from the Promised Land.

In 1871 A.D., some Jews began to return to the Promised Land. Within about 10 years, about 25,000 Jews settled in the land, but there was no official announcement nor approval. The Jews' return was always met by social and ethnic oppositions. There were frequent riots and terrorist attacks from the Arabs who tried to obstruct the population growth and the economic revival of the Jews.

In 1897, at the First Zionist Congress convened in Basel, Switzerland, Theodor Herzl, who is called "the father of modern Israel," publicly advanced the idea of establishing a Jewish State by restoring the Promised Land, the homeland of the Jews.

World War I (1914-1917) completely changed the political situation and borders in the Middle East. The Ottoman Empire's control over the Middle East ended in exactly 400 years. In 1917, the British government publicly issued the Balfour Declaration drafted by Foreign Secretary Balfour, declaring their support for the establishment of the Jewish State in the land of Palestine. Meanwhile, through the Battle of Jerusalem in 1917, the British forces took control of Jerusalem from the Ottoman Empire. In this battle, 18,000 British soldiers and 25,000 Turkish soldiers died.

On May 14, 1948, the Jewish people, who had been scattered all over the world for about 1,900 years, finally reestablished their own nation. The prophecy in Isaiah 66:7-8 was fulfilled in history.

According to an official document from 1864, Jews were the most numerous inhabitants of Jerusalem at that time. The full-fledged Zionist Movement commenced in earnest from the 1897 meeting in Basel, Switzerland, held under the leadership of Theodor Herzl.

120 Years of the History of Zionism

1897	First Zionist Congress in Basel, Switzerland, is led by Theodor Herzl.
1917	The Balfour Declaration promises to establish the Jewish Nation.
1920	The San Remo Conference promises to build the Jewish Nation (Magna Carta of Israel).
1922	The League of Nations' Resolution provides Britain with the authority to build the Jewish Nation.
1928	At the Évian Conference, 30+ western nations refused to accept escaped Jewish refugees.
1939-1945	6 million Jews killed.
1947	U.N. Partition Plan for Palestine (Jerusalem is an open international city.)

1948	Israel's Independence and the 1st Middle East War (May 1948 to March 1949)
1956	Suez Crisis
1967	Six-Day War (June 5 to 10) and Jerusalem's restoration (Israel gives the Temple Mount to the Muslims.)
1973	Yom Kippur War
2017	U.S. President Trump approves Jerusalem as Israel's capital and announces the plan to move the U.S. Embassy to Jerusalem on December 6, 2017 (70 years after the U.N. resolution for Israel's Independence from November 29, 1947)
2018	U.S. President Trump moves the U.S. Embassy to Jerusalem on May 14, 2018 (70 years after Israel's Independence on May 14, 1948)

Question 27 **Does the State of Israel have the legitimacy to remain in the land under international law historically, diplomatically, and militarily? And what should be our attitude toward Israel?**

With U.N. approval in 1947, the Israeli Declaration of Independence in 1948 and subsequent victories in Israel's War of Independence led to the international community's recognition of the State of Israel. Therefore, it is right and just for free democratic nations to protect and support Israel. Israel is the only country in the Middle East that is governed by democracy and the rule of law. All residents in Israel have their fundamental human rights ensured by the law. To support Israel is to stand by the side of legitimate justice. Following God's promise, "I will bless those who bless you," given to Abraham

(Gen. 12:3), standing with Israel is the way for any individual, people, or nation to receive blessings from God.

Even in the 21st century today, there are many acts of widespread and indiscriminate terrorism perpetrated against Israel. Israel is being targeted by the greatest new weaponry and is surrounded by enemies that constantly casts threats of total annihilation. However, Israel has been miraculously surviving and has been developing brilliantly. Israel's population has been continuously increasing and reached about 9.7 million in 2023, with the Jewish population being around 7.1 million.[15] More than one million Russian Jews immigrated to Israel and a considerable number of Ethiopian Jews as well. These Jewish groups show a great interest in the Christian gospel.

If we trace the Jewish population in the land of Israel from 1882 to 2020, we can readily ascertain how quickly it has been increasing (See the following table).

Jewish Return (Aliyah) and Population (1882 to 2020)

Year	Jewish Return (Aliyah) Details		How many?
1882-1903	Czarist Russia (Includes part of Yemen)		about 35,000
1904-1914	Russian persecution (pogrom)	First Kibbutz built	about 40,000
1917	Balfour Declaration/beginning of British Mandate		

1919-1923	Eastern Europe (Aftermath of W.W. I)	Palestine	about 40,000
1924-1929	Poland/Hungary-Anti-Semitism	Many from the middle class	about 82,000
1929-1939	Germany - Nazism	Many professionals	about 250,000
Arabs/Jews tension increase/demand of independence from the Arabs - revolt 1940, Jewish Population - about 450,000			
1945-1951	New wave in Europe/ Arab nations	Influence of Holocaust	about 688,000
1948	Jewish Population at the time of Independence, 650,000		
1949-1950	Yemen Jews - life-threatening crisis	Operation Magic Carpet	about 49,000
1951-1952	Iraq (plane)	Operation Ezra/ Nehemiah	about 120,000
1952-1964	North Africa		about 240.000
1948-1970	Arab nations	(immigration or exile)	about 900,000
1967-1973	North America (Victory from the 6 Day War)		about 60,000
1979	Iranian Revolution		about 30.000
1984-1985	Sudan-Ethiopia Jews	(plane)	about 7,000
1991	Ethiopia Jews	(plane)	14,325
1948-1967	Soviet Union (after 6 Day War –diplomatic break)		about 22,000
1989	Gorbachev, General Secretary of the Soviet Union – lifted the restraint in the number of Jewish immigration		
After 1991	Jews from the old Soviet Union	Soviet Union Collapse	about 1,000,000
1999-2002	Argentina/Uruguay	Political, economic crisis	about 12,000

2000-2009	France – Anti-Semitism		about 13,000
2009	American Jews (world economic crisis)	(the most after the Yom Kippur War)	3,324
2013-2014	France – Anti-Semitism/Pro-Palestinism/ Violence/Economic Depression		about 6,000
2015	Editor of French weekly magazine, Charlie Hebdo, shot to death, by IS		about 8,000
2016-2020	Trend of global increase of anti-Semitism	Every year, about 30,000	about 150.000
1882-2020	Over 70 nations, all over the world	Immigration to Israel	about 3.9 M
2020 Jewish Population	world	Israel	USA
	14,800,000	6,870,000	5,700,000

Sources: Cheol-hwan Cho, 하나님은 이스라엘을 버리셨는가? [Has God Cast Away Israel?] (Seoul, South Korea: Elijah, 2016), 87-91; Jewish Virtual Library, "Demographics of Israel: Jewish Population of Israel Relative to World Jewish Population (1882 - Present)," December 29, 2022, accessed September 3, 2023, https://www.jewishvirtuallibrary.org/jewish-population-of-israel-relative-to-world-jewish-population; Pew Research Center, "Jewish Americans in 2020," May 11, 2021, accessed September 3, 2023, https://www.pewresearch.org/religion/2021/05/11/the-size-of-the-u-s-jewish-population/.

Question 28 How many more Jews will return to their homeland?

Ezek. 39:28   Then they will know that I am the LORD their God, for though I sent them into exile among the nations, I will gather them to their own land, not leaving any behind.

Hosea 11:10   They will follow the LORD; he will roar like a lion. When he roars, his children will come trembling from the west.

The people of Israel have kept a faith oriented to Zion. With dreams of returning to Zion, they have overcome dark realities. Nevertheless, about half of the Jewish people in the world still live outside Israel. Looking back in history, we find that most Jews did not want to return to Palestine. Only a small number of Jews deeply desired to return, so if the work of returning to their homeland had been left entirely to the Jews, only a very few Jews would have returned. Then, the Holocaust struck. It is heartbreaking to think of the pain and fear of those who suffered the Holocaust, and, due to those horrors, God's plan accelerated. The Holocaust, like nothing else, compelled the Jews to leave the land of Europe, where they had been living for hundreds of years. Suffering the tribulations of the Holocaust, the Jews could not but look, once again, toward the ancient land of promise.

Recently, hate crimes against Jews living in the western world have increased by 74% in France, 60% in Germany, 16%

in Britain, and 37% in the U.S.[16] Outside of Israel, the largest number of Jews live in the U.S. Most Jews in the U.S. do not want to return to Palestine. However, some Jews are returning either in obedience to God's Word or for other various reasons. In the future, when God roars like a lion, many Jews will return to their land trembling to escape terrifying things.

Stages of the Restoration of Israel Foreseen by Ezekiel

Stage 1	Ezek. 36:24	Return to the ancient land	Restoration of the people
Stage 2	Ezek. 36:25	Purified by clean water	Spiritual Restoration (Repentance)
Stage 3	Ezek. 36:26-27	Receive new heart and new spirit	Spiritual Restoration (Holy Spirit)
Stage 4	Ezek. 36:28	Relationship between God and His people is restored	Restoration of the relationship
Stage 5	Ezek. 36:34-35	The desolate land is transformed like Eden	Restoration of the land
Stage 6	Ezek. 37:17	The two will become one	Restoration as a nation
Stage 7	Ezek. 37:24-28	David will be their King forever	Messianic Kingdom

God's love is unfathomably deep, and, at times, God can be fearsome in carrying out His predestined plan. Throughout Israel's history, God has been accomplishing what He revealed to His prophet Ezekiel and, ultimately, will fulfill it.

Question 29 Is the ministry of Jewish Return (Aliyah) the mission of Gentile Christians?

Jer. 31:10   "Hear the word of the LORD, O nations; proclaim it in distant coastlands: 'He who scattered Israel will gather them and will watch over his flock like a shepherd.'

Isa. 49:22   This is what the Sovereign LORD says: "See, I will beckon to the Gentiles, I will lift up my banner to the peoples; they will bring your sons in their arms and carry your daughters on their shoulders.

Yes. God gave the Gentiles the calling to hear God's Word and proclaim it to the whole world. The banner of God is the nation of Israel. Through the reestablishment and protection of a nation that had disappeared for 1,900 years, God is waving this banner as a sign for the Jews to return to their ancient land and for believing Gentiles to help the Jews return. The mission is to assist in the national restoration of Israel. We must proclaim that the global return of the Jews to their homeland and the restoration of Jerusalem are signs of the last days. Thus, we must help the restoration of the Jewish nation through the global return of the Jews.

Isa. 66:20   And they will bring all your brothers, from all the nations, to my holy mountain in Jerusalem as an offering to the LORD

– on horses, in chariots and wagons, and on mules and camels," says the LORD. "They will bring them, as the Israelites bring their grain offerings, to the temple of the LORD in ceremonially clean vessels.

Helping the Diaspora Jews return to Jerusalem (Aliyah) is precious work akin to giving God a gift that brings Him joy.

We are all pilgrims, living to fulfill God's will in this world, while looking forward to God's eternal Kingdom of the New Heaven and the New Earth and the New Jerusalem. The Jews are the most representative diaspora in history. The national tragedy of being scattered all over the world is a blessing in disguise that is now becoming the strength to protect Israel. In fact, Apostle Paul, who was a descendant of the Jewish Diaspora, began world missions through the dispersed Jews.

The Korean people, with a 5,000-year history, likewise have 7.5 million Koreans living scattered in 180 countries around the world. The establishment of 5,000 Korean Diaspora churches was also God's work. Currently, about 28,000 Korean missionaries are serving in 169 nations all over the world. Now, the Korean people, who are more widely scattered than any other country in the world, must become one in the Holy Spirit and fulfill the mission of awakening and helping the approximately 7 million Diaspora Jews, who are still living scattered in 108 countries, to return to the Promised Land. The ministry of West Hills (Korean) Presbyterian Church (WHPC), where I served as the Senior Pastor, began to support Aliyah through the Ebenezer Emergency Fund (EEF) since 2005, after long years of intercessory prayers for the restoration of Israel, and, since 2014, has been continuously supporting Aliyah through the Jewish Agency. These days, witnessing many Korean churches, both domestic and abroad, actively helping the ministry of Aliyah, I sincerely thank God for answering our prayers.

Question 30 Is the ministry of comforting the Jews the mission of Gentile Christians?

Isa. 40:1-2   1 Comfort, comfort my people, says your God. 2 Speak tenderly to Jerusalem, and proclaim to her that her hard service has been completed, that her sin has been paid for, that she has received from the LORD's hand double for all her sins.

We should inform the church and the nations about God's will toward Israel as revealed in the Bible, and we should comfort and bless the nation and people of Israel. The European countries that proudly claimed to be Christian nations yet persecuted the Jews through Crusades and the Inquisition, etc., must repent of their Anti-Semitism. We must tenderly care for the Jewish people's deep scars from the cruel massacres of the Holocaust that murdered 6 million innocent lives simply for being a Jew. To bless Israel and stand by them is an important teaching of the Bible. God loves the Israelites to this day and leads them upon good paths, and so we too must bless and comfort them. We must put on the clothes of faith and humility and in obedience go toward the Lord of history, Almighty God.

Question 31 Is the ministry of praying for Jerusalem and Israel the mission of Gentile Christians?

Ps. 122:6　　Pray for the peace of Jerusalem: "May those who love you be secure.

Isa. 62:6-7　　6 I have posted watchmen on your walls, O Jerusalem; they will never be silent day or night. You who call on the LORD, give yourselves no rest, 7 and give him no rest till he establishes Jerusalem and makes her the praise of the earth.

We ought to discern the Last Days, rejoice with God's people, remain awake, and pray. We should become the watchmen on the walls and pray for the peace of Jerusalem. We should pray for the Holy Spirit's anointing upon Jerusalem's residents and for the realization of true peace by the Prince of Peace's return.

We should pray for our leaders to fear God, rely on Him fully, and thereby be bold and strong. We should pray for Israel, as a democracy, to become a nation where the Gospel can be freely preached and to have a stronger national defense. We should pray for God's protection over Israel from the threat of war and terrorism by the surrounding Arab nations.

We should pray for the return of the scattered Jews and an open door to evangelize to them. Israel is a potential Christian nation for "all Israel will be saved" (Rom. 11:26) in God's time. From the historical viewpoint acknowledging God's sovereign reign, God's work is for Israel securing the land to which the Lord will return (Zech. 12:4-5) and enduring in the struggle to guard it through tough fights. Satan is attacking Israel in various ways to destroy the foothold for the Lord's return. Whoever is looking forward to the return of the Lord should thank Israel, pray for them, and help them with every means.

This world is a battleground between Light and darkness. We should pray for the growth of the Kingdom of Light around the globe led by Biblical faith and values. And we should pray that nations of Light will protect and help the children of Light who are suffering in nations of darkness in the world that rejects God and pray for the numerous souls locked in the Kingdom of darkness to be drawn into the Kingdom of Light. We should pray earnestly, desperately, and continuously that the Kingdom of Light may prepare the way for our Lord's return, first, by warding off the attacks of the spirit of darkness, deception, harlotry, violence, and apostasy which tries to shake them and, second, by filling the numbers of the children of Light.

Question 32 Is the ministry of evangelizing the Jews the mission of Gentile Christians?

Isa. 40:9-10   9 You who bring good tidings to Zion, go up on a high mountain. You who bring good tidings to Jerusalem, lift up your voice with a shout, lift it up, do not be afraid; say to the towns of Judah, "Here is your God!" 10 See, the Sovereign LORD comes with power, and his arm rules for him. See, his reward is with him, and his recompense accompanies him.

Isa. 52:7-8   7 How beautiful on the mountains are the feet of those who bring good news, who proclaim peace, who bring good tidings, who proclaim salvation, who say to Zion, "Your God reigns!" 8 Listen! Your watchmen lift up their voices; together they shout for joy. When the LORD returns to Zion, they will see it with their own eyes.

Matt. 23:39   For I tell you, you will not see me again until you say, 'Blessed is he who comes in the name of the Lord.' "

The only Way for the Jews and Gentiles to be reconciled is the saving faith in Jesus, the Messiah. If there is no Christ, there is no peace. We should boldly inform, teach, and proclaim to the Jews that Jesus is the Messiah.

Israel restored Jerusalem through their victory in the Six-Day War in 1967. The times of the Gentiles are full. Now Israel is returning. The Jewish population has increased from about 50,000 in 1881 to about 650,000 at the time of Israel's Independence in 1948, and to about 7,145,000 in 2023.[17]

Spiritual revival is taking place in Israel. When the number of believing Jews is filled, the Lord will come again.

Question 33 Is there a special calling for the Korean people regarding Israel's restoration?

Isa. 55:5   Surely you shall call a nation you do not know, And nations who do not know you shall run to you, Because of the LORD your God, And the Holy One of Israel; For He has glorified you." (NKJ)

Here, a nation (גוֹי, goy) refers to a Gentile nation which has well organized structures and systems. Today, there are only 38 nations, including Korea, that are sufficiently organized in structures and systems to join the OECD (Organization for Economic Cooperation and Development). Among them, "a nation that does not know you," a nation which has no experience of living with any Jewish communities, is Korea alone. After the destruction by Rome in A.D. 70, the scattered Jews have been living in more than 100 nations, forming Diaspora Jewish communities, but Korea is not included among those nations. The increased request for cooperation from Messianic Jewish congregations and Jewish organizations in recent days is a voice calling the Korean people.

These days, due to the influence of the "Korean Wave" and similar historical experiences of national suffering, the Jewish people have open hearts toward the Korean people, and many Jewish students are learning Korean. Many people of faith say Koreans are called to save the Jews. If we visit Ben Yehuda Street in Jerusalem, a place like Myung Dong in Seoul, we can hear Koreans singing praise songs. In the Last Days, the Korean people must go to the ends of the earth and all the way to Jerusalem to preach the gospel and be used by God as His instruments for the final great harvest that will save all Israel's remnants. The Korean church's participation in Israel's restoration is the calling of this age and the way to revival and blessings.

God promised that He will bless those who bless Abraham (Gen. 12:3). "Pray for the peace of Jerusalem: May they prosper who love you" (Ps. 122:6). is also a blessing that God promised. If the Korean church with a sincere faith aids the full restoration of the descendants of Abraham, Israel, we will receive the amazing blessings God promised. In this respect, the Korean church's active cooperation with and prayers for Israel's restoration will bring new revival to the Korean church and will open a way to establish a free, democratic, unified, Christian Korea, which has been our long-awaited national task.

Conclusion

The church must remember. God has never forsaken Israel as He promised. Israel's rebirth, Jerusalem's restoration, the Jews' return to their ancient land which remains ongoing, and their spiritual restoration are the most realistic and concrete proof that God's Word, the Bible, is true. The church must repent of its anti-Semitism for the past 2,000 years and change Replacement Theology to Restoration Theology. God's covenants made with Israel must be understood and their sure fulfillments must be expected. We must protect the Jewish people from all forms of anti-Semitism and stand by Israel. We must thank, pray for, comfort, and serve Israel with acts of love so that they may fulfill their calling.

Chapter 5

God's People

Introduction

The Bible is the story of God and His people Israel. After Jesus the Messiah, who came through Israel, died and rose again, the church was born through the Descent of the Holy Spirit. Peter described the church as God's people (1 Pet. 2:10). As the body of Christ, the church is organically connected and must obey Christ Who is its Head. Christ commands the church to form "one new man," a community of saints made whole by the unity of believing Gentiles and Jews. It is a commandment to make a perfected community of God's people in Christ.

Question 1 What identity should Israel have as God's people?

Exod. 19:5-6   5 Now if you obey me fully and keep my covenant, then out of all nations you will be my treasured possession. 6 Although the whole earth is mine, you will be for me a kingdom of priests and a holy nation.' These are the words you are to speak to the Israelites."

Isa. 49:6   he says: "It is too small a thing for you to be my servant to restore the tribes of Jacob and bring back those of Israel I have kept. I will also make you a light for the Gentiles, that you may bring my salvation to the ends of the earth."

Rom. 11:21-24 21 For if God did not spare the natural branches, he will not spare you either. 22 Consider therefore the kindness and sternness of God: sternness to those who fell, but kindness to you, provided that you continue in his kindness. Otherwise, you also will be cut off. 23 And if they do not persist in unbelief, they will be grafted in, for God is able to graft them in again. 24 After all, if you were cut out of an olive tree that is wild by nature, and contrary to nature were grafted into a cultivated olive tree, how much more readily will these, the natural branches, be grafted into their own olive tree!

The identity Israel should have as God's people is three-fold: God's treasured possession, God's Kingdom of priests, and God's holy nation. Their identity as God's treasured possession reveals Israel's status. Their identity as God's Kingdom of priests explains Israel's mission to be "a light for the Gentiles." And their identity as a holy nation reveals their lifestyle. Paul viewed Israel's identity as the original branch of the cultivated olive tree. He saw that the broken branches will be regrafted to it to bear abundant fruit in God's time.

Question 2 What is the church's identity as God's people?

1 Pet. 2:9-10   9 But you are a chosen people, a royal priesthood, a holy nation, a people belonging to God, that you may declare the praises of him who called you out of darkness into his wonderful light. 10 Once you were not a people, but now you are the people of God; once you had not received mercy, but now you have received mercy.

Rom. 11:17-18 17 If some of the branches have been broken off, and you, though a wild olive shoot, have been grafted in among the others and now share in the nourishing sap from the olive root, 18 do not boast over those branches. If you do, consider this: You do not support the root, but the root supports you.

The church is called "a chosen people" because God chose 120 people, who were gathered in an attic in Jerusalem on the Feast of Pentecost, to use them for the work of His redemption plan and poured the Holy Spirit upon them. The church is "a royal priesthood" because we must live as servant leaders in this age and will rule the nations as kings with the King, Christ, in the coming age (2 Tim. 2:12; Rev. 5:10, 20:6, 22:5). The church, as priests, should be channels for sharing God's message of love and grace to the world. We should be a bridge connecting unbelieving people to God. The church is called to be "a holy nation" set apart from worldly people, and we choose to serve Jesus Christ as Lord and live according to the law of love. The church is different from unbelievers in every aspect. The church is God's treasured possession that He purchased with a price (1 Cor. 6:20). Paul considered the church as the branches of a wild olive tree grafted onto a cultivated olive tree to share the nourishing sap from its root. He considered it a mystery to be fulfilled in the "one new man" that will be formed by the grafted branches being united with the natural branches in God's time.

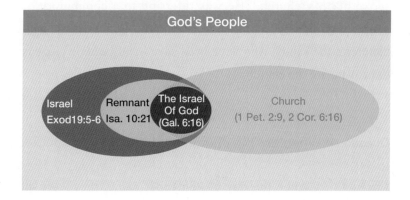

Question 3 What does Jesus mean by "My Church" in Matthew 16:18?

Matt. 16:16   Simon Peter answered, "You are the Christ, the Son of the living God."

Matt. 16:18   And I tell you that you are Peter, and on this rock I will build my church, and the gates of Hades will not overcome it.

In response to Peter's confession of faith to Him that "You are the Christ, the Son of the living God," Jesus said, "on this rock I will build my church." For the first time in human history, Jesus established an organic body called the church. Then, what is the church? Many think that it refers to a building or sanctuary for worship, but instead the church (ἐκκλησία, ekklésia) is a community of people who have been called. When Jesus spoke of "My church," He was referring to a community of people who have been called by Him Who is the Christ, and, therefore, the saints, who have been saved and became citizens of heaven, are the church.

Question 4 When did the church commence?

Acts 2:1-4   1 When the day of Pentecost came, they were all together in one place. 2 Suddenly a sound like the blowing of a violent wind came from heaven and filled the whole house where they were sitting. 3 They saw what seemed to be tongues of fire that separated and came to rest on each of them. 4 All of them were filled with the Holy Spirit and began to speak in other tongues as the Spirit enabled them.

Jesus commanded His early followers, "Do not leave Jerusalem, but wait for the gift my Father promised, which you have heard me speak about. For John baptized with water, but in a few days you will be baptized with the Holy Spirit" (Acts 1:4-5). In obedient response to Him, 120 saints gathered in an attic during the Feast of Pentecost, prayed, received the fullness of the Holy Spirit, and became one body, the church. Having one faith in one Lord, those saints were baptized by one Spirit to form one body, and Christ's body, the church, was born (Eph. 4:3-5).

Question 5 What are the visible church and the invisible church?

Rev. 21:27   Nothing impure will ever enter it, nor will anyone who does what is shameful or deceitful, but only those whose names are written in the Lamb's book of life.

The visible church constitutes the people who are registered in local churches. The invisible church constitutes the people whose names are written in the Book of Life. The church is visible, and, at the same time, invisible. The invisible church is hidden from mankind's eyes.

Question 6 The church is the body of Christ. Then, Who is the head of the Church?

Eph. 1:22-23   22 And God placed all things under his feet and appointed him to be head over everything for the church, 23 which is his body, the fullness of him who fills everything in every way.

Eph. 5:30   for we are members of his body.

1 Cor. 12:27   Now you are the body of Christ, and each one of you is a part of it.

Col. 1:18   And he is the head of the body, the church; he is the beginning and the firstborn from among the dead, so that in everything he might have the supremacy.

The church is the body of Christ which consists, like a human body, of many members. Every member is closely interconnected to each other in an organic relationship. Jesus Christ is the head of the church. The head and body analogy represents a relationship not only of life but also of obedience as well. He is the head, the chief, the Lord, and the ruler. Those who have been saved through faith in Jesus should give Him absolute obedience and the glory of which He is worthy.

Question 7 What is the new self?

Eph. 4:22-24   22 You were taught, with regard to your former way of life, to put off your old self, which is being corrupted by its deceitful desires; 23 to be made new in the attitude of your minds; 24 and to put on the new self, created to be like God in true righteousness and holiness.

To put off the old self and to put on the new self means repenting and believing in Jesus. To move from the state of being the old self to being the new self is salvation. We believers became new selves by receiving the forgiveness of our sins and justification through Christ's redemptive work on the cross.

Question 8 What is the one new man (one new people)?

Eph. 2:15   by abolishing in his flesh the law with its commandments and regulations. His purpose was to create in himself one new man out of the two, thus making peace,

Rom. 10:12 For there is no difference between Jew and Gentile – for the same Lord is Lord of all and richly blesses all who call on him,

Gal. 3:28-29 28 There is neither Jew nor Greek, slave nor free, male nor female, for you are all one in Christ Jesus. 29 If you belong to Christ, then you are Abraham's seed, and heirs according to the promise.

The Greek word translated as "new" here is καινός (kainos), which refers to something totally different from the previous one in kind and characteristic. Spiritually, any "new man" in Christ is neither a Jew nor a Gentile and is only a Christian. The Jewish "new man" and the Gentile "new man" becoming one is the "one new man" (one new people). However, the oneness and absence of discrimination in Christ does not mean that the differences in male and female and in racial identities vanish. In Christ there is no more discrimination, but differences remain to glorify God with the beautiful diversity He created.

Question 9 What were the Gentiles like?

Eph. 2:11-12 11 Therefore, remember that formerly you who are Gentiles by birth and called "uncircumcised" by those who call themselves "the circumcision" (that done in the body by the hands of men) – 12 remember that at that time you were separate from Christ, excluded from citizenship in Israel and foreigners to the covenants of the promise, without hope and without God in the world.

In the past, the Gentiles were outside Christ and in darkness, full of sins, and awaiting God's wrath. Gentiles did not have the living Word of God. The expression "without God in the world" reveals the Gentiles' miserable status. Those without Father God are indeed pitiful. The Gentiles, not knowing Father God existed, were miserable.

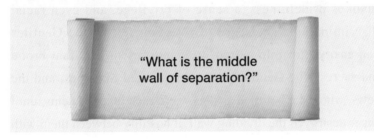

"What is the middle wall of separation?"

Question 10 **How can Jews and Gentiles become close to each other?**

Eph. 2:13   But now in Christ Jesus you who once were far away have been brought near by the blood of Christ.

The Jews and Gentiles, who were unable to become one in the past, have now become close to each other by the precious blood of the Lamb, Jesus Christ, Who was slain on the cross.

Question 11 What is "the barrier," described as "the dividing wall of hostility," between Jews and Gentiles?

Eph. 2:14   For he himself is our peace, who has made the two one and has destroyed the barrier, the dividing wall of hostility,

The Jewish nation's chosen status necessarily involves exclusivity. The moment some are chosen, the rest are not chosen. Due to the sinfulness of man, such a choice always invokes pridefulness, a sense of privilege, and even racial discrimination. The sense of rejection felt by the Gentiles can easily turn into hatred, fury, and resentment that brood massacres. The Gentiles, who were treated like dogs, and the Jews, who were belittled as pigs, were each other's enemy, until Jesus destroyed the dividing wall of hostility between them with His own body on the cross and made the two into one, making peace.

Question 12 What is the "the law with its commandments and regulations?"

Eph. 2:15   by abolishing in his flesh the law with its commandments and regulations. His purpose was to create in himself one new man out of the two, thus making peace,

Col. 2:14   having canceled the written code, with its regulations, that was against us and that stood opposed to us; he took it away, nailing it to the cross.

Col. 2:20-21   20 Since you died with Christ to the basic principles of this world, why, as though you still belonged to it, do you submit to its rules (δόγμα, dogma): 21 "Do not handle! Do not taste! Do not touch!"?

Col. 2:16-17   16 Therefore do not let anyone judge you by what you eat or drink, or with regard to a religious festival, a New Moon celebration or a Sabbath day. 17 These are a shadow of the things that were to come; the reality, however, is found in Christ.

The commandments in the Torah that are called "the written code" or "rules" (δόγμα, dogma) include at least the following: rules related to the calendar such as kosher (food) laws, Sabbath laws, the Sabbath day, Feasts, and the new moon, etc., and rules related to touch such as purification laws for priests and laws about unclean things, etc. These commandments clearly distinguished Jews from other peoples or nations. Hebrew writer and philosopher Asher Zvi Hirsch Ginsberg (pen name Ahad Ha'am) wrote, "More than Israel preserved the Sabbath, the Sabbath preserved Israel."[18] Jesus broke down the wall of separation, ripping the dogma with His body on the cross, to establish peace between Jews and Gentiles.

Question 13 How did the church, born on Pentecost, grow?

Acts 21:20   When they heard this, they praised God. Then they said to Paul: "You see, brother, how many thousands of Jews have believed, and all of them are zealous for the law.

Jerusalem/Pentecost	120	Acts 1:15, 2:1-4
Peter's Sermon	3,000	Acts 2:41
The Number of Men	5,000	Acts 4:4
Men and Women	More and more	Acts 5:14
Disciples	Increasing	Acts 6:1
Disciples/Priests	Increasing rapidly	Acts 6:7
Judea, Galilee, Samaria	Growing in numbers	Acts 9:31
Churches	Growing daily	Acts 16:5
Jews Believers	How many thousands	Acts 21:20

Question 14 Who was the first Gentile to accept the gospel after the Descent of the Holy Spirit?

Acts 8:35-36   35 Then Philip began with that very passage of Scripture and told him the good news about Jesus. 36 As they traveled along the road, they came to some water and the eunuch said, "Look, here is water. Why shouldn't I be baptized?"

Some say that the first Gentile to accept the gospel was the eunuch who oversaw the entire treasury of the Ethiopian Queen Candace. However, he was likely a Diaspora Jew who was returning to Ethiopia after worshiping in Jerusalem.

Acts 10:44-46 44 While Peter was still speaking these words, the Holy Spirit came on all who heard the message. 45 The circumcised believers who had come with Peter were astonished that the gift of the Holy Spirit had been poured out even on the Gentiles. 46 For they heard them speaking in tongues and praising God. Then Peter said,

One of the first Gentiles who accepted the gospel was Cornelius. The same Holy Spirit, who came upon the 120 Jewish disciples gathered to pray in an attic in Jerusalem on the Feast of Pentecost, came upon the house of Cornelius as well. The Jewish believers who came with Peter had been taught that all the promises in the Bible were only for the elect people of God. However, they were astonished to witness the Gentiles receiving and being filled with the Holy Spirit.

Question 15 What happened to the church at Antioch, which formed the first Jewish and Gentile community of believers?

Acts 13:1   In the church at Antioch there were prophets and teachers: Barnabas, Simeon called Niger, Lucius of Cyrene, Manaen (who had been brought up with Herod the tetrarch) and Saul.

Acts 15:1   Some men came down from Judea to Antioch and were teaching the brothers: "Unless you are circumcised, according to the custom taught by Moses, you cannot be saved."

Acts 15:5   Then some of the believers who belonged to the party of the Pharisees stood up and said, "The Gentiles must be circumcised and required to obey the law of Moses."

At the church in Antioch, some believing men, who had come down from Judea and belonged to the Pharisees, insisted that the Gentiles must be circumcised and required to obey the law of Moses. Not every believer understood in the beginning that the atoning work through the death and resurrection of Jesus Christ fulfilled the Law. Circumcision is a promise to keep the Law in the Old Testament. Those believing men had been taught that man can only be saved by receiving circumcision and keeping the Law. This sort of idea is called legalism. Due to this erroneous teaching, there were considerable conflicts and controversies among members in the church at Antioch.

Question 16 What decisions were made at the Jerusalem Council to advance the gospel to the Gentiles?

Acts 15:8-11   8 God, who knows the heart, showed that he accepted them by giving the Holy Spirit to them, just as he did to us. 9 He made no distinction between us and them, for he purified their hearts by faith. 10 Now then, why do you try to test God by putting on the necks of the disciples a yoke that neither we nor our fathers have been able to bear? 11 No! We believe it is through the grace of our Lord Jesus that we are saved, just as they are."

Acts 15:28-29   28 It seemed good to the Holy Spirit and to us not to burden you with anything beyond the following requirements: 29 You are to abstain from food sacrificed to idols, from blood, from the meat of strangled animals and from sexual immorality. You will do well to avoid these things. Farewell.

The Jerusalem Council confirmed that salvation can only be received by the grace of the Lord Jesus Christ. The doctrinal defense finally led to ideological unity among the churches of the apostolic age. The time of confusion and heartache had beneficial results. Through the guidance of the Holy Spirit, the apostles, elders, and church members were convinced of God's will. It was to "abstain from food sacrificed to idols, from blood, from the meat of strangled animals and from sexual immorality." The decision maintained the duty to keep core parts of the Torah related to life and excluded circumcision, the Sabbath day, the Feasts including the Passover, the new moon and kosher food laws.

Question 17 What should be the stance of Gentile Christians toward the Feasts?

Gal. 4:10-11   10 You are observing special days and months and seasons and years! 11 I fear for you, that somehow I have wasted my efforts on you.

Observing special days, months, seasons, and years is legalism. We do not keep the ceremonial laws of the Old Testament because Jesus Christ delivered us from the law and set us free. By reminding the church members in Galatia of the truth of the gospel, Paul hoped to prevent them from falling into the fallacy of legalism.

Col. 2:16-17   16 Therefore do not let anyone judge you by what you eat or drink, or with regard to a religious festival, a New Moon celebration or a Sabbath day. 17 These are a shadow of the things that were to come; the reality, however, is found in Christ.

The ceremonial laws in the Old Testament were a shadow of things to come, and their substance was fulfilled by Jesus

Christ. They were fulfilled by Jesus Christ's redemptive work. Therefore, the saints of the New Testament were no longer under obligation to keep those laws. The ceremonial laws in the Old Testament were finished in Christ. The meanings of the Passover and the Day of Atonement in the Old Testament, which drew the Jews closer to God, were fulfilled by the Lord's Supper, in which both Jews and Gentiles remember Jesus' broken body and shed blood (1 Cor. 11:20). We now hope in the Lord's promises of a Second Advent, resurrection, and heaven.

1 Cor. 7:18-20   18 Was a man already circumcised when he was called? He should not become uncircumcised. Was a man uncircumcised when he was called? He should not be circumcised. 19 Circumcision is nothing and uncircumcision is nothing. Keeping God's commands is what counts. 20 Each one should remain in the situation which he was in when God called him.

To saints, whether to receive or not receive circumcision is not important. Even baptism is not important in form but rather in meaning. True religion is not in form but rather in content that is faith and obedience.

However, many parts of the Torah (Moses' Law) contain prophetic dimensions. This is especially so in the Feasts of the LORD. The Lord's First Advent occurred during the Spring Feasts, which are the Passover, the Feast of Unleavened Bread, the Feast of Firstfruits, and the Pentecost. Likewise, by studying the Fall Feasts, we can learn much about the timing and method of His Second Advent. It is not important to keep the Feasts at fixed times like the Judaists. What is important is to learn the deep prophetic and typological truths from them and how they are fulfilled.

Question 18 When Gentiles become Abraham's descendants by believing in Christ, do they need to keep the Law?

Gal. 3:29   If you belong to Christ, then you are Abraham's seed, and heirs according to the promise.

The observance of dogma and commandments does not define individual and corporate sanctity anymore. Gentiles can be brought into Abraham's family with their cultures and identities fully respected. The Lord's body is the seat of reconciliation, love, and blessed identity for all Jews and Gentiles from every nation, tribe, people, and language who worship and accept God. God calls out the Gentiles from every nation, tribe, people, and language exactly as they are and transforms each of them into a new creation.

Question 19 Did Paul oppose the observance of the law?

Rom. 10:2-4   2 For I can testify about them that they are zealous for God, but their zeal is not based on knowledge. 3 Since they did not know the righteousness that comes from God and sought to establish their own, they did not submit to God's righteousness. 4 Christ is the end of the law so that there may be righteousness for everyone who believes.

Paul points out that to try to establish one's own righteousness by keeping the law is to not believe in Jesus, Who finished the law for the righteousness of all believers. After the Lord's death, resurrection, and ascension, and the Holy Spirit's descent, acquiring righteousness (salvation, justification, sanctification) through observing the law became impossible. If one accepts the teaching that keeping the law is valid for obtaining holiness, righteousness, and sanctification, she or he has the obligation to keep the entire law perfectly. Paul was not against the law but rather against legalism.

Question 20 What does fulfilling the law mean?

Matt. 5:17   "Do not think that I have come to abolish the Law or the Prophets; I have not come to abolish them but to fulfill them.

Matt. 22:37-40 37 Jesus replied: "'Love the Lord your God with all your heart and with all your soul and with all your mind.' 38 This is the first and greatest commandment. 39 And the second is like it: 'Love your neighbor as yourself.' 40 All the Law and the Prophets hang on these two commandments."

The fundamental spirit of the Law is to love God and to love one's neighbors. For every law, the fundamental spirit behind its enactment is always vital. If the fundamental spirit of a law is neglected, that law becomes nothing but a husk. We Christians are cleansed from sins and live freely by the grace of the gospel in accordance with the Holy Spirit. Through the help of the Holy Spirit, we should be able to keep the fundamental spirit of the Law.

Question 21 Do Gentile believers need to learn and practice Jewish culture?

Rom. 11:29   for God's gifts and his call are irrevocable.

Lev. 24:8   This bread is to be set out before the LORD regularly, Sabbath after Sabbath, on behalf of the Israelites, as a lasting covenant.

If God's "gifts and call" for Israel are "irrevocable," the Jewish identity and uniqueness cannot disappear in Christ. The declaration that in Christ "there is neither Jew nor Gentile" is a personal and spiritual statement about our relationship with God. It is not to repetitively point out whether the Jewish identity or any other ethnic identity is valid or not. It is wrong for Gentile Christians to assume any sort of quasi-Jewish identity that dilutes the uniqueness of the Jewish people.

Question 22 Are we required to give up the uniqueness of each nation and people group to become one in Christ?

Acts 10:14-15　14 "Surely not, Lord!" Peter replied. "I have never eaten anything impure or unclean." 15 The voice spoke to him a second time, "Do not call anything impure that God has made clean."

Before realizing God's will through a vision as described in the above text, Peter and most Jews in his days were racists. All Jews believed that they were different, chosen, holier, and superior. The gifts and call bestowed on Israel are clearly a great privilege and the source of the blessed identity of the Jews. However, Israel's ultimate purpose is to convey the blessing of becoming God's children to all nations. That is the ultimate fulfillment of the promise given to Abraham. Each nation and people group has its own uniqueness and possesses God's redemptive gifts and call.

Question 23 Are there absolute and relative moral laws?

Matt. 19:17-19 17 "Why do you ask me about what is good?" Jesus replied. "There is only One who is good. If you want to enter life, obey the commandments." 18 "Which ones?" the man inquired. Jesus replied, " 'Do not murder, do not commit adultery, do not steal, do not give false testimony, 19 honor your father and mother,' and 'love your neighbor as yourself.' "

1 Cor. 9:21   To those not having the law I became like one not having the law (though I am not free from God's law but am under Christ's law), so as to win those not having the law.

The unchangeable fundamental message of the Gospel is that salvation can be obtained only through faith and grace (Eph. 2:8). The absolute moral law is to love God and love one's neighbors (Matt. 22:37-39). The commandments to keep that lead to life are: "Do not murder, do not commit adultery, do not steal, do not give false testimony, honor your father and mother, and love your neighbor as yourself." Lighter moral laws are ethical things to do in our daily lives. The Biblical symbols, such as baptism, Communion, Feasts, and anointing with oil, are still spiritually important and beneficial. Understanding and participating in cultural traditions is to be done with love (1 Cor. 9:19-23).

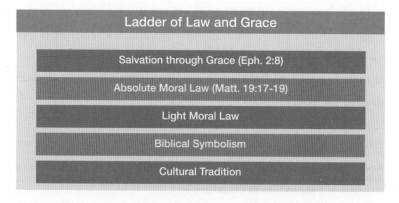

Source: Asher Intrater, Alignment (Frederick, MD: Revive Israel Media, 2017), 115-122.

Question 24 Is it a mutual blessing to form "one new man?"

Missiologists today stress the contextualization of the Gospel. In the mission field, it is imperative to guard the essence of the Gospel by forbidding idol worship and maintaining Biblical ethics and, at the same time, it is important to respect the culture and circumstances of the people. The loving God Himself needed Incarnation to go into the culture and circumstances of mankind to save us sinners. Mission presupposes the existence of a particular people group, tribe, place, and culture. Sharing the Gospel transcends all boundaries but, at the same time, requires respecting those boundaries. Furthermore, we must understand that diversity is a blessing to one another just as the rainbow composed of seven colors is beautiful.

Question 25 What blessings do the Gentiles enjoy through the Gospel?

Eph. 3:6   This mystery is that through the gospel the Gentiles are heirs together with Israel, members together of one body, and sharers together in the promise in Christ Jesus.

"Heirs together" in Greek is συγκληρονόμος (synklēronomos), which means co-heirs. Two blood-related siblings in unity are receiving their father's inheritance, hope, and success, etc. together.[19] In Christ, Jewish believers will receive their ultimate inheritance only when the Gentile nations receive theirs, and vice versa.

"Members together" in Greek is σύσσωμος (syssōmos), which means people of one body. It is a living body with Christ as the Head. The Jews and Gentiles are one living organism, united by Christ's blood. The two are now one family with the same spiritual DNA (John 1:13). If something occurs to one member of the body, the entire body is affected.[20]

"Sharers together" in Greek is συμμέτοχος (symmetochos),

which means fellow partakers. They are those who participate in the same promise in Jesus Christ, the promise of blessings given to Abraham.

In Jesus Christ, Jews and Gentiles are co-heirs of the promise given to Abraham. We are members of one family in the Messiah. And all this is in accordance with the promise that our Father God gave to our forefather Abraham.

Question 26 Is the precursor for all Israel's salvation the full number of the Gentiles or the fullness of the Gentiles?

Rom. 11:25-26   25 I do not want you to be ignorant of this mystery, brothers, so that you may not be conceited: Israel has experienced a hardening in part until the full number of the Gentiles (the fullness of the Gentiles, KJV) has come in. 26 And so all Israel will be saved...

Rom. 11:12   But if their transgression means riches for the world, and their loss means riches for the Gentiles, how much greater riches will their fullness bring!

Rom. 11:15   For if their rejection is the reconciliation of the world, what will their acceptance be but life from the dead?

When the fullness of the Gentiles is reached, all Israel will be saved. The "one new man" dynamic arises between Jews and Gentiles and between Israel and the nations. "The fullness of the Gentiles" is not only the fullness in number but also the vision of the one new man and obedience in faith. Full obedience and maturity in faith among the nations will stir up the Jews' jealousy, leading to Israel's salvation. Here, "all Israel will be saved" refers to Israel's great national conversion. God's historical work of renewal among the Jews and Gentiles, Israel and the nations, is mutual and simultaneous.

Question 27 How is Jerusalem's restoration related to the fulfillment of the "one new man?"

Luke 21:24   They will fall by the sword and will be taken as prisoners to all the nations. Jerusalem will be trampled on by the Gentiles until the times of the Gentiles are fulfilled.

Israel's return to their ancient land about 1,800 years after their scattering was an unprecedented event in human history. Zionism, which was advocated in the 1880s, gained more urgency during and after the First and Second World Wars. After the Holocaust, in 1948, Israel was reestablished with U.N. approval. Despite incessant attacks from Arabs and Muslims, millions of Jews are returning from all over the world. This is preparation of the foothold for the Messiah's Second Advent in the Last Days. Jerusalem's restoration through the Six-Day War in 1967 demonstrates that the times of the Gentiles are largely fulfilled, even though the Temple Mount was given up to the Muslims at that time. The accelerated fulfillment of the "one new man" is deeply anticipated.

Question 28 What is the difference between the Gospel of Salvation and the Gospel of the Kingdom of Heaven?

Matt. 24:14   And this gospel of the kingdom will be preached in the whole world as a testimony to all nations, and then the end will come.

The Gospel of Salvation is to receive eternal life through repentance and faith. The Gospel of Salvation is the door through which one can join God's people and enter heaven. The Lord said that the Gospel of the Kingdom should be proclaimed to all nations before His return. The Gospel of the Kingdom is the Gospel of His reign over His Kingdom. With the Gospel of God's reign, individuals, families, churches, societies, nations, and peoples must be transformed, and the spread of the gospel must be accelerated. All this constitutes the "fullness of the Gentiles." They are the conditions for all Israel's salvation and Jesus' return. Only when the Bible is translated into a people group's language can the Gospel of the Kingdom reach them deeply. In 1999, both Wycliffe International (predecessor of the Wycliffe Global Alliance) and partner organization, SIL

International, announced their vision "that by the year 2025 a Bible translation project will be in progress for every people group that needs it."[21]

Question 29 How is the fullness of the Gentiles progressing?

According to the Lausanne Statistical Task Force, which distinguished born-again Christians from nominal Christians, "it took 18 centuries for dedicated believers to grow from 0% of the world's population to 2.5% in 1900, only 70 years to grow from 2.5% to 5%" in 1970," and only another "30 years to grow from 5% to 11.2% of the world population" by 2000.[22] At the turn of the millennium, for the first time in history, there was one true believer for every nine unbelieving people worldwide.[23] In A.D. 100, the ratio of congregations of active believers per unreached people group was 1:12.[24] This ratio became 1:5 in A.D. 1000, 1:1 in 1500, 20:1 in 1900, 150:1 in 1970, 650:1 in 2000, and 1000:1 in 2010.[25] During the past 120 years, there has been an amazing and explosive growth in the number of Christians. We see that there has been a remarkable acceleration in world evangelism and tremendous growth of the Christian population since 1900.

Percentage of True Christians in the World

Early Church	0%	Elapsed time
AD 1900	2.5%	1800 years
AD 1970	5%	70 years
A.D. 2000	11.2%	30 years

Source: Ralph D. Winter and Bruce A. Koch, "Finishing the Task: The Unreached Peoples Challenge," International Journal of Frontier Missions 16, no. 2 (Summer, 1999): 67.

According to research from January 2018 to June 2020 conducted by the Center for the Study of Global Christianity at Gordon-Conwell Theological Seminary and their partners, Pentecostal and charismatic Christians are a little over one fourth of all Christians worldwide.[26] This can be called the Third Era. The First Era began with the early church and continued with the Catholic and Eastern Orthodox churches until the 1500s, the Second Era was the Reformation, and the Third Era is the past 120 years to today of the Pentecostal and charismatic age.

The Flow of Church Growth

Early Church	beginning	elapsed time
Catholic/Easten Oxthodox Church	the first age	1500 yrs
Reformation Era	the second age	1900 yrs
Pentecost/Charismatic (1/4 of all Christians)	the third age	last 120 yrs

Question 30 What are the percentages of the world's religious populations in 2023?

According to the Center for the Study of Global Christianity at Gordon-Conwell Theological Seminary, Christians broadly defined (not distinguishing between being born-again and nominal) were trending to 32.4% of the world population in mid-2023, which is a decrease of 0.5 percentage points from 32.9% in 1970.[27] In contrast, in mid-2023, Muslims were trending to 25% of the world population, increasing by 9.5 percentage points from 15.5% in 1970, which is a noticeably larger increase compared to other religions.[28]

Christianity is the largest religion in the world as of mid-2023, but Islam, currently in second place, is projected to increase and greatly reduce the differential.[29] The difference between Christianity and Islam was 17.4 percentage points in 1970 but diminished to 7.4 percentage points in mid-2023; as the gap has narrowed significantly, it appears necessary to take measures to be on guard and prevent Christianity from declining. The third largest world religion in mid-2023 is Hinduism (14%), followed by Buddhism (7%).[30]

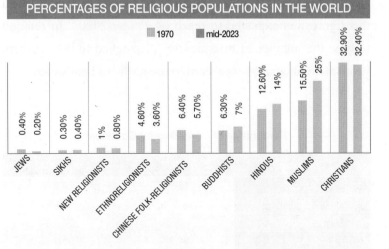

PERCENTAGES OF RELIGIOUS POPULATIONS IN THE WORLD

1970   mid-2023

	1970	mid-2023
JEWS	0.40%	0.20%
SIKHS	0.30%	0.40%
NEW RELIGIONISTS	1%	0.80%
ETHNORELIGIONISTS	4.60%	3.60%
CHINESE FOLK-RELIGIONISTS	6.40%	5.70%
BUDDHISTS	6.30%	7%
HINDUS	12.60%	14%
MUSLIMS	15.50%	25%
CHRISTIANS	32.90%	32.40%

Source: Center for the Study of Global Christianity at Gordon-Conwell Theological Seminary, "Status of Global Christianity, 2023, in the Context of 1900-2050," accessed September 4, 2023, https://www.gordonconwell.edu/wp-content/uploads/sites/13/2023/01/Status-of-Global-Christianity-2023.pdf. Data from the Center for the Study of Global Christianity was utilized to calculate these percentages.

Question 31 **What are the trending percentages of Christians by continent as of mid-2023, and what have been the anticipated rankings of countries by Christian population around 2020?**

According to the Center for the Study of Global Christianity at Gordon-Conwell Theological Seminary, in 1970, 41.3% of Christians (broadly defined, not distinguishing between being born-again and nominal) were in Africa, Asia, and Latin America, and this figure was expected to reach 64.7% by 2020.[31] In relation to this, the number of missionaries dispatched to the southern hemisphere increased compared to the northern hemisphere.

Percentage of Christians by Continent

Continent	1970	mid-2023
Africa	38.7 %	49.2 %
Asia	4.5 %	8.6 %
Europe	75 %	76.3 %
Latin America	94.2 %	91.9 %
North America	91.2 %	71.8 %
Oceania	92.5 %	66 %
Globe	33.2 %	32.4 %

Source for 1970 data: Center for the Study of Global Christianity at Gordon-Conwell Theological Seminary, Christianity in its Global Context, 1970-2020: Society, Religion, and Mission (South Hamilton, MA: Center for the Study of Global Christianity at Gordon-Conwell Theological Seminary, 2013). 9, https://www.gordonconwell.edu/wp-content/uploads/sites/13/2019/04/2Christianityinits GlobalContext.pdf.

Source for 2023 data: Center for the Study of Global Christianity at Gordon-Conwell Theological Seminary, "Status of Global Christianity, 2023, in the Context of 1900-2050," accessed September 4, 2023, https://www.gordonconwell.edu/wp-content/uploads/sites/13/2023/01/Status-of-Global-Christianity-2023.pdf; Worldometer, "Regions in the world by population (2023)," accessed September 4, 2023, https://www.worldometers.info/world-population/population-by-region/. Data from the Center for the Study of Global Christianity and Worldometer were utilized to calculate the 2023 data.

In mid-2023, Christians (including Roman Catholics) were trending to 91.9% of the population in Latin America, which is the largest Christian population by continent. It is followed by Europe (76.3%), North America (71.8%), and Oceania (66%). In Europe, where the church was reported to be decaying, the Christian population has been increasing by a trend of 1.3 percentage points since 1970, and, by contrast, the Christian populations have been decreasing in Latin America, North America, and Oceania. The decreases are attributed to increasing individualism in Europe, increasing atheism in North America, and increasing secularization in Oceania.

In Asia, where only about 8.6% of its population are Christians in mid-2023, the Christian population has been trending toward doubling relative to 4.5% in 1970. This result was greatly influenced by the evangelization of China, which was not even ranked in Christian populations in 1970 but rose to fifth place in 2010 and was anticipated to rise to third place in 2020.[32] Given that China was projected to rise to third place despite only 10.6% of its population being projected to be Christian in 2020, there is anticipation of revival there in the future. The country with the largest Christian population in 2020 was expected to be the U.S. (263 million), followed by Brazil (190 million), which maintained high numbers since 1970.[33] Third place in 2020, as already noted, was anticipated to be China (148 million), fourth place was anticipated to be Mexico (120 million), and fifth place was anticipated to be

Russia (119 million).[34] Britain, Italy, France, and Spain, which were the European countries ranked within the top 10 in 1970 in Christian populations, were not expected to rank in 2020, and, instead, the Congo, Nigeria, and Ethiopia were expected to enter the top 10, indicating noticeable church growth in Africa.[35]

Question 32 What should be the mission strategy given the Christian demographics by continent?

Acts 16:6-9   6 Paul and his companions traveled throughout the region of Phrygia and Galatia, having been kept by the Holy Spirit from preaching the word in the province of Asia. 7 When they came to the border of Mysia, they tried to enter Bithynia, but the Spirit of Jesus would not allow them to. 8 So they passed by Mysia and went down to Troas. 9 During the night Paul had a vision of a man of Macedonia standing and begging him, "Come over to Macedonia and help us."

Apostle Paul laid the foundation for early Christianity. He went on three mission trips. He first chose to go to Asia, but, during the mission in Asia Minor, the Holy Spirit appeared to him and commanded him to turn the mission toward Europe. Therefore, the evangelism in East Asia was moved to Western Europe. This is called the gospel's westward movement. The evangelical movement that changed its direction to the west first

Christianized Rome then Christianized the European continent, then moved to England and Scotland, and, after the 17th century, crossed the Atlantic Ocean to reach North America and South America. Protestantism became predominant in North America, while Catholicism became predominant in South America. Protestantism took root in the U.S. and Canada, continued its westward movement, and spread the gospel to China, Japan, and Korea. The Gospel spread from Europe, crossing the Atlantic Ocean to set its roots in North America, and continued to move westward, crossing the Pacific Ocean to finally advance to Asia. Korea became the first country in Asia where the Protestant church's missionary efforts were successful.

In addition to Apostle Paul, the rest of Jesus' disciples, including His 12 apostles, spread the Gospel from Jerusalem to the east, west, south, and north, and established numerous churches. In this way, the Gospel was transmitted.

The U.S. is still the country that sends out the greatest number of missionaries in the world. Even at this very moment, many missionaries from the U.S. and from other countries are departing from their homes for missions to the east, west, north, and south. Korea, ranked second in number of missions, has dispatched missionaries to 168 countries. Still, the westward movement of the Gospel should not be underestimated. It is a historical fact that one large stream of evangelism has traveled westward from Jerusalem to Antioch to Rome to Europe to England to North America to Korea. The evangelical mission needs to break through Asia (especially Islamic regions) and reach Jerusalem. This is because only when the Gospel of the Kingdom is preached to all nations (Matt. 24:14), and when Israel is restored (Matt. 23:39; Rom. 11:26), will the Lord return to Jerusalem (Zech. 14:4).

As evident in the prior reference table, the evangelization rate is the lowest in Asia, even though more than half of the world's population live there. Given the fact that Korea was the first country in Asia where Christianity and the church flourished, Korea has a great calling for Asia's future. The Korean Church must lead the era of a unified Korea and become the center for missions across Asia. The Korean Church should continue to send missionaries across the globe for world evangelism while fulfilling the calling to take a central role in the westward movement of world missions.

Question 33 How are the end times related to the fulfillment of the "one new man?"

Rev. 19:11   I saw heaven standing open and there before me was a white horse, whose rider is called Faithful and True. With justice he judges and makes war.

Rev. 19:14-15   14 The armies of heaven were following him, riding on white horses and dressed in fine linen, white and clean. 15 Out of his mouth comes a sharp sword with which to strike down the nations. "He will rule them with an iron scepter." He treads the winepress of the fury of the wrath of God Almighty.

Zech. 12:10   "And I will pour out on the house of David and the inhabitants of Jerusalem a spirit of grace and supplication. They will look on me, the one they have pierced, and they will mourn for him as one mourns for an only child, and grieve bitterly for him as one grieves for a firstborn son.

Zech. 14:3-4   3 Then the LORD will go out and fight against those nations, as he fights in the day of battle. 4 On that day his feet will stand on the Mount of Olives, east of Jerusalem, and the Mount of Olives will be split in two from east to west, forming a great valley, with half of the mountain moving north and half moving south.

Although the revelation about the "one new man," a community of unified and perfected saints, has been clearly present in the writings of the Lord and the Apostles, it has been preserved without being fulfilled until the Last Days of this age. Jesus proclaimed on the cross, "It is finished" (John 19:30). Jesus' finished work will be fully fulfilled throughout the entire Christian era and will reach its climax as it is intensively, holistically fulfilled during the end times. Therefore, Jews and Gentiles fulfilling the "one new man" is a sign of the coming age and the completion of the church.

In the Last Days, heaven will open, and Jesus will return riding on a white horse, accompanying countless heavenly hosts and resurrected saints, and He will strike the nations with a sharp sword from His mouth and personally rule over them with an iron scepter. He will wage a war against the combined forces of all the nations that came against Israel and attacked Jerusalem. It will seem like Israel and the Jews may be annihilated, but Jesus will intervene. His intervention is described in detail in Zechariah 12-14 in terms of the earthly part and in Revelation 19 in terms of the heavenly part. Then God will pour out a spirit of grace and supplication upon all Israel, and they will look upon Him whom they had pierced and mourn for Him just as one does for an only child and grieve bitterly for Him as one grieves for a firstborn son. In this way, "all Israel will be saved" (Rom 11:26), and the "one new man" will be fulfilled. The global church, the bride of Christ, should

Completion of the Church
Achievement of the One New Man

Gentile Salvation
(Matt. 24:14)

Jewish Salvation
(Matt. 23:39)

One New Man
(Eph. 2:15)

intercede for Jerusalem and Israel, and pray eagerly for Jesus' Second Advent (Rev. 22:21).

Question 34 When did the early church's "one new man" spirit disappear?

The first Gentile-centered Antioch church (Acts 11:19-21, 15:22-35) served as the "one new man" mission center for the early churches (Acts 13:1-3, 14:26, 18:22). At the time, James the brother of Jesus (Matt. 13:55), as the first overseer of the Jewish-centered Jerusalem Church, the mother church of the early churches, practiced the "one new man" spirit (Acts 15:13-29, 21:18; Gal. 1:19, 2:9). Church historian Josephus states that, until A.D. 135, the overseers of the early Jerusalem church were all Jewish.[36] Until that time, the Gospel spirit of the "one new man" was well preserved. However, after the Bar Kokhba revolt, Rome renamed Jerusalem to Aelia Capitolina and turned it into a Gentile city, banning all Jews. After this, all 15 overseers of the Jerusalem church were Gentiles, and, from this time, the Gentile bishop system continued. Under these circumstances, Replacement Theology gained power, gradually belittling and excluding the Jewish Messiah and the legacy of the Old Testament.

Question 35 What was the greatest obstacle to the "one new man" vision?

First, the number of Jews in the church decreased, while the number of Gentiles in the church increased. Second, due to the destruction of Jerusalem in A.D. 70 and A.D. 135, some believed that God forsook Israel. Third, through the influence of allegorical interpretation, a theology was born that argues that the promises given to Israel have been replaced by spiritual blessings for the church. There was tension between replacement theology and restoration theology, with varying viewpoints expressed by Justin Martyr (A.D. 100-166), Clement of Alexandria (A.D. 150-215), Tertullian (A.D. 160-220), Cyprian (A.D. 200-258), Roman emperor Constantine (A.D. 272–337), Augustine (A.D. 354–430), and, during the Middle Ages (c. 450-1517), allegorical interpretation and amillennialism were predominant. And sadly, Martin Luther, the initiator of the Reformation, promoted a harsh Replacement Theology. This is because Jerusalem was still in a ruined state at that time. Luther considered that grave reality as evidence that God abandoned Israel. Luther's brutal anti-Semitic statements later provided Hitler the political and social excuse to murder 6 million Jews.

Question 36 Who most influenced the anti-Semitism that hinders the fulfillment of the "one new man?"

Ignatius (2nd century) said that whoever celebrates the Passover with the Jews and accepts the symbols of Jewish Feasts is an accomplice of those who killed the Lord and His disciples. Chrysostom (A.D. 349-407) argued, "To hate the Jews is the duty of a Christian. The Jews are possessed by the devil and are like greedy pigs. God always hates the Jews."[37] Augustine (A.D. 354-430) said, "Even though the Jews deserve to die, instead they were destined to roam the face of the earth as the witness of God's punishment and the victory of the church over the synagogue."[38] Luther (1483-1546), who raised up the torch of German Reformation in 1517, wrote in 1543 in his book, *On the Jews and Their Lies:* "Burn the synagogues, destroy Jewish homes, confiscate their prayer books and Talmud, forbid Rabbis to teach, execute the violators, deprive their travel right, ban usury, impose forced labor."[39] Later, quoting Luther's anti-Semitic statements, Hitler perpetrated the Holocaust, persecuting and annihilating the Jews.

Weissmandl, a Polish Jewish Rabbi, sent a letter to the Vatican pleading for the rescue of innocent young Jewish children, but he received the anti-Semitic reply: "There is no such thing as the innocent blood of Jewish children. All Jewish blood is guilty, and the Jews must die because that is their punishment for that sin." [40]

Question 37 In what form does the anti-Semitism that hinders the fulfillment of the "one new man" appear today?

Christian Anti-Semitism is becoming a large stumbling block to the fulfillment of the "one new man." Recently, there was a shooting in the U.S. in which a 19-year-old youth opened fire at a Jewish synagogue, killing 1 and wounding 3 people. The suspect who sprayed bullets was a member of a church and was firmly convinced that killing Jews was doing God's will. Just as Satan hates Christ's followers, Satan's hatred against Jews is persistent. Satan, who failed to prevent the Messiah's first Advent, is now actively obstructing His Second Advent, because he knows his own fate. Satan has been making the memory of the Holocaust dimmer and dimmer for over 70 years. Many young people are ignorant of the Holocaust, and some deny it as false information or a conspiracy. Some refuse to believe that the rebirth of the modern state of Israel and Jerusalem's restoration are God's miracles. Some are wrongly labeling and attacking Israel as a nation of occupying forces, genocide, and racial discrimination. And Satan is causing many Christians to think that the church has replaced Israel and that God has no plan whatsoever for modern Jews anymore. The church must change Replacement Theology to Restoration Theology, repent of its past sins against the Jews, and actively resist the world's hatred against Jews. Then the fulfillment of the "one new man" will be ignited.

"One New Man's Purpose?"

Question 38 What is the purpose of the "one new man"?

Eph. 2:15   by abolishing in his flesh the law with its commandments and regulations. His purpose was to create in himself one new man out of the two, thus making peace,

Eph. 2:18   For through him we both have access to the Father by one Spirit.

Eph. 2:22   And in him you too are being built together to become a dwelling in which God lives by his Spirit.

The "one new man" is a community in which Jews and Gentiles are being built together in the Holy Spirit to become God's dwelling place. The purpose of the "one new man" is to complete a dwelling place for God.

Question 39 What is the mystery of God in the process of salvation?

Rom. 11:17   If some of the branches have been broken off, and you, though a wild olive shoot, have been grafted in among the others and now share in the nourishing sap from the olive root,

Rom. 11:23   And if they do not persist in unbelief, they will be grafted in, for God is able to graft them in again.

Rom. 11:25-26 25 I do not want you to be ignorant of this mystery, brothers, so that you may not be conceited: Israel has experienced a hardening in part until the full number of the Gentiles has come in. 26 And so all Israel will be saved, as it is written: "The deliverer will come from Zion; he will turn godlessness away from Jacob.

The completion of God's work of salvation consists of the branches of the cultivated olive tree (Jewish believers) with Abraham being its root and the branches of the wild olive trees (Gentile believers) that have been grafted onto it, so when the full number of Gentiles comes in, we expect the eschatological completion of all Israel being saved (Rom. 11:25-26a).

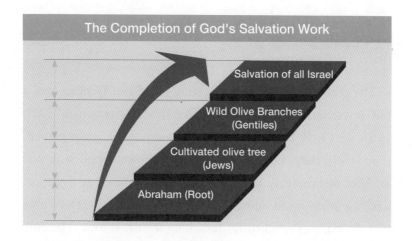

The Completion of God's Salvation Work

Salvation of all Israel

Wild Olive Branches
(Gentiles)

Cultivated olive tree
(Jews)

Abraham (Root)

Question 40 Was the church at Ephesus a church that achieved the "one new man?"

Eph. 2:15   by abolishing in his flesh the law with its commandments and regulations. His purpose was to create in himself one new man out of the two, thus making peace,

Acts 20:21   I have declared to both Jews and Greeks that they must turn to God in repentance and have faith in our Lord Jesus.

Rev. 2:2-4   2 I know your deeds, your hard work and your perseverance. I know that you cannot tolerate wicked men, that you have tested those who claim to be apostles but are not, and have found them false 3 You have persevered and have endured hardships for my name, and have not grown weary. 4 Yet I hold this against you: You have forsaken your first love.

The church at Ephesus, consisting mostly of Gentiles and a few Jews, was a church that realized the "one new man" (Acts 19:10, 19:17, 19:21). With God's "incomparably great power" (Eph. 1:19), they worshiped God and fellowshipped with one another in brotherly love. However, the church at Ephesus, which was strong for more than 40 years to Apostle John's time (c. A.D. 95), was rebuked for forsaking their first love. The only reprimand against the church at Ephesus, "You have forsaken your first love," likely means that they forsook the first love with which they, Jews and Gentiles together, had realized the "one new man."

Question 41 Where will the ultimate fulfillment of the "one new man" be visibly affirmed?

Rev. 21:12-14   12 It had a great, high wall with twelve gates, and with twelve angels at the gates. On the gates were written the names of the twelve tribes of Israel. 13 There were three gates on the east, three on the north, three on the south and three on the west. 14 The wall of the city had twelve foundations, and on them were the names of the twelve apostles of the Lamb.

The ultimate fulfillment of the "one new man" will be visibly affirmed in the New Jerusalem as described in Revelation 21. The twelve gates of the New Jerusalem, on which the names of the twelve tribes of Israel are inscribed, and its twelve foundations, on which the names of the twelve Apostles are inscribed, robustly shows the completed image of the "one new man." Likewise, the complete unification of Jews and Gentiles in Christ is the fulfillment of the "one new man" and an indispensable element of the fulfillment of God's Kingdom.

Question 42 Where was God during the Holocaust?

During World War II, about 6 million Jews, including about 1.5 million children, were murdered. Many people ask, "Where was God?" Israel's God, Who was there when a young Jew named Jesus, the Son of God, was dying a miserable death on the cross, was there when the Jews, His people, were being massacred, and He was also there at the U.N. General Assembly held on November 29, 1947, when voting was underway to decide upon the Palestine partition plan for the reestablishment of the modern state of Israel.

Question 43 Will the national, corporate salvation of Israel be possible?

Exod. 19:6   you will be for me a kingdom of priests and a holy nation.' These are the words you are to speak to the Israelites."

Isa. 42:6   "I, the LORD, have called you in righteousness; I will take hold of your hand. I will keep you and will make you to be a covenant for the people and a light for the Gentiles,

Israel's calling is to become a blessing to the nations (Gen. 12:3), a kingdom of priests, and a light for the Gentiles. To fulfill this calling, they must gather again. Only through regathering can their national salvation be achieved (Rom. 11:26). Is it not possible for the One Who enabled Israel's independence to save all the Jews in Israel (as of 2020, about 6.8 million) in an instant?

Question 44 Can we expect reconciliation between Arabs and Jews?

Isa. 19:24-25   24 In that day Israel will be the third, along with Egypt and Assyria, a blessing on the earth. 25 The LORD Almighty will bless them, saying, "Blessed be Egypt my people, Assyria my handiwork, and Israel my inheritance."

God's Word foretells that Egypt, Assyria, and Israel will together become a blessing on the earth. Reconciliation between Arabs and Jews through the love of Jesus has the potential to heal all kinds of racial, political, and religious divisions.

Question 45 What is the difference between Arabs and Jews as Abraham's descendants?

Gen. 12:2-3   2 "I will make you into a great nation and I will bless you; I will make your name great, and you will be a blessing. 3 I will bless those who bless you, and whoever curses you I will curse; and all peoples on earth will be blessed through you."

Gen. 17:4   "As for me, this is my covenant with you: You will be the father of many nations.

Gen. 21:12   But God said to him, "Do not be so distressed about the boy and your maidservant. Listen to whatever Sarah tells you, because it is through Isaac that your offspring will be reckoned.

A father desires the most for his children to love him and to love one another. The blessings of Abraham were equally given to Arabs as well. They are preserving the ancient culture of the Middle East more abundantly than the Jews. Their population is over 25 times greater than the Jewish population, and their land is 500 times vaster than that of the Jews. God has blessed them with land, wealth, and resources.

However, Arabs are excluded from two special aspects of the covenant related to the Messiah. To protect the Messiah's genealogy, God had to separate the descendants of Isaac from those of Ishmael (Gen. 21:12). And for fulfilling that calling, God gave Isaac ownership of the land of Israel. Nevertheless, this does not exclude Arabs from the love of God for them. Abraham's spiritual blessings are equally available to Arabs through their faith in Jesus Christ. God said that He would make the Jews jealous through His saving relationship with Gentiles. The Gentiles who can best serve in making Israel jealous are Arabs!

Question 46 How are Muslims converting to Christianity today?

Muslims are increasing more rapidly in number than Christians. Today, Europe is rapidly becoming Islamized. However, cruel acts of violence by radical Islamic militant groups are causing many Muslims to leave Islam in horror, and they are becoming interested in Christian messages of God's love, salvation, hope, peace, and joy. As a result, even under horrible persecutions, Muslims are explosively converting to Christianity. These days, millions of Arabs are being exposed to Christianity through TV, the radio, or the internet. And many Muslims are encountering God through visions, dreams, or miracles. The number of Arabs starting to read the Bible are increasing, and the Gospel is being rapidly spread through refugees. They are converting upon realizing the truth that Jesus provides hope that can never be found in Islam. This is God's mystery.

While Muslims use violence and cruelly kill people for their beliefs, Christians die peacefully out of love for their faith. In 2015, on a beach in Syria, 21 Egyptian Coptic Christians were cruelly beheaded by a radical Islamic militant terrorist group called IS, and the people of the victims' village are proud of their martyrdom. The mothers, who lost their sons at the hands of IS, know that their sons are now in heaven wearing crowns. They too are resolved to be martyred, are waiting for martyrdom, and are proud of the martyrs. "The blood of martyrs is the seed of the church."[41] As long as there are believers willing to become martyrs for Christ, the church is alive and will never die. Christians, who are living in the Last Days, should be filled with the Holy Spirit to proclaim the gospel even to the point of martyrdom and show their love for God and their neighbors.

Question 47 What is the true solution to the Israeli-Palestinian conflict?

The Israeli-Palestinian conflict is impossible to resolve with any political, economic, or military approach. The Israelis and Palestinians today most urgently need the turmoil to subside, but, due to Satan's hatred, the deep enmity cannot be broken by political power. Only Jesus can demolish the wall of hostility between Jews and Arabs and change their hearts of stone to forgiveness, understanding, and love. Whether Jew or Arab, whether individually or corporately, all must serve Jesus Christ. Only the Prince of Peace, Jesus Christ, can provide true peace and enable Israel and Palestine to live in peace. The only solution is in God the Creator's Word of Truth.

An Arab pastor, who remains anonymous due to safety concerns, says, "I know for sure that the Bible is revealing God's plan for Israel. The land that the Jews and Palestinians are now fighting over is what God promised to give to the Jews, not to Ishmael's descendants. It is impossible to resolve the Israel and Palestine issue at the political level, which is widely off from God's Word. The Bible is the living Word of God, and it makes clear who is entitled to the right of succession of the land. This land is the one promised to the Jews, and no one else."

Question 48 What kind of church is a glorious, evangelical church?

Matt. 24:14   And this gospel of the kingdom will be preached in the whole world as a testimony to all nations, and then the end will come.

An evangelical church teaches, enjoys, and preaches the Gospel. The Gospel is the victory of Jesus Christ on the cross confirmed by His resurrection. The Gospel restores in Christ what Adam lost. Salvation is enjoying the Gospel in all aspects of life. Evangelism is helping people to live abundant lives through the Gospel.

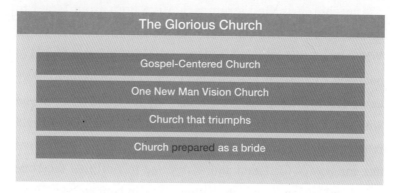

The Glorious Church

Gospel-Centered Church

One New Man Vision Church

Church that triumphs

Church prepared as a bride

Question 49 What kind of church is the glorious, "one new man" vision church?

Eph. 2:13-15   13 But now in Christ Jesus you who once were far away have been brought near through the blood of Christ. 14 For he himself is our peace, who has made the two one and has destroyed the barrier, the dividing wall of hostility, 15 by abolishing in his flesh the law with its commandments and regulations. His purpose was to create in himself one new man out of the two, thus making peace,

Eph. 2:18   For through him we both have access to the Father by one Spirit.

Eph. 2:22   And in him you too are being built together to become a dwelling in which God lives by his Spirit.

The church is God's representative born from Israel to demonstrate His love and grace for the salvation of the world. While Israel was geographically and spiritually far away and in pain, the church was grafted onto the root of Abraham to serve as a priest to the nations. Now is the time for Israel to return and with the church fulfill the "one new man" together. Until Israel returns, the church is not yet whole. The glorious church loves and intercedes for Israel and is devoted to fulfilling the "one new man" vision, in which the two of them come to the Father in one Spirit and are built together in Jesus to become God's dwelling place.

Question 50 What kind of church is the glorious, victorious church?

Eph. 6:18-19   18 And pray in the Spirit on all occasions with all kinds of prayers and requests. With this in mind, be alert and always keep on praying for all the saints. 19 Pray also for me, that whenever I open my mouth, words may be given me so that I will fearlessly make known the mystery of the gospel,

The church is a house of prayer. We must pray continually. If we pray continually, God also works continually. Overpower Satan with a victorious prayer that breaks through all difficulties and troubles to fulfill God's will on earth. Victory in prayer enables us to overcome ourselves and the world and fulfill our calling. With earnest, fervent prayers, let us burn down all obstacles and open heaven's path. If we kneel with poor and humble hearts to pray fervently and intensely, relying on Jesus' precious blood, the fire of the Holy Spirit will come down. When the fire of the Holy Spirit comes down, we can overcome ourselves and the world and be used as a church to fulfill the mission. Let us pray fervently for the outpouring of the Holy Spirit, for spiritual victory, and for the strength to fulfill the mission. The glorious, victorious church in the Last Days prays, full of the Holy Spirit, and sparks the most powerful revival in history, transforms society in diverse areas, and will be used for gathering the great harvest in the Last Days.

Question 51 What kind of church is adorned as a glorious bride?

Rev. 19:7-8   7 Let us rejoice and be glad and give him glory! For the wedding of the Lamb has come, and his bride has made herself ready. 8 Fine linen, bright and clean, was given her to wear." (Fine linen stands for the righteous acts of the saints.)

Paul described his evangelical mission as matchmaking between the Groom, Jesus Christ, and the saints, His Bride (2 Cor. 11:2). Saints need to become a pure Bride who adore only one Groom, Jesus Christ. The Bride's robe will be bright, clean fine linen. The clean fine linen granted by God's grace is only Jesus Christ's righteousness. Since the saints' righteous acts will make the fine linen shine even brighter, the saints must live righteous lives in Christ. Saints have been washed by Jesus' precious blood shed on the cross, proclaim the Gospel by the anointing of the Holy Spirit, and live as lights in the world. The glorious church adorns itself as the Bride for the Wedding of the Lamb. The glory of heaven that the saints will enjoy is described as a wedding party because heaven will be full of true joy, delight, and satisfaction. The Bride who participates in the Wedding of the Lamb will enjoy the utmost satisfaction and perfect joy.

Conclusion

Through the Gospel of the Kingdom, the Jews and Gentiles becoming "one new man" in Jesus Christ is the mystery of God, the pinnacle of all kinds of God's wisdom, and the essence of God's master plan. To overcome the dark forces, believing Jews and believing Gentiles, with the help of the Holy Spirit, must in unity, humility, and self-denial look to the Lord alone. The beautiful image of God's people is the glorious church. The image of the most glorious church is all Jews and Gentiles who are called Christians fulfilling the "one new man" and is a pure, beautifully adorned Bride waiting for her Groom, Jesus.

Chapter 6

God's Time

Introduction

God's master plan to save mankind has been unfolding according to His timetable. God presides over individuals, communities, nations, and people groups. God created the heavens and the earth, and time and history, for mankind. Days added together form a week, weeks added together form a month, months added together form a year, and years added together form a life. Life involves sleeping every night and waking up every morning, constituting daily experiences of death and resurrection. During the week, mankind works for 6 days, and, on the Lord's Day, mankind worships God, fellowships, and enjoys rest. The Lord's Day is when mankind experiences in advance the rest in heaven to be enjoyed after life on earth. God has revealed several kinds of timetables for mankind's salvation.

Question 1 Are the Feasts of the LORD God's timetable?

Gen. 1:14   And God said, "Let there be lights in the expanse of the sky to separate the day from the night, and let them serve as signs to mark seasons (מוֹעֵד, moed) and days and years,

Lev. 23:2   "Speak to the Israelites and say to them: 'These are my appointed feasts (מוֹעֵד, moed), the appointed feasts of the LORD, which you are to proclaim as sacred assemblies.

1 Sam. 20:35   In the morning Jonathan went out to the field for his meeting (מוֹעֵד, moed) with David. He had a small boy with him,

Many translators have translated the Hebrew word מוֹעֵד(mô'ēḏ) in Genesis 1:14 into "seasons" and in 1 Samuel 20:35 into "meeting."

The word "feast" is also a translation of מוֹעֵד (mô'ēḏ), meaning appointed time, appointment, season, congregation, assembly, and sign. The Feasts are sacred assemblies. The Hebrew word for assembly is מִקְרָא (miqrâ'), which also means rehearsal. Israel is the kingdom of priests commanded to keep the Feasts. Since the main character of the Old and New Testaments is Jesus, the essence of the Feasts is all about Jesus the Savior. The Feasts of the LORD are God's promises fulfilled precisely to the date by the ministry of Jesus the Savior.

The Spring Feasts that God gave to Israel are the Passover,

the Feast of Unleavened Bread, the Feast of Firstfruits, and Pentecost. The Spring Feasts represent Jesus' First Advent and has already been fulfilled by His first coming. Jesus died as the Passover Lamb, resurrected on the day of the Feast of Firstfruits, and sent the promised Holy Spirit on the day of Pentecost. Israel had been rehearsing the First Advent until the time became full for its fulfillment by Jesus' coming. The Fall Feasts that symbolize the Lord's Second Advent are the Feast of Trumpets, the Day of Atonement, and the Feast of Tabernacles. The Fall Feasts are a rehearsal for the Lord's Second Advent. Therefore, the Jews must gather and keep the Feasts at the Temple before the Lord returns. God is gathering the Jews back to the Promised Land to restore the Feasts to rehearse the Lord's Second Coming. The King of kings Jesus, Who is the Lord of the Feast of Tabernacles, will return and reign in the Millennial Kingdom. God's salvation is achieved through the Savior. The Feasts are shadows providing hope for the substance to come and the basis for recognizing the substance when it arrives.

Feasts of Spring

Feast	Commemoration	Jewish Calendar	Solar
Passover	Crucifixion of Jesus	Jan. (Nisan) 14	3-4
Unleavened Bread	Sanctification	Jan. 15 (one week)	3-4
Firstfruits	Resurrection	Jan. 17	3-4
Harvest Pentecost	Giving of the Torah Descent of the Holy Spirit	Sivan 6	5-6

Feasts of Autumn

Feast	Commemoration	Jewish Calendar	Solar Calendar
Trumpets	King's Coming Judgment begins	July 1	9-10
Atonement (Yom Kippur)	National repentance	July 10	9-10
Tabernacles Ingathering	Messianic Reign God with us	July 15 (one week)	9-10

Question 2 What does the Passover Feast signify?

Lev. 23:4-5   "These are the LORD's appointed feasts, the sacred assemblies you are to proclaim at their appointed times: The LORD's Passover begins at twilight on the fourteenth day of the first month.

Exod. 12:13   The blood will be a sign for you on the houses where you are; and when I see the blood, I will pass over you. No destructive plague will touch you when I strike Egypt.

1 Cor. 5:7   Get rid of the old yeast that you may be a new batch without yeast – as you really are. For Christ, our Passover lamb, has been sacrificed.

John 13:1   It was just before the Passover Feast. Jesus knew that the time had come for him to leave this world and go to the Father. Having loved his own who were in the world, he now showed them the full extent of his love.

John 1:29   The next day John saw Jesus coming toward him and said, "Look, the Lamb of God, who takes away the sin of the world!

John 18:28   Then the Jews led Jesus from Caiaphas to the palace of the Roman governor. By now it was early morning, and to avoid ceremonial uncleanness the Jews did not enter the palace; they wanted to be able to eat the Passover.

John 18:39   But it is your custom for me to release to you one prisoner at the time of the Passover. Do you want me to release 'the king of the Jews'?"

John 18:38   "What is truth?" Pilate asked. With this he went out again to the Jews and said, "I find no basis for a charge against him.

John 18:32   This happened so that the words Jesus had spoken indicating the kind of death he was going to die would be fulfilled.

Passover commemorates Nisan 14 at the time of the Exodus when each Israelite household killed a lamb and smeared its blood on the doorposts of their houses. The angel of death passed over every Israelite house due to the blood of the lamb. This is because the judgment of death had already been made. Through the sacrifice of the sinless Son of God, the angel of death passes over believers. Sinners receive salvation through the shed blood of the innocent Lamb, Jesus Christ. Through the sacrifice of the Savior, sinners obtain salvation. Without His sacrifice, no one can obtain salvation. On Passover Day, the LORD God redeemed the people of Israel from the bondage of Egypt, and, in the New Testament era, Jesus Christ fulfilled the prophetic symbol of the Old Testament as the Passover Lamb. In history, at the predetermined time on Passover Day and the predetermined place in Jerusalem, Jesus died on the cross to fulfill salvation.

Question 3 What does the Feast of Unleavened Bread signify?

Lev. 23:6   On the fifteenth day of that month the LORD's Feast of Unleavened Bread begins; for seven days you must eat bread made without yeast.

1 Cor. 5:8   Therefore let us keep the Festival, not with the old yeast, the yeast of malice and wickedness, but with bread without yeast, the bread of sincerity and truth.

On Nisan 15, Israel escaped from Egypt's bondage and began the Exodus, and, likewise, in the New Testament era, the saints who were redeemed by the eternal sacrifice of the Passover Lamb began their journey of sanctification by removing the old yeast from their lives. Beginning on Nisan 15 and lasting for 7 days, the Feast of Unleavened Bread is when homes are searched to remove, burn, and discard any leaven to cleanse the house, and unleavened bread is eaten. The unleavened bread represents sinless Jesus Christ. By believing in Jesus, we live with the life of Jesus. Jesus' blood and flesh become ours. The Passover signifies salvation through faith, and the Feast of Unleavened Bread symbolizes sanctification.

Question 4 What does the Feast of Firstfruits signify?

Lev. 23:10-11 10 "Speak to the Israelites and say to them: 'When you enter the land I am going to give you and you reap its harvest, bring to the priest a sheaf of the first grain you harvest. 11 He is to wave the sheaf before the LORD so it will be accepted on your behalf; the priest is to wave it on the day after the Sabbath.

Matt. 28:1   After the Sabbath, at dawn on the first day of the week, Mary Magdalene and the other Mary went to look at the tomb.

Luke 24:1   On the first day of the week, very early in the morning, the women took the spices they had prepared and went to the tomb.

1 Cor. 15:20   But Christ has indeed been raised from the dead, the firstfruits of those who have fallen asleep.

The Feast of Firstfruits is when the firstfruits of the first harvest in the new year are offered to God. It was observed on the day after the Sabbath during the Feast of Unleavened Bread. At the beginning of the barley harvest, the sheaf of the first grain was brought to the priest, and the priest offered the sheaf as a wave offering to God. At that time, the burnt offering, meal offering, and drink offering were offered together. On the Feast of Firstfruits, Jesus resurrected after three days in the tomb, as prophesied in the Bible (1 Cor. 15:4, 15:20) and became the firstfruits of those who have fallen asleep. Lord Jesus resurrected on the very day of the Feast of Firstfruits, ascended into heaven, and is now seated at the right hand of the throne of God (Luke 22:69; Heb. 12:2). The Feast of Firstfruits requires believers to have resurrection faith.

The Feast of Firstfruits on Nisan 17 was when Noah's Ark rested on Mount Ararat (Gen. 8:4) and coincides with when God's new creation work began, which signifies that we who will be resurrected will begin the new creation life. The Feast of Firstfruits was also when Israel crossed the Red Sea (Exod. 13:20, Succoth and Etham; Exod. 14:2, Baal Zephon), which represents freedom from sins and the beginning of a new life of resurrection.

Question 5 What does the Feast of Pentecost (the Feast of Weeks, the Feast of Harvest) signify?

Lev. 23:16-17 16 Count off fifty days up to the day after the seventh Sabbath, and then present an offering of new grain to the LORD. 17 From wherever you live, bring two loaves made of two-tenths of an ephah of fine flour, baked with yeast, as a wave offering of firstfruits to the LORD.

Exod. 19:16-18 16 On the morning of the third day there was thunder and lightning, with a thick cloud over the mountain, and a very loud trumpet blast. Everyone in the camp trembled. 17 Then Moses led the people out of the camp to meet with God, and they stood at the foot of the mountain. 18 Mount Sinai was covered with smoke, because the LORD descended on it in fire. The smoke billowed up from it like smoke from a furnace, the whole mountain trembled violently,

After a very loud trumpet blast was heard, God descended on Mount Sinai and gave the Ten Commandments.

Eph. 2:15   by abolishing in his flesh the law with its commandments and regulations. His purpose was to create in himself one new man out of the two, thus making peace,

Matt. 5:17   "Do not think that I have come to abolish the Law or the Prophets; I have not come to abolish them but to fulfill them.

Acts 2:1-4   1 When the day of Pentecost came, they were all together in one place. 2 Suddenly a sound like the blowing of a violent wind came from heaven and filled the whole house where they were sitting. 3 They saw what seemed to be tongues of fire that separated and came to rest on each of them. 4 All of them were filled with the Holy Spirit and began to speak in other tongues as the Spirit enabled them.

Pentecost, occurring the day after the seventh Sabbath following the Feast of Firstfruits which is the 50th day after the Feast of Firstfruits, is when the first of the wheat harvest is offered to God as two loaves made of fine flour for a wave offering. Through the outpouring of the Holy Spirit on Pentecost, the beginning of the harvest for God's Kingdom was proclaimed through His power and strength. Pentecost was when the Law was given on Mount Sinai and later when the law of the Spirit of new life was given to enable believers to keep the Law.

Jesus died on the cross as the Passover Lamb on Nisan 14 in the Jewish calendar, for the forgiveness of sins, and resurrected at dawn on Nisan 17, the Feast of Firstfruits, to provide eternal life. Thereafter, for 40 days He revealed His glorious, resurrected body and taught about the Kingdom of God, and then He ascended into heaven. 10 days after ascension, on Pentecost, He sent the promised Holy Spirit to provide the power to fulfill the mission for God's Kingdom. God's people who fulfill the mission for His Kingdom will reign with Jesus when He returns.

Question 6 What does the Feast of Trumpets signify?

Lev. 23:24 "Say to the Israelites: 'On the first day of the seventh month you are to have a day of rest, a sacred assembly commemorated with trumpet blasts.

The Feast of Trumpets falls on the first day of the first month in the civil calendar, so it was also called Rosh Hashanah (הַשָּׁנָה רֹאשׁ, New Year's Day). Each year, on the first day of the seventh month in their religious calendar, the Israelites blew trumpets to signify a new beginning. Israel blew trumpets when calling for repentance, when announcing a war, and when welcoming a king. During the Feast of Trumpets, the Israelites confessed their sins and reconciled with each other to purify themselves.

Just as God descended on Mount Sinai with trumpet blasts (Exod. 19:16-18), the Lord Jesus will return with trumpet blasts. Rosh Hashanah is also when the Messiah will rise to the throne. The Messiah will begin to exercise His kingship and judicial power.

Rev. 8:6   **Then the seven angels who had the seven trumpets prepared to sound them.**

Rev. 10:7   **But in** the days when the seventh angel is about to sound his trumpet, **the mystery of God will be accomplished, just as he announced to his servants the prophets.**

Rev. 11:15   The seventh angel sounded his trumpet, **and there were loud voices in heaven, which said: "The kingdom of the world has become the kingdom of our Lord and of his Christ, and he will reign for ever and ever."**

1 Thess. 4:16 For the Lord himself will come down from heaven, with a loud command, with the voice of the archangel and with the trumpet call of God, and the dead in Christ will rise first.

The New Testament tells us that the Messiah will return with the final trumpet blast and, at that time, resurrection and rapture will occur.

Question 7 What does the Day of Atonement (יום כיפור, Yom Kippur) signify?

Lev. 23:27 "The tenth day of this seventh month is the Day of Atonement. Hold a sacred assembly and deny yourselves, and present an offering made to the LORD by fire.

Heb. 9:7 But only the high priest entered the inner room, and that only once a year, and never without blood, which he offered for himself and for the sins the people had committed in ignorance.

Heb. 9:28 so Christ was sacrificed once to take away the sins of many people; and he will appear a second time, not to bear sin, but to bring salvation to those who are waiting for him.

The Day of Atonement is the tenth day of the seventh month in the Jewish calendar and the only day of the year when Israel's high priest was allowed to enter the Holy of Holies. It is the day when the sins of the entire nation are removed for the past year, opening the way to boldly come before God again. The high priest cast lots over two goats to determine which one to sacrifice as a sin offering to God and which one to send into the wilderness as the scapegoat carrying sins. God's grace provides not only atonement for sins but also release from guilt.

Jesus Christ, as the atoning sacrifice for all mankind, offered His own body and shed His precious blood to obtain eternal redemption for us once and for all. Therefore, the work on the Day of Atonement foreshadowed the cross of Jesus Christ. The moment Jesus died on the cross, the veil of the Holy Temple was torn from top to bottom, opening the barrier caused by sin. The Holy of Holies, where the Ark of the Covenant was seated, became accessible.

Question 8 What is the relationship between the last trumpet and the Day of Atonement?

Rev. 11:15   The seventh angel sounded his trumpet, and there were loud voices in heaven, which said: "The kingdom of the world has become the kingdom of our Lord and of his Christ, and he will reign for ever and ever."

Rev. 11:18   The nations were angry; and your wrath has come. The time has come for judging the dead, and for rewarding your servants the prophets and your saints and those who reverence your name, both small and great – and for destroying those who destroy the earth."

The seventh angel blows his trumpet, and the reign of Christ is announced in heaven.

Matt. 24:31   And he will send his angels with a loud trumpet call, and they will gather his elect from the four winds, from one end of the heavens to the other.

1 Cor. 15:51-52 51 Listen, I tell you a mystery: We will not all sleep, but we will all be changed 52 in a flash, in the twinkling of an eye, at the last trumpet. For the trumpet will sound, the dead will be raised imperishable, and we will be changed.

The last trumpet announces Jesus' Second Advent as well as resurrection and rapture. In a word, the lesson of the Feast of Trumpets is Jesus Christ's Second Advent. It is the event that completes God's history of redemption. Of course, there will be judgment on the day of Christ's return, but, for Christians, it is the day of completion, joy, and renewal.

The seventh trumpet will lead to the most staggering judgment against the world that killed God's prophets. This is because, in the Jewish tradition, the Feast of Trumpets (Rosh Hashanah) is also when God's judgment is declared. Therefore, the period between the Feast of Trumpets (Rosh Hashanah) and the Day of Atonement (Yom Kippur) is known as the "Days of Awe." In the Jewish tradition, these days are the time for God's judgment as well as His vengeance against the unrepentant.

Question 9 What does the Feast of Tabernacles (Ingathering, Tents) signify?

Lev. 23:34   "Say to the Israelites: 'On the fifteenth day of the seventh month the LORD's Feast of Tabernacles begins, and it lasts for seven days.

Zech. 14:9   The LORD will be king over the whole earth. On that day there will be one LORD, and his name the only name.

Zech. 14:16   Then the survivors from all the nations that have attacked Jerusalem will go up year after year to worship the King, the LORD Almighty, and to celebrate the Feast of Tabernacles.

For seven days beginning on the fifteenth day of the seventh month in the Jewish calendar, the Feast of Tabernacles was held by building and dwelling in temporary shelters to commemorate Israel's forty years of wandering in the wilderness after the Exodus. It was also a thanksgiving feast at the close of the year's harvest to thank God for His grace in providing an abundant harvest in the Promised Land. While the Day of Atonement was to atone for Israelites' sins, the Feast of Tabernacles was to atone for all nations' sins in the world. Given the 70 clans delineated in Genesis 10, 70 bulls representing all nations in the world were offered to God in prayer and blessing for them (Num. 29:12-34). The Feast of Tabernacles represents the Messianic Millennial Kingdom ruled by Christ Himself. During the Feast of Tabernacles, Solomon's Temple was dedicated, becoming God's dwelling place in Israel (1 Kings 9:3). In the future, when Jesus returns and reigns over the Millennial Kingdom, Israel and other nations will observe this Feast.

Question 10 What is meant by "He must remain in heaven until the time comes for God to restore everything?"

Acts 3:20-21   20 and that he may send the Christ, who has been appointed for you – even Jesus. 21 He must remain in heaven until the time comes for God to restore everything, as he promised long ago through his holy prophets.

Isa. 61:2   to proclaim the year of the LORD's favor (First Advent) and the day of vengeance of our God (Second Advent), to comfort all who mourn,

Luke 4:19   to proclaim the year of the Lord's favor."

John 12:47-48　47 "As for the person who hears my words but does not keep them, I do not judge him. For I did not come to judge the world, but to save it (First Advent). 48 There is a judge for the one who rejects me and does not accept my words; that very word which I spoke will condemn him at the last day (Second Advent).

Jesus is in heaven until the time for the restoration of all things, and, when He returns, He will restore all things. God will send Christ, Who has been appointed for us, again. In the First Advent, Jesus came to save believers by bearing our sins and being crucified. In the Second Advent, Jesus will also come for believers. He will return to complete His work of salvation that He began on the cross and by His resurrection to save sinners.

When reading Isaiah 61:1-2, Jesus quoted only up to the first part of verse 2, "to proclaim the year of the LORD's favor." However, Jesus' return will be "the day of vengeance of our God," the latter part of verse 2, and unbelievers will be judged. Jesus will return to judge the sins of those who refused to believe Him and lived as they pleased, and He will make them pay the price for their sins.

Question 11 What is meant by "until the land is utterly forsaken?"

Isa. 6:11-12　11 Then I said, "For how long, O Lord?" And he

answered: "Until the cities lie ruined and without inhabitant, until the houses are left deserted and the fields ruined and ravaged, 12 until the LORD has sent everyone far away and the land is utterly forsaken.

The Bible informed us in advance that after God scatters the children of Israel all over the nations by His judgment and providence, and after the land becomes utterly forsaken, Israel's restoration will begin. After Israel's destruction in A.D. 70 by Rome, the devastation of the land continued for about 1900 years under seven great powers (the Romans, Byzantines, Arabs, Crusaders, Mamluks, Ottomans, and the British) that controlled the land in turns. In 1866, W.M. Thomson wrote that the Holy Land was utterly desolate, with no home, no footsteps of inhabitants, and no shepherd to lessen monotony and boredom. Mark Twain also wrote, after traveling to the land in the 1860s, that it was "desolate and unlovely," with "miles of desolate country whose soil is rich enough, but is given over wholly to weeds—a silent, mournful expanse" and the "hush of a solitude that is inhabited only by birds of prey and skulking foxes."[42] However, because it was a desolate land, the Jews were able to return to live in the Holy Land without expelling anyone. If the land had been well cultivated and inhabited, there would have been no place for them to come and live when God brought the Jews back to their land in His time.

In the 1880s during the pogroms in Russia, about 25,000 to 35,000 diaspora Jews, mostly university students, returned to the land of Israel. The Zionist movement that followed encouraged many Jews to return to the Promised Land. Traditionally, at the close of the annual Passover commemoration, the Jews expressed their dream of returning to their ancient land by exchanging the greeting "Next year in Jerusalem!" This is because, for Diaspora Jews, the land of Israel is the land God promised their ancestors as an everlasting covenant, and there are numerous Bible verses about their prophesied return to that land.

As of 2021, there are about 6.8 million Jews who returned and are living in the land. Ministries around the globe are helping Jews return to the land. In present-day Israel, the wastelands have been transformed into vast grasslands, where many agricultural products are produced and exported. Through wide-ranging international cooperation programs, hundreds of Israeli doctors, engineers, teachers, agronomists, irrigation experts, and youth counselors are imparting their know-how and experience to the people of many developing countries. Israel's GDP per capita has now surpassed that of Britain, France, South Korea, and Japan.

Question 12 When will the Israelites shout "He Who comes in the Name of the Lord?"

Matt. 23:37-39 37 "O Jerusalem, Jerusalem, you who kill the prophets and stone those sent to you, how often I have longed to gather your children together, as a hen gathers her chicks under her wings, but you were not willing. 38 Look, your house is left to you desolate. 39 For I tell you, you will not see me again until you say, 'Blessed is he who comes in the name of the Lord.' "

Jesus knew that the Jewish people would be scattered all over the world for nearly 1900 years, that the Jewish nation would be reestablished, and that Jews would return to Jerusalem. Jesus will return as well, before a great crowd who will be shouting, "Baruch Haba B'shem Adonai!" (Blessed is He Who comes in the name of the Lord!).

The stage is finally being set with the return of the Jews to their reestablished Israel and their restored Jerusalem. God's people are waiting for the arrival of the hero who will transform the frightening and terrible phase on the stage of this chaotic world into a happy ending. Jesus, who once humbly rode the colt of a donkey from Bethpage on the Mount of Olives to enter Jerusalem, will return to the Mount of Olives (Zech. 14:4) to enter Jerusalem from the east. Ezekiel also saw the glory of God returning and coming in from the east (Ezek. 43:1-7).

The text, "you will not see me again until you say, 'Blessed is he who comes in the name of the Lord' " (Matt. 23:39), contains the hope that in the future Israel will accept Jesus as their Messiah, the One "who comes in the name of the Lord." When the time is full, Jesus will enter Jerusalem as Israel's Messiah amid the welcoming shouts of Jerusalem's residents. Ultimately, the Messiah's Second Advent is inseparably connected with the spiritual restoration of Israel through which they lift up praises to Him. Israel's spiritual restoration is clearly evident in the Messianic Jewish churches that continue to grow rapidly since Israel's independence. Messianic Jews in Jerusalem are waiting for the Lord as they sing, "Baruch Haba B'shem Adonai!" (Blessed is He Who comes in the name of the Lord!).

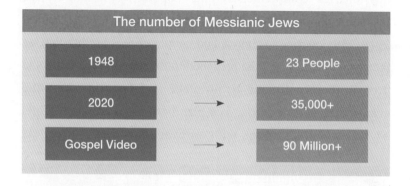

The number of Messianic Jews	
1948 →	23 People
2020 →	35,000+
Gospel Video →	90 Million+

Question 13 When will the Gospel of the Kingdom be preached to all nations?

Matt. 24:14   And this gospel of the kingdom will be preached in the whole world as a testimony to all nations, and then the end will come.

The Wycliffe Bible Translators' goal is to translate the Bible into all the languages of those who do not yet have the

Bible in their native tongue by 2025. Missions for unreached people groups have been the focus of the global church since the Lausanne International Congress held in Manila in 1989. Since then, due to the united missionary efforts of churches around the world, there have been remarkable achievements in pioneering missions for unreached people groups. In 2000, experts reported that there were about 3,000 unreached people groups with no church planter and no church. As the result of missionaries' comprehensive and cooperative mission efforts, the number of unreached people groups decreased to 260 by 2019. Missionaries for unreached people groups predict that, as the gospel continues to be preached to the remaining 260 people groups, there will soon be no place in the world where the evangelization rate is 0%. The plan is to focus mission efforts on 4,738 people groups with an evangelization rate of less

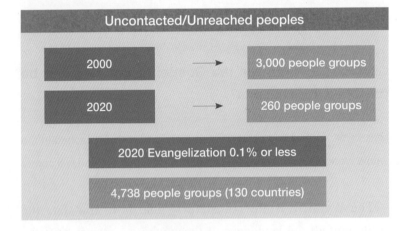

Uncontacted/Unreached peoples

2000 → 3,000 people groups

2020 → 260 people groups

2020 Evangelization 0.1% or less

4,738 people groups (130 countries)

than 0.1% in about 130 countries. The goal is to increase their evangelization rate up to 2% by mobilizing churches around the world to participate in the mission.

We do not know the day nor hour when the Gospel of the Kingdom will be preached to all nations, but that time is certainly getting closer.

Question 14 What is meant by "until the times of the Gentiles are fulfilled?"

Luke 21:23-24 23 How dreadful it will be in those days for pregnant women and nursing mothers! There will be great distress in the land and wrath against this people. 24 They will fall by the sword and will be taken as prisoners to all the nations. Jerusalem will be trampled on by the Gentiles until the times of the Gentiles are fulfilled.

The destruction of Jerusalem in A.D. 70 by Roman general Titus caused the Jews to be scattered throughout the world. This was the beginning of the times of the Gentiles. Jerusalem was ruled by the Romans and then the Byzantines, Arabs, Crusaders, Mamluks, Ottomans, and the British in turn. However, Israel's independence on May 14, 1948, and the restoration of Jerusalem on June 7, 1967, revealed that the times of the Gentiles are nearing their completion. They are also the evidence that Jesus' Second Advent is drawing near. Jesus' Second Advent will be the ultimate proof that the times of the Gentiles are fulfilled.

The restoration of Jerusalem reveals that the times of the Gentiles have started to end. Israel, which gained independence in 1948, continues to grow. Control over Jerusalem was restored to Israel due to the Six-Day War in 1967. Defying all predictions, Israel won an unexpected victory in six days. As a result, Israel recovered the West Bank and Jerusalem from Jordan, the Golan Heights from Syria, and Gaza and the Sinai Peninsula from Egypt. After acquiring control over Jerusalem for the first time in 2,000 years, Israel pronounced Jerusalem as its capital, including East Jerusalem. However, Israel conceded the jurisdiction of the Temple Mount area, where the Old Temple once stood, to the Muslims. Although Israel appears to have regained control of Jerusalem, the actual jurisdiction of Jerusalem's core, the Temple Mount, remains in Arab hands. Considering this, the restoration of Jerusalem, which reveals that "the times of the Gentiles" are almost over, should be received as a strong warning for believers from the Lord to stay awake.

Question 15 What is the significance of U.S. President Trump's acknowledgment of Jerusalem as Israel's capital?

U.S. President Trump announced that it was time for the

world to recognize Jerusalem as Israel's capital based on reality and history. Here, "reality" refers to Israel's effective control over Jerusalem, and "history" refers to the fact that Israel never gave up Jerusalem as its capital since King David designated Jerusalem as the capital of the unified kingdom of Israel about 3,000 years ago. In 1947, U.S. President Truman actively supported the U.N. Partition Plan for Palestine and played the leading role in its passing. As a successor to the U.S. presidency which had led the U.N. Partition Plan, Trump officially acknowledged Jerusalem as Israel's capital on December 6, 2017, 50 years after its restoration, and thus provided a new turning point for the political restoration of Jerusalem. The following year, Trump moved the U.S. Embassy to Israel's capital, Jerusalem, on May 14, 2018, the 70th anniversary of Israel's independence. Following the U.S., Guatemala, Paraguay, Honduras and Kosovo moved their embassies to Jerusalem.

Question 16 What is meant by "the full number of the Gentiles has come in?"

Rom. 11:25-27 25 I do not want you to be ignorant of this mystery, brothers, so that you may not be conceited: Israel has experienced a hardening in part until the full number of the Gentiles has come in. 26 And so all Israel will be saved, as it is written: "The deliverer will come

from Zion; he will turn godlessness away from Jacob. 27 And this is
my covenant with them when I take away their sins."

Paul defined "the times of the Gentiles" as the time period
"until the full number of the Gentiles has come in" and stated
that the Jews have "experienced a hardening in part" during that
period (Rom. 11:25). For the Jews, the "times of the Gentiles"
are an unfortunate period of being blind to the Gospel, but, for
the Gentiles, it is a blessed period during which the Gospel is
fully proclaimed. Paul emphasized the multilayered meaning of
"the times of the Gentiles" as a "mystery" (μυστήριον, mustérion),
God's provident work.

Jesus said, "And the gospel must first be preached to all
nations," (Mark 13:10) and "Therefore go and make disciples of
all nations, baptizing them in the name of the Father and of the
Son and of the Holy Spirit" (Matt. 28:19). In those two verses,
"the times of the Gentiles" refers to when the full number of the
Gentiles comes in. In those verses, "all nations" refers to the
Gentiles. Translating "the full number of the Gentiles" as "the
fullness of the Gentiles" is closer to the original text. Thus, this
can be seen as the Gospel being fully proclaimed to all nations.
When the Gospel is preached to all nations (Matt. 24:14), the end
will come, which is Jesus' Second Advent.

Question 17 What is meant by "to become a dwelling in which God lives?"

Eph. 2:15   by abolishing in his flesh the law with its commandments and regulations. His purpose was to create in himself one new man out of the two, thus making peace,

Eph. 2:18   For through him we both have access to the Father by one Spirit.

Eph. 2:22   And in him you too are being built together to become a dwelling in which God lives by his Spirit.

This era is the age of the "one new man." By the tearing of His flesh on the cross, Jesus broke down the wall that divided the Jews and the Gentiles in history when they were being debased as "pigs" (Judensau) and "dogs" (Caleb), respectively. Both the Jews and Gentiles can approach Father God boldly through the Messiah Jesus in one Spirit (Eph. 2:18). The Jews have been entrusted with God's Word, and theirs is the adoption as God's children, the Divine glory, the covenants, the receiving of the law, temple worship, the promises, and the human ancestry leading to Christ's birth (Rom. 9:4-5). In Jesus, the Gentiles partake in the blessings of Abraham as his descendants and as heirs of God's inheritance (Gal. 3:29). The wild olive tree has been grafted into the cultivated olive tree (Rom. 11:17).

When the full number of Gentiles is reached, all Israel will be free from their partial hardening and be saved (Rom. 11:25-26). This is how the "one new man" (Eph. 2:15) will be fulfilled. The original branches, the Jews, will be re-grafted into the cultivated olive tree and enjoy more abundance. Thus, God's dwelling place will be built in Jesus (Eph. 2:22). When the dwelling place is ready, the Lord will return and reign with believers.

Question 18 What is God's timetable as revealed by the seventy sevens?

Dan. 9:24-27   24 "Seventy 'sevens' are decreed for your people and your holy city to finish transgression, to put an end to sin, to atone for wickedness, to bring in everlasting righteousness, to seal up vision and prophecy and to anoint the most holy. 25 "Know and understand this: From the issuing of the decree to restore and rebuild Jerusalem until the Anointed One, the ruler, comes, there will be seven 'sevens,' and sixty-two 'sevens.' It will be rebuilt with streets and a trench, but in times of trouble. 26 After the sixty-two 'sevens,' the Anointed One will be cut off and will have nothing. The people of the ruler who will come will destroy the city and the sanctuary. The end will come like a flood: War will continue until the end, and desolations have been decreed. 27 He will confirm a covenant with many for one 'seven.' In the middle of the 'seven' he will put an end to sacrifice and offering. And on a wing [of the temple] he will set up an abomination that causes desolation, until the end that is decreed is poured out on him."

Matt. 24:15 "So when you see standing in the holy place 'the abomination that causes desolation,' spoken of through the prophet Daniel – let the reader understand –

2 Thess. 2:3-4 3 Don't let anyone deceive you in any way, for that day will not come until the rebellion occurs and the man of lawlessness is revealed, the man doomed to destruction. 4 He will oppose and will exalt himself over everything that is called God or is worshiped, so that he sets himself up in God's temple, proclaiming himself to be God.

The mystery of the seventy sevens that God revealed to Daniel is about Jesus coming to this earth to complete His redemption work on the cross (Dan. 9:24). The seventy sevens in the Book of Daniel is subdivided into seven sevens, sixty-two sevens, and one seven (Dan. 9:25). These subdivisions show that Daniel's prophecy of seventy sevens, which began with Jesus' First Advent, will be fulfilled when Jesus returns to judge the nations and establish God's Kingdom (The Millennial Kingdom) on earth.

The seven sevens and sixty-two sevens refer to Israel's history "From the issuing of the decree to restore and rebuild Jerusalem until the Anointed One, the ruler, comes" (Dan.

9:25). Rebuilding Jerusalem was decreed in 445 B.C. by King Artaxerxes of Persia to his cupbearer Nehemiah (Neh. 2:1-8) and was fulfilled. The seven sevens refer to the 49 years from 445 B.C. when the decree to rebuild Jerusalem was issued to 397 B.C. when the last Old Testament prophet Malachi was active. After the seven sevens, the intertestamental period of about 400 years in Israel followed, during which no prophet of God appeared. That was the sixty-two sevens (434 years). At the end of that period, Daniel's prophecy that "the Anointed One, the ruler, comes" (Dan. 9:25) was accurately fulfilled when Jesus entered Jerusalem riding on a donkey to then bear the cross. Daniel also prophesied that after the sixty-two sevens, "the Anointed One will be cut off and will have nothing. The people of the ruler who will come will destroy the city (Jerusalem) and the sanctuary" (Dan. 9:26). This prophecy has been accurately fulfilled in history as well by Jesus' death on the cross and the destruction of Jerusalem by the Roman army in A.D. 70.

The last subdivision of Daniel's seventy sevens prophecy is one seven, which is equivalent to 7 years. According to Daniel's prophecy, a ruler (antichrist) will appear and make a covenant (peace treaty) with Israel for one seven. In the covenant with Israel, the ruler will promise peace and guarantee the construction of the Holy Temple. However, after half of the seven years (3 ½ years) passes, he will forbid sacrifices and offerings at the Temple and will instead set himself up in God's Temple, proclaiming himself to be God. From that time on, a

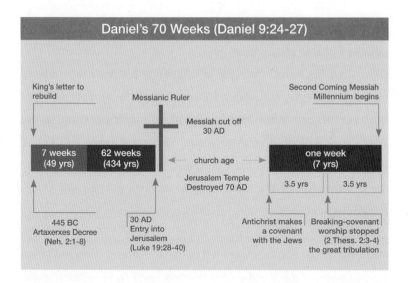

Daniel's 70 Weeks (Daniel 9:24-27)

| King's letter to rebuild | Messianic Ruler | | Second Coming Messiah Millennium begins |

Messiah cut off
30 AD

| 7 weeks (49 yrs) | 62 weeks (434 yrs) | church age | one week (7 yrs) |

Jerusalem Temple
Destroyed 70 AD

3.5 yrs | 3.5 yrs

445 BC
Artaxerxes Decree
(Neh. 2:1-8)

30 AD
Entry into
Jerusalem
(Luke 19:28-40)

Antichrist makes
a covenant
with the Jews

Breaking-covenant
worship stopped
(2 Thess. 2:3-4)
the great tribulation

full-fledged tribulation upon Israel will begin and culminate with the Armageddon War. Then, Jesus' Second Advent will occur to judge all His enemies and to commence His reign over the Messianic Kingdom.

Question 19 When will rapture occur?

Matt. 24:8   **All these are** the beginning of birth pains.

The "birth pains" (ὠδίν, ódin) described in the Book of Matthew include deceptions, wars, famines, pestilences, and earthquakes. The tribulation in the Last Days will be like the pains of childbirth, which begins weakly and occasionally at first, then becomes stronger and weaker for a while, only to become stronger and more frequent. Just as childbirth does not take place without labor and pain, the tribulation in the Last Days will give birth to Jesus' Second Advent and God's Kingdom. Overcoming the tribulation triumphantly will become the last mission of the saints who have been praying for God's Kingdom to come.

Matt. 24:21-22 21 **For then there will be** great distress, unequaled from the beginning of the world until now – and never to be equaled again. 22 **If those days had not been cut short, no one would survive, but for the sake of the elect those days will be shortened.**

Extreme disasters will occur at the climax of the tribulation. The saints will need to patiently endure until the end. The elect will receive a way of escape for they are not the objects of God's wrath. For the sake of the elect, God will shorten those days and protect them.

Matt. 24:29-31 29 **"Immediately** after the distress of those days **"'the sun will be darkened, and the moon will not give its light; the stars will fall from the sky, and the heavenly bodies will be shaken.' 30 "At that time the sign of the Son of Man will appear in the sky, and all the nations of the earth will mourn. They will see the Son of Man coming** on the clouds of the sky, with power and great glory. 31 And he will send his angels with a loud trumpet call, and they will gather his elect from the four winds, from one end of the heavens to the other.

The signs of the Lord's Second Advent and the end times include: persecution, apostasy, rampant lawlessness, cooling of love, world evangelization, appearance of the antichrist, and the Great Tribulation. After the distress of those days, there will be abnormal phenomena from the sun, moon, and stars. All the peoples of the earth will see the Lord's return while mourning, and the elect will experience rapture.

Question 20 What is God's timetable as revealed by the parable of the fig tree?

Jer. 24:5-7   5 "This is what the LORD, the God of Israel, says: 'Like these good figs, I regard as good the exiles from Judah, whom I sent away from this place to the land of the Babylonians 6 My eyes will watch over them for their good, and I will bring them back to this land. I will build them up and not tear them down; I will plant them and not uproot them. 7 I will give them a heart to know me, that I am the LORD. They will be my people, and I will be their God, for they will return to me with all their heart.

Matt. 21:19   Seeing a fig tree by the road, he went up to it but found nothing on it except leaves. Then he said to it, "May you never bear fruit again!" Immediately the tree withered.

Matt. 24:32-34   32 "Now learn this lesson from the fig tree: As soon as its twigs get tender and its leaves come out, you know that summer is near. 33 Even so, when you see all these things, you know that it is near, right at the door. 34 I tell you the truth, this generation will certainly not pass away until all these things have happened.

While speaking about His Second Advent, Jesus taught the parable of the fig tree. Here, the fig tree symbolizes Israel (Mic. 7:1; Hosea 9:10). Here, summer signifies the day of the Second Advent that is nearing when the fig tree's "twigs get tender and its leaves come out" (Matt. 24:32), which refers to Israel's independence (1948) and Jerusalem's restoration (1967) after about 1900 years of withering and dying.

The budding of a fig tree in the spring serves as a reminder that summer is approaching. In Israel, summer is the last season of the year. The appearance of a fig tree's leaves signals the arrival of the last season, summer. Therefore, Israel's independence is an event signaling that the day of the Lord's return is near. "When you see all these things" refer to the signs recorded in Matthew 24:4-24, which include the appearance and activities of the antichrist and false prophets, wars, famines, earthquakes, world evangelization, and persecutions against the saints and the church. "This generation," in the sentence "this generation will certainly not pass away until all these things have happened," can be seen as referring to our generation, for we have witnessed Israel's independence and Jerusalem's restoration.

Question 21 Who is the antichrist, and when will he appear?

2 Thess. 2:3-4   3 Don't let anyone deceive you in any way, for that day will not come until the rebellion occurs and the man of lawlessness is revealed, the man doomed to destruction. 4 He will oppose and will exalt himself over everything that is called God or is worshiped, so that he sets himself up in God's temple, proclaiming himself to be God.

Dan. 7:25   He will speak against the Most High and oppress his saints and try to change the set times and the laws. The saints will be handed over to him for a time, times and half a time.

Rev. 13:1-2   1 And the dragon stood on the shore of the sea. And I saw a beast coming out of the sea. He had ten horns and seven heads, with ten crowns on his horns, and on each head a blasphemous name. 2 The beast I saw resembled a leopard, but had feet like those of a bear and a mouth like that of a lion. The dragon gave the beast his power and his throne and great authority.

The man of lawlessness or the man doomed to destruction is the antichrist (1 John 2:18, 4:3), not an abstract force nor a collective concept but a clear eschatological man. He will exalt himself above the gods, sit in God's temple, and make himself known as God. The Roman emperors or popes cannot be the man of lawlessness, because he will appear shortly before Christ's Second Advent (2 Thess. 2:3) and will be killed by Christ's breath at the time of His glorious return (2 Thess. 2:8). As the last conqueror of the world who opposes God and the Messiah, the antichrist will desecrate the Jerusalem Temple and attempt to usurp the place of worship. He will reject God's reign by all means possible and reflect the anti-Semitic and anti-Biblical spirit of the age. Like his predecessors who demonstrated negative traits, the antichrist will be a despicable man, who will do whatever he wants and will exalt himself. Christ will return to destroy the antichrist's works and army, to establish a righteous government, and to reign for the next thousand years.

Christians should keep an eye on the European Union (E.U.) because the last ruler of the world, the antichrist, will emerge from the vestiges of the ancient Roman Empire (Dan. 7:7-8). The birth of the European Union is like the resurrection of the Roman Empire. The development of the European Union into a strong centralized structure appears to be setting the stage for antichrist's dictatorship. International cooperation, international conflicts, and global structures centered on the European Union will form a single type of anti-Christian world government. This anti-Christian world government will make the antichrist an invincible leader.

Question 22 What is the War of Gog and Magog?

Ezek. 38:2-6   2 "Son of man, set your face against Gog, of the land of Magog, the chief prince of Meshech and Tubal; prophesy against him 3 and say: 'This is what the Sovereign LORD says: I am against you, O Gog, chief prince of Meshech and Tubal. 4 I will turn you around, put hooks in your jaws and bring you out with your whole army – your horses, your horsemen fully armed, and a great horde with large and small shields, all of them brandishing their swords. 5 Persia, Cush and Put will be with them, all with shields and helmets, 6 also Gomer with all its troops, and Beth Togarmah from the far north with all its troops – the many nations with you.

Gog's allies are Persia, Cush, Put, Gomer and Beth Togarmah, and this alliance corresponds to modern day Russia, Iran, Pakistan, Afghanistan, Ethiopia, Sudan, Libya, Algeria, Tunisia, Turkey, and Islamic nations in central Asia, which are pro-Russia, pro-Islam, and anti-Israel. This war against Israel will be initiated by one of the northern powers along with the Arab-Islamic world. Under the influence of Russia's (Gog's) leader from the north, the nations attacking Israel will form an alliance led by Russia, Iran, and Turkey as the central axis. However, God's miraculous intervention will destroy the enemies of Israel to a degree unprecedented in the history of war. God will reveal His greatness and holiness so that all nations will know that He alone is the King of kings and Lord of lords.

Question 23 What is the War of Armageddon?

Zech. 14:1-3   1 A day of the LORD is coming when your plunder will be divided among you. 2 I will gather all the nations to Jerusalem to fight against it; the city will be captured, the houses ransacked, and the women raped. Half of the city will go into exile, but the rest of the people will not be taken from the city. 3 Then the LORD will go out and fight against those nations, as he fights in the day of battle.

The War of Armageddon will be the darkest, most painful, and brutal war in world history. It will occur when many Jews from around the world, still in disbelief, return to their ancient land. After a momentary period of peace and prosperity, a great crisis will suddenly come upon them, leading to the final hour. The peace treaty between Israel and the antichrist will be broken in three and half years. As the antichrist breaks his promise and decides to commit genocide against Israel, many nations in the world will join him and come against Israel and Jerusalem. They will surround Jerusalem for attack, but that crisis will become the day of God's grace and salvation for the house of David and the inhabitants of Jerusalem (Zech. 12:10-13:6).

"On that day His feet will stand on the Mount of Olives, east of Jerusalem" (Zech. 14:4). Some view the Mount of Olives mentioned in this verse as a symbolic place where God's judgment will come on the Day of the LORD, but Jesus will literally return to the Mount of Olives, east of Jerusalem across the Kidron Valley. Jesus' return will be exactly as the two men in white robes taught the disciples after Jesus' resurrection and His ascension to heaven from the Mount of Olives: "Men of Galilee, why do you stand here looking into the sky? This same Jesus, who has been taken from you into heaven, will come back in the same way you have seen him go into heaven" (Acts 1:11). When the Lord returns on the Mount of Olives, many amazing things will occur. The center of the Mount of Olives will be split into two from east to west, with half of the mountain moving north and the other half moving south, forming a valley through which survivors of the attack against Jerusalem will flee (Zech. 14:4-5). The LORD God, the hope of Israel and the Church, will come in majesty with "all the holy ones" (Zech. 14:5). On that day, the LORD God will be the only King in the whole world, and those who worship the LORD God will exalt His Name alone.

Question 24 **What is the judgment of all the nations in the end times, and by what standard will the judgment be made?**

Matt. 25:31-33 31 "When the Son of Man comes in his glory, and all the angels with him, he will sit on his throne in heavenly glory. 32 All the nations will be gathered before him, and he will separate the people one from another as a shepherd separates the sheep from the goats. 33 He will put the sheep on his right and the goats on his left.

Matt. 25:40   "The King will reply, 'I tell you the truth, whatever you did for one of the least of these brothers of mine, you did for me.'

Joel 3:1-3   1 'In those days and at that time, when I restore the fortunes of Judah and Jerusalem, 2 I will gather all nations and bring them down to the Valley of Jehoshaphat. There I will enter into judgment against them concerning my inheritance, my people Israel, for they scattered my people among the nations and divided up my land. 3 They cast lots for my people and traded boys for prostitutes; they sold girls for wine that they might drink.

The Old and New Testaments record that the LORD will return to gather and judge all nations. The first criterion for judging the nations is whether they scattered Israel. The scattering of the Jews occurred several times in history, but the largest scattering of the Jews occurred at the hands of Rome upon

Israel's failed independence movements in A.D. 70 and A.D. 135. The Jews, who were scattered across the nations, were unable to settle down and were repeatedly exiled. It is not an exaggeration to say that Israel's history of suffering is a history of exile. The second criterion for judging the nations is whether they divided the land that God gave to Israel. The League of Nations, the United Nations, Islamic nations, secular nations, and even many Christians are ignoring God's sovereignty over the land that He gave Israel. God is emphasizing that He gave the land of Canaan to Israel as the portion they will inherit, in accordance with His command for a thousand generations: the covenant He made with Abraham, the oath He swore to Isaac, the decree He confirmed to Jacob, to Israel, as an everlasting covenant (Ps. 105:8-11). The third criterion for judging the nations is their attitude toward the Jews, who are "one of the least of these brothers of mine" and who are the apple of God's eye. Jews were sold into slavery, were killed by the Crusades and the Spanish Inquisition, and experienced Pogroms and the Holocaust. However, the Jews survived through a history of great suffering and reestablished their own nation after about 1,900 years. As soon as Israel declared independence, it was attacked by Islamic nations. Israel has been through several more wars and continues to be threatened with extinction by the threat of wars, terrorist attacks, international isolation, and injustice.

God will judge the nations in His time. Any acts against

God's will, due to the failure to understand Israel's special calling as revealed in Genesis 12:3, will not escape God's judgment. Nations that do not give up their hostility against Israel and the Jews will be categorized as goat nations and will face destruction as a result of God's final judgment. Even if an individual belongs to a goat nation, his or her personal salvation will not be affected.

Question 25 Is God's judgment of the nations and people only enforced in the future?

Jer. 25:15   This is what the LORD, the God of Israel, said to me: "Take from my hand this cup filled with the wine of my wrath and make all the nations to whom I send you drink it.

Gen. 12:3   I will bless those who bless you, and whoever curses you I will curse; and all peoples on earth will be blessed through you."

Gen. 27:29   May nations serve you and peoples bow down to you. Be lord over your brothers, and may the sons of your mother bow down to you. May those who curse you be cursed and those who bless you be blessed."

Num. 24:9   Like a lion they crouch and lie down, like a lioness – who dares to rouse them? "May those who bless you be blessed and those who curse you be cursed!"

Matt. 25:40   "The King will reply, 'I tell you the truth, whatever you did for one of the least of these brothers of mine, you did for me.'

Mark 3:35   Whoever does God's will is my brother and sister and mother."

God's judgment of the nations and people existed in the past (Jer. 25:13-31; Ezek. 25-26, 29) and continues into the present. Nations that refused mercy for the Jews will not receive God's mercy. Israel is the apple of God's eye. To attack Israel is to attack God. We can see God's words being fulfilled in time periods not far from ours.

Spain was an empire that dominated Europe in the 15th and 16th centuries with its powerful army and navy, occupying a territory that extends across both hemispheres of the earth. However, less than a century after evicting the Jews from its territory, Spain declined rapidly, becoming a weaker nation.

In July 1938, an international conference was held in Evian, France. 15 weeks after Hitler's annexation of Austria, representatives from 32 nations were gathered to discuss rescuing Jews in Germany and Austria. At the time, thousands of Jews were lining up in front of every embassy in Austria to request a visa to escape Hitler's imminent persecution. George Rublee, the Chair of the Mediation Committee of the conference, proposed that 16 of the 32 nations should each accept 25,000 Jews but was rejected. The international community's indifference to Jews further fueled Hitler's ambitions for aggression. If the representatives of those nations had strongly condemned Hitler's inhumane treatment and had welcomed Jewish refugees into their countries, Hitler would not have dared to massacre the Jews. And ultimately, World War II may have been prevented. Only one month after the conference in August of that year, the Holocaust intensified. In the following year, World War II broke out, killing more than 50 million people. Germany was defeated in the deadliest war in human history, with an estimated 6.6 to 8.7 million Germans deaths.

Great Britain remained the largest empire in human history, while leading its allies through two world wars into victory. Britain governed Palestine and was mandated by the League of Nations to establish a Jewish state. However, in 1947 to 1948, at the crucial moment to act in favor of Israel's independence, Britain instead objected and interfered. Since then, Britain declined with surprising rapidity. Britain's decline cannot simply be explained by international political, military, or economic factors. About one generation later, today, Britain, like Spain, became weaker.

"These brothers of mine" in Matthew 25:40 refers to Jesus' brothers, who were born by blood and who were born by the Holy Spirit. Today, Islam and atheistic Communism even more vehemently oppose Christianity. Christians and Jews now face a common enemy. Even at this very moment, anti-Semitism is occurring all over the world, and persecution against Christians is also rising over time and will be further aggravated in the future. In 2007, about 100 million Christians were experiencing high levels of persecution. More than 10 years later, in recent days, 245 million Christians, one eighth of the world's Christian population, are suffering high levels of persecution. This figure had more than doubled in 10 years. People often think that persecution against Christians will decrease as modern society globalizes further, but that is not the case. Satan's strategy of deception is obstructing Israel's restoration and persecuting Christians to block the prophetic events pointing to the Lord's return (Matt. 24:14, 23:39). However, as promised in God's Word, the day will come when the Lord returns, judges His enemies, and reigns.

Question 26 Will the elect's rapture at the time of Jesus' Second Advent occur before or after the tribulation?

1 Thess. 4:15-17 15 According to the Lord's own word, we tell you that we who are still alive, who are left till the coming (παρουσία, parousia) of the Lord, will certainly not precede those who have fallen asleep. 16 For the Lord himself will come down from heaven, with a loud command, with the voice of the archangel and with the trumpet call of

God, and the dead in Christ will rise first. 17 **After that,** we who are still alive **and are left will be caught up together with them in the clouds to** meet (ἀπάντησις, apantēsis) the Lord in the air. And so we will be with the Lord forever.

Acts 28:15   The brothers there had heard that we were coming, and they traveled as far as the Forum of Appius and the Three Taverns to meet (ἀπάντησις, apantēsis) us. At the sight of these men Paul thanked God and was encouraged.

Matt. 24:29-31   29 "Immediately after the distress of those days "'the sun will be darkened, and the moon will not give its light; the stars will fall from the sky, and the heavenly bodies will be shaken.' 30 "At that time the sign of the Son of Man will appear in the sky, and all the nations of the earth will mourn. They will see the Son of Man coming on the clouds of the sky, with power and great glory. 31 And he will send his angels with a loud trumpet call, and they will gather his elect from the four winds, from one end of the heavens to the other.

Rev. 3:10   Since you have kept my command to endure patiently, I will also keep you from the hour of trial that is going to come upon the whole world to test those who live on the earth.

The theory of pre-tribulation rapture divides 1 Thessalonians 4:16-17 into two parts: Christ's Advent in the air and Christ's Advent on the earth, occurring 7 years apart. However, Advent (παρουσία, parousia) and meeting (ἀπάντησις, apantésis) in 1 Thessalonians 4:16-17 are meant to be paired. This means that, when a king or high official visits, the people inside the class come out to welcome him and return. Because Jesus will come after the tribulation to gather His elect, the rapture cannot occur before the tribulation. "Keep you from" in Revelation 3:10 means that He will keep and protect.

Question 27 According to Matthew's Gospel, how will the events in the Last Days progress?

1. Beginning of Israel's restoration (Matt. 24:32-34)

2. Beginning of birth pains (Matt. 24:4-12)
   • Deceptions, turmoil, wars, famines, pestilences, earthquakes, persecutions, false prophets, lawlessness, cooling of love

3. Global spread of the Gospel of the Kingdom of Heaven (Matt. 24:14)

4. Rebuilding the Third Temple in Jerusalem (Matt. 24:15)

5. Appearance of the antichrist (Matt. 24:15)

6. Great tribulation (Matt. 24:21-28), salvation of all Israel (Matt. 23:39; Rom. 11:26; Zech. 12:10)

7. Anomalies among the heavenly bodies (Matt. 24:29), Jesus' Second Advent and rapture (Matt. 24:30-31)

Question 28 Can we ascertain when the Last Days will occur?

Acts 1:7   He said to them: "It is not for you to know the times (χρόνος, chronos) or dates (καιρός, kairos) the Father has set by his own authority.

1 Thess. 5:1   Now, brothers, about times and dates we do not need to write to you,

Matt. 24:36   "No one knows about that day or hour, not even the angels in heaven, nor the Son, but only the Father.

Chronos (χρόνος) is objective and natural time. It is chronological time determined by the rising and setting of the sun. Kairos (καιρός) is subjective time, a time of opportunity, and a set time. It is a significant time when an event or opportunity occurs. Jesus Christ entered mankind's regular chronos time and lived a special kairos time. We cannot know the time nor season, nor the day nor hour. However, we can observe the progress and be discerning.

Question 29 Who are the good and faithful servants in the Last Days?

Matt. 24:44   So you also must be ready, because the Son of Man will come at an hour when you do not expect him.

Matt. 24:45-47 45 "Who then is the faithful and wise servant, whom the master has put in charge of the servants in his household to give them their food at the proper time? 46 It will be good for that servant whose master finds him doing so when he returns. 47 I tell you the truth, he will put him in charge of all his possessions.

A faithful servant is one who is trusted by the Master as well as people. A wise servant is one who prepares for the future. The faithful and wise servant Noah was warned of the future and prepared an ark to save his whole family (Gen. 6-8). The faithful and wise servants in the Last Days are discerning, eagerly awaiting the Lord's appearance (2 Tim. 4:8), and doing their best to distribute spiritual food in accordance with the times. The faithful and wise servants are blessed servants, who fully believe and obey the Lord's promises, obediently share them to rescue their neighbors, and receive great rewards upon the Lord's return.

Question 30 How should we live the Last Days?

Matt. 25:13   "Therefore keep watch, because you do not know the day or the hour.

2 Tim. 3:1-5   1 But mark this: There will be terrible times in the last days. 2 People will be lovers of themselves, lovers of money, boastful, proud, abusive, disobedient to their parents, ungrateful, unholy, 3 without love, unforgiving, slanderous, without self-control, brutal, not lovers of the good, 4 treacherous, rash, conceited, lovers of pleasure rather than lovers of God – 5 having a form of godliness but denying its power. Have nothing to do with them.

Heb. 10:24-25   24 And let us consider how we may spur one another on toward love and good deeds. 25 Let us not give up meeting together, as some are in the habit of doing, but let us encourage one another – and all the more as you see the Day approaching.

Heb. 3:12-14   12 See to it, brothers, that none of you has a sinful, unbelieving heart that turns away from the living God. 13 But encourage one another daily, as long as it is called Today, so that none of you may be hardened by sin's deceitfulness. 14 We have come to share in Christ if we hold firmly till the end the confidence we had at first.

During these confusing and rapidly changing times, we frequently receive the question "How should we live?" To answer in one sentence, we should live like the saints of the early church. They overcame persecutions and lived victorious lives with the faith of Maranatha. Maranatha, which means "Come, Lord Jesus" (Rev. 22:20) or "Come, O Lord" (1 Cor. 16:22), is the summation of the faith and spirit of the early church's saints. It was the daily prayer and greeting of the early church's saints, who felt the imminence of the Lord's return and preached the gospel with the power of the Holy Spirit even to martyrdom. The faith of Maranatha enabled them to live with a sense of urgency about the Last Days and with a sincere, responsible faith that devotes their whole beings to God. Proclaiming the gospel with the power of the Holy Spirit is the life and substance of the church. Living as if today is our last day, we should be loyal to God in truth, faith, and love, stay awake and pray, purify ourselves, and serve in the Lord's work with the power of the Holy Spirit. We should also live diligently each day in preparation for our eternal lives. This is because we do not know the day nor the hour of Christ's return (Matt. 25:13). Maranatha! "Amen. Come, Lord Jesus" (Rev. 22:20)!

Conclusion

History is the process of fulfilling God's master plan for mankind's salvation and the restoration of all things. God is telling His children about His timetable in various ways. However, by not telling us the exact day and hour, He wants His children to always stay awake. Despite numerous attacks and conflicts by enemies, God re-established Israel and restored Jerusalem after 1,900 years, fulfilling His promises in the fullness of His time. Our Lord, the King of kings, is now preparing the foothold for His return to transform the world into His Kingdom and reign forever and ever. All God's covenants and promises will surely be fulfilled. Let us discern the times with the Holy Spirit's guidance, fulfill the mission of these times with the Holy Spirit's power, and reign together with the Lord.

Chapter 7

God's Kingdom

Introduction

God's Kingdom is the most important theme that runs through the entire Bible. The Bible begins and ends with God's Kingdom. Jesus' greatest interest has been God's Kingdom. Jesus commenced His public ministry by proclaiming God's Kingdom. During the 40 days after His resurrection, Jesus taught about God's Kingdom work. The core of the Gospel that Paul preached was God's Kingdom. The Book of Revelation ends with the story of the completed, everlasting Kingdom of God.

Question 1 What is God's Kingdom?

  The expression "Kingdom of God" appears 39 times in the Synoptic Gospels, 2 times in John's Gospel, and 37 times in Matthew's Gospel. The word "Kingdom" (βασιλεία, basileia) means Kingship, King's reign, or Kingdom. God's Kingdom is God's sovereignty over His creatures. God's Kingdom is the realization of His reign in redemptive history within the history of the world.

Question 2 What are the five stages of God's Kingdom project?

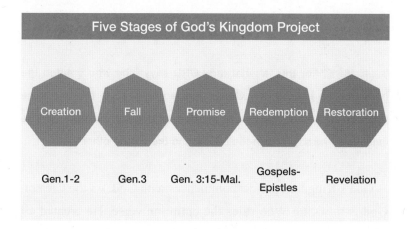

Five Stages of God's Kingdom Project				
Creation	Fall	Promise	Redemption	Restoration
Gen.1-2	Gen.3	Gen. 3:15-Mal.	Gospels-Epistles	Revelation

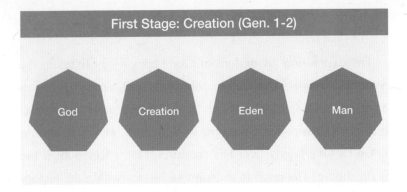

First Stage: Creation (Gen. 1-2)

God   Creation   Eden   Man

In God's Kingdom, God Who is King dwells with His creatures. In addition, human beings, who bear God's image and rule over creatures, are with Him.

Question 3 What is God's role in His Kingdom project?

Isa. 45:18   For this is what the LORD says – he who created the heavens, he is God; he who fashioned and made the earth, he founded it; he did not create it to be empty, but formed it to be inhabited – he says: "I am the LORD, and there is no other.

God's Kingdom project commences with God. As the Creator, God is the King Who rules the entire universe. He created all things, material and immaterial, for His Name and glory. Even the rebellious acts of angels and men fall under God's sovereign

reign.[43] For His purposes, God governs by appointing mankind as His vice regent or steward.

The plot of the Bible is the process of God restoring His first Kingdom, Eden, that the first Adam failed, to a New Eden through His Son, Messiah Jesus. When Messiah Jesus successfully completes the Kingdom and lifts it to Father God (1 Cor. 15:24), the eternal Kingdom of God will begin.[44] God will dwell with the people on the New Earth, where people will see God face to face, enjoying true fellowship with Him (Rev. 21:3, 22:4).

Question 4 What is creation like in God's Kingdom project?

Gen. 1:31   God saw all that he had made, and it was very good. And there was evening, and there was morning – the sixth day.

Rom. 8:20-21 20 For the creation was subjected to frustration, not by its own choice, but by the will of the one who subjected it, in hope 21 that the creation itself will be liberated from its bondage to decay and brought into the glorious freedom of the children of God.

God created a world that was "very good" in His sight. However, mankind's sin and fall caused creation to be cursed and subjected to futility, and corruption and death entered the world. Creation yearns for restoration in which God makes all things new (Matt. 19:28; 2 Pet. 3:10-13). Creation's restoration is universal and includes cultural pursuits that glorify God (Isa. 11:4-9, 65:21-25). This expected restoration was verified through Jesus' miracles (Luke 7:15; Matt. 8:26-27, 14:19-21). Although Jesus has been revealed as the King already, Jesus' reign will be full only after His second coming ushers in the Millennial Kingdom and culminates in the eternal Kingdom of God (Rev. 20:6, 22:3-5).

Question 5 What is mankind's role in God's Kingdom project?

Gen. 1:26   Then God said, "Let us make man in our image, in our likeness, and let them rule over the fish of the sea and the birds of the air, over the livestock, over all the earth, and over all the creatures that move along the ground."

Mankind was created in God's image to be God's vice regents or stewards over His creation that He had declared to be very good (Gen. 1:26-28). Mankind has both a material body and an immaterial soul. Mankind was commissioned to fill the earth and rule over God's creation for His glory. Given free will, mankind had the choice to serve God or to disobey Him. Adam sinned, was separated from God, was subjected to death, and plunged the world into disaster. God has been carrying out His plan of salvation through Jesus, Who is the offspring of a woman, the last Adam and the life-giving Spirit (1 Cor. 15:45). To prevent mankind's unified rebellion against Him, God scattered mankind across the face of the earth, instituting different nations and various languages (Gen. 11:9). The last Adam will successfully rule the earth and succeed where the first Adam failed. Those who believe in Jesus will be restored and live forever as kings in the New Earth (Rev. 22:5). Unbelievers will experience eternal punishment in the lake of fire (Rev. 21:8). Anyone who desires to participate in God's kingdom needs to be born again through the Word and by the Holy Spirit (John 3:5).

Question 6 Was the Garden of Eden the first Kingdom of God?

Ps. 24:1   The earth is the LORD's, and everything in it, the world, and all who live in it;

Ps. 10:16   The LORD is King for ever and ever; the nations will perish from his land.

Gen. 3:8   Then the man and his wife heard the sound of the LORD God as he was walking in the garden in the cool of the day, and they hid from the LORD God among the trees of the garden.

Eden was the first Kingdom of God because the earth and everything in it, all who live in it, belonged to God. Moreover, it was where God enjoyed dwelling with man.

God was interested in filling the earth with Godly people and making it His dwelling place. Thus, mankind received the blessing of being created in God's image so that we can have fellowship with God the Creator, fill the earth, and rule over it (Gen. 1:27-28).

Gen. 2:9   And the LORD God made all kinds of trees grow out of the ground – trees that were pleasing to the eye and good for food. In the middle of the garden were the tree of life and the tree of the knowledge of good and evil.

Eden was God's Kingdom because the tree of life was there. The tree of life supplied mankind with life, strength, and capability. Whenever one eats from the fruit of this tree in the eternal Kingdom of God, one will realize that the source of life is in God (Rev. 22:1-2).

Gen. 2:17   but you must not eat from the tree of the knowledge of good and evil, for when you eat of it you will surely die."

Eden was God's Kingdom because mankind, as the crown of God's creation, were worshippers. The tree of the knowledge of good and evil distinguished the Creator from His creatures, so that they can obey and glorify God the Creator. In addition, Eden was God's Kingdom because it was a place for living together and helping one another (Gen. 2:18).

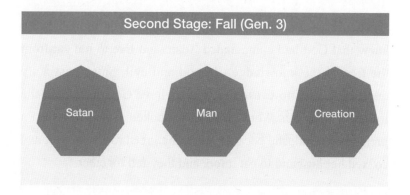

Second Stage: Fall (Gen. 3)

Satan   Man   Creation

The Fall marks mankind's failure to rule over God's creation. Both mankind created in God's image and other creatures became subjected to the devastating effects of the Fall.

Question 7 What are the causes and consequences of mankind's Fall?

Gen. 3:1 Now the serpent was more crafty than any of the wild animals the LORD God had made. He said to the woman, "Did God really say, 'You must not eat from any tree in the garden'?"

Gen. 3:6 When the woman saw that the fruit of the tree was

good for food and pleasing to the eye, and also desirable for gaining wisdom, she took some and ate it. She also gave some to her husband, who was with her, and he ate it.

Satan used a serpent to tempt mankind. Even though Satan knew that God had commanded Adam and Eve to not eat from the tree of the knowledge of good and evil, Satan cast a sly question to Eve to cause her to disbelieve God and doubt the truthfulness of His Word. When Eve looked at that tree with a prejudiced mind, she became driven by greed to eat its fruit and coaxed her husband to eat it too, and they fell together.

Gen. 3:16-19 16 To the woman he said, "I will greatly increase your pains in childbearing; with pain you will give birth to children. Your desire will be for your husband, and he will rule over you." 17 To Adam he said, "Because you listened to your wife and ate from the tree about which I commanded you, 'You must not eat of it,' "Cursed is the ground because of you; through painful toil you will eat of it all the days of your life. 18 It will produce thorns and thistles for you, and you will eat the plants of the field. 19 By the sweat of your brow you will eat your food until you return to the ground, since from it you were taken; for dust you are and to dust you will return."

God punished the woman with labor and pain in childbirth, continual desire for her husband, and being under her husband's authority. God punished man with difficult, lifelong labor to eat the produce of the land and eventual return to the soil from which he was created. Because they disobeyed God and sinned, they tasted inevitable death (Rom. 6:23). The land was cursed by God because of mankind's fall and produced many thorns and thistles that harm human life. Thus, mankind's fall as the representative of the whole created world did not end with mankind's suffering and caused the natural world to also groan in suffering (Rom. 8:22). Thus, before the Fall, mankind lived amid the benefits and abundance of nature, but, after the Fall, mankind has only been able to survive through a constant struggle with devastated nature.

Question 8 How does Satan oppose God's Kingdom project?

Eph. 2:2   in which you used to live when you followed the ways of this world and of the ruler of the kingdom of the air, the spirit who is now at work in those who are disobedient.

Satan was one of the archangels and the first to challenge God's authority. Although God has sovereignty over all things, mankind's sin temporarily gave Satan kingship over this world (John 12:31; 2 Cor. 4:4; Eph. 2:2). Since then, history became a cosmic war between God's Kingdom and Satan's kingdom.[45] Satan was fatally defeated by Jesus' death on the cross and no longer has any authority over those who believe in Jesus (Eph. 2:15; James 4:7). However, in this age before Jesus' return, Satan promotes evil to actively try to deceive and kill, and he persecutes God's saints (Eph. 6:11-12). Satan plans to establish a permanent, earthly kingdom with his last ruler, the antichrist, but, when Jesus returns, the antichrist and false prophets will ultimately be cast into the fiery lake of burning sulfur, and Satan will be imprisoned in the Abyss for a thousand years (Rev. 19:20, 20:3). On that day, the earth and its people will be liberated from Satan. Although Satan will be released from the Abyss after a thousand years and will attack Jerusalem again, he will be immediately defeated by God and ultimately cast into the eternal, fiery lake of burning sulfur (Rev 20:7-10).[46]

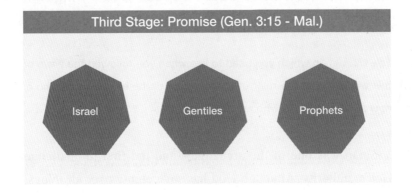

God's promise guarantees that the woman's offspring will victoriously defeat the serpent (Satan). The Fall will be reversed, and mankind will effectively rule over creation. God chose Abraham as the channel for the woman's offspring to come, and He re-established the nation of Israel. He gave a series of covenants and many promises and will fulfill them all when the time becomes full.

Question 9 What is Israel's role in God's Kingdom project?

Deut. 4:5-6   5 See, I have taught you decrees and laws as the LORD my God commanded me, so that you may follow them in the land you are entering to take possession of it. 6 Observe them carefully, for this will show your wisdom and understanding to the nations, who will hear about all these decrees and say, "Surely this great nation is a wise and understanding people."

Israel is a nation born from the lineage of Abraham, Isaac, and Jacob. After the Exodus from Egypt, Israel received the Mosaic Covenant, becoming a kingdom of priests (Exod. 19:5-6). Although God chose Israel, God's purpose was not Israel itself but rather Israel as His channel to bless all nations (Gen. 12:2-3). This blessing was to be realized only when Israel proclaimed the Messiah to the nations and revealed God's greatness by obeying the Mosaic Covenant. However, Israel disobeyed God and, consequently, was scattered across the nations where they were supposed to be a light and became the objects of mockery and proverbs. Nevertheless, God promised that the Israelites would regather to the land according to His covenant (Deut. 30:1-5). Israel rejected their Savior Jesus, was scattered, and suffered persecution at the hands of the nations (Matt. 23:37-38). While many Gentiles are being saved in Christ, the Jews have been experiencing a temporary, partial hardening (Rom. 11:25). However, there is a "remnant" among Israel who believe in Jesus as their Messiah, and their existence testifies to God's continued faithfulness to Israel (Rom. 11:5). Israel's unbelief will be reversed on the Day of the LORD that is approaching, and God will save and restore all Israel in connection with Messiah Jesus' return (Zech. 12:10; Rom. 11:26). When Israel believes in Messiah Jesus as a nation, the Messianic Kingdom will be established, and abundant blessing will flow to all the nations. The land of Israel and the city of Jerusalem will become the headquarters of the global Messianic Kingdom, and Israel will become a leader and a priestly nation among the nations that worship the Messiah (Mic. 4:1-3).

Question 10 Why did God establish Israel as a theocracy?

Exod. 19:5-6   5 Now if you obey me fully and keep my covenant, then out of all nations you will be my treasured possession. Although the whole earth is mine, 6 you will be for me a kingdom of priests and a holy nation.' These are the words you are to speak to the Israelites."

God raised up a new nation through Abraham, Isaac, and Jacob. God created Israel for His Name, for the salvation of the world, and as His foothold for the restoration of His Kingdom (Deut. 7:6).

Isa. 44:6   "This is what the LORD says – Israel's King and Redeemer, the LORD Almighty: I am the first and I am the last; apart from me there is no God.

Isa. 49:6   he says: "It is too small a thing for you to be my servant to restore the tribes of Jacob and bring back those of Israel I have kept. I will also make you a light for the Gentiles, that you may bring my salvation to the ends of the earth."

As a theocracy, Israel was supposed to serve God as its King, obey Him, and, under God's protection, proclaim His salvation to the ends of the earth, becoming a light for the Gentiles.

1 Sam. 8:6-7   6 But when they said, "Give us a king to lead us," this displeased Samuel; so he prayed to the LORD. 7 And the LORD told him: "Listen to all that the people are saying to you; it is not you they have rejected, but they have rejected me as their king.

From the moment Israel sought a king, Israel rebelled against God's will and rejected His sovereignty. They rejected theocracy, the only form of government that pleases God and brings happiness to mankind.

Question 11 Did God forsake Israel when Israel asked for a king?

2 Sam. 5:9-10   9 David then took up residence in the fortress and called it the City of David. He built up the area around it, from the supporting terraces inward. 10 And he became more and more powerful, because the LORD God Almighty was with him.

God never gave up on His master plan and will ultimately establish His Kingdom on earth. Since theocracy is the only form of government that pleases God and brings happiness to mankind, God's master plan will continue to move forward, even if it is temporarily sidelined.

Question 12 Israel's history records many failures thus far. Historically, when was Israel the closest to fulfilling its mission?

1 Kings 4:24   For he ruled over all the kingdoms west of the River, from Tiphsah to Gaza, and had peace on all sides.

1 Kings 10:21-25 21 All King Solomon's goblets were gold, and all the household articles in the Palace of the Forest of Lebanon were pure gold. Nothing was made of silver, because silver was considered of little value in Solomon's days. 22 The king had a fleet of trading ships at sea along with the ships of Hiram. Once every three years it returned, carrying gold, silver and ivory, and apes and baboons. 23 King Solomon was greater in riches and wisdom than all the other kings of the earth. 24 The whole world sought audience with Solomon to hear the wisdom God had put in his heart. 25 Year after year, everyone who came brought a gift-articles of silver and gold, robes, weapons and spices, and horses and mules.

During King Solomon's reign, when God's reign was with him, Israel was a powerful and prosperous nation and was widely known through trade with many distant nations in all directions. The promises to bless the land, descendants, and nations were being well fulfilled. Many surrounding nations admired Jerusalem, and the queen of Sheba visited Jerusalem from Ethiopia. King Solomon's sins, recorded in 1

Kings 11, reveals that Israel would not yet be able to fulfill its calling. After King Solomon's death, Israel was divided into the northern and southern kingdoms. Israel's worsening sins eventually led to God's judgment and their exile. The northern kingdom perished in 722 B.C. with many people being taken as captives to Assyria, the southern kingdom was destroyed in 586 B.C. with many people being taken as captives to Babylon.

Question 13 How can David's Kingdom be preserved forever when it was destroyed by Babylon?

2 Sam. 7:16   Your house and your kingdom will endure forever before me; your throne will be established forever.' "

Dan. 2:44   "In the time of those kings, the God of heaven will set up a kingdom that will never be destroyed, nor will it be left to another people. It will crush all those kingdoms and bring them to an end, but it will itself endure forever.

David was a king after God's own heart. This is why God intends to establish the throne of David forever. God intends and prophecies His eternal Kingdom that will be established through David's Offspring, Jesus Christ.

Question 14 What is the nations' role in God's Kingdom project?

Isa. 49:6   he says: "It is too small a thing for you to be my servant to restore the tribes of Jacob and bring back those of Israel I have kept. I will also make you a light for the Gentiles, that you may bring my salvation to the ends of the earth."

Isa. 19:24-25   24 In that day Israel will be the third, along with Egypt and Assyria, a blessing on the earth. 25 The LORD Almighty will bless them, saying, "Blessed be Egypt my people, Assyria my handiwork, and Israel my inheritance."

The nations listed in Genesis 10 emphasize the importance of nations in God's Kingdom project. Although people tried to glorify themselves by building the Tower of Babel to reach heaven, God confused their languages and scattered them across the face of the earth (Gen. 11:9). Israel was chosen to bless all nations but disobeyed that calling. God sent Jesus to restore Israel and bring blessings to the nations. Through Jesus' First Advent, Gentiles who believe in Him experience Messianic salvation.

Jews who believe in Jesus as their Messiah, called "God's Israel," (Gal. 6:16) and believing Gentiles are joined together as God's people (Eph. 3:6). The mission of this age is to proclaim the Gospel of the Kingdom so that all nations can believe in

Jesus as the Messiah (Matt. 24:14). But, the nations continue to rebel against God and His Word (Ps. 2:1-3). However, when Jesus returns to establish God's Kingdom, the nations of the world will worship God with redeemed Israel (Isa. 19:24-25). During the Messianic Kingdom, many Gentiles will go up to Jerusalem to learn the Way of the Lord. Under the Messiah's reign, they will live in peace with other nations (Mic. 4:1-4). In God's eternal Kingdom, all nations will live in harmony through the leaves of the tree of life (Rev. 22:2). The nations and their kings will worship God and bring their own cultural contributions to the New Jerusalem (Rev. 21:24, 21:26).

Question 15 What is the prophets' role in God's Kingdom project?

Isaiah prophesies with great reliance on the Davidic Covenant. The day will come when all nations will gather in Jerusalem to worship God and will learn His word. The Lord will rule over the nations, and weapons for war will be transformed into tools for peace (Isa. 2:4). The coming Kingdom with the Messiah at its center will have abundant peace. He will sit upon the throne of David, and His Kingdom, characterized by justice and righteousness, will have no end (Isa. 9:7). The earth will be restored like Eden, and there will be peace among the animal as well (Ps. 11:6-9). The restoration of God's Kingdom comes through the Suffering Servant Who atones (Isa. 53:3-5). When He judges the forces of Satan, there will be a global tribulation upon all the nations of the earth. However, after this judgment, God's Kingdom will be established, and God will be enthroned as King in Jerusalem (Isa. 24:19-23).

Jeremiah prophesies that Judah will experience judgment and captivity by Babylon due to disobeying God's covenant. God's faithfulness to the Abrahamic Covenant will lead to the re-gathering of God's people to the Promised Land from the nations, and they will live there in peace and prosperity forever. The New Covenant guarantees that the Israelites will be redeemed and will have new hearts that obey the Lord. Upon the fulfillment of the Davidic Covenant, the Son of David will rule over restored Israel. Even amid judgment, there is a message of hope based on God's Name and His faithfulness to His covenant promises. Both Israel and the nations will see this and will give glory to God Who made the heavens and the earth.

Ezekiel provides detailed information about the coming Kingdom of God. He gives hope for restoration from judgment and exile and for advancement toward the Kingdom. This hope is centered on the blessings of the New Covenant under the righteous King David.

Daniel prophesies about the Gentile nations that will exist before God's Kingdom is established on the earth. He also prophesies that Israel's Messiah will be killed and that there will be great tribulation upon Israel before His kingship is established.

Zechariah prophesies that, when Jerusalem is besieged, captured, plundered, and insulted by the nations, the Lord will return to the Mount of Olives to rescue the city and its residents. On that day, along with cosmic signs, there will be great geographical changes, and God will be King over the whole earth (Zech. 14:1-9).

Although Israel has returned from exile, it remains under Gentile influences and suffers the consequences of its disobedience. However, the prophets kept proclaiming the coming Kingdom in which Israel will be saved, be restored, and experience both spiritual and physical blessings. The Gentiles will ultimately participate in the Kingdom under King David. Since the Kingdom of God prophesied by the prophets is both spiritual and physical in nature, it will be established on the earth.

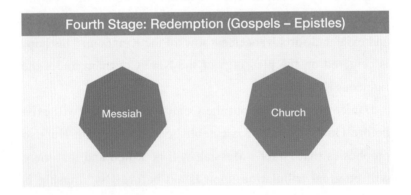

The prophets comfort Israel and proclaim hope by reaffirming the hope of the Davidic Covenant. They repeatedly prophesy the hope that Israel will experience the blessings of the Abrahamic Covenant under the Son of David's Kingdom and reign.

Jesus the King brings redemption through atonement, and His death is the foundation for the restoration of all things.

Question 16 What is Jesus the Messiah like in God's Kingdom project?

Matt. 25:31   "When the Son of Man comes in his glory, and all the angels with him, he will sit on his throne in heavenly glory.

Rev. 11:15   The seventh angel sounded his trumpet, and there were loud voices in heaven, which said: "The kingdom of the world has become the kingdom of our Lord and of his Christ, and he will reign for ever and ever."

Jesus is the hero in God's plan for His Kingdom, and the central theme of the Bible is Jesus Who is to come, has come, and will come again. Jesus, the Son of David, will defeat Satan and restore all things from the curse into blessings. Jesus, the last Adam, will rule over all nations from Jerusalem. Jesus, a Jewish man, is God's Servant Who restores the nation of Israel and brings blessings to the Gentiles. The foundation of God's

Kingdom is the precious blood of Jesus shed on the cross (Rev.1:5-6). Through His earthly ministry, Jesus offered God's Kingdom and revealed it through miracles and blessings (Matt. 12:28). After His resurrection and ascension, Jesus sent the Holy Spirit to dwell in the saints to help them obey God. Jesus is now seated at the right hand of Father God and has all authority in heaven and on earth (Heb. 12:2; Matt. 28:18). Jesus will return and rule over the earth with the saints for a thousand years through the Messianic Kingdom (Rev. 20:6). Jesus will successfully rule His Messianic Kingdom and will eventually hand it to Father God (1 Cor. 15:24). Jesus will rule over the eternal Kingdom with Father God and the saints (Rev. 22:5).

Question 17 What is the church's role in God's Kingdom project?

Col. 1:18   And he is the head of the body, the church; he is the beginning and the firstborn from among the dead, so that in everything he might have the supremacy.

The church is important in God's Kingdom project. God's Kingdom itself is broader in scope than the church and is where God's sovereignty is fully exercised over every aspect of creation, both spiritual and physical. The church is the New Covenant community of believing Jews and believing Gentiles in this age between Jesus' First and Second Advents. While Israel is temporarily suffering spiritual blindness in this age, the church has the mission to proclaim Jesus Christ's message. Although the church is not God's Kingdom, it is connected to God's Kingdom project in several important ways. First, the church is a gathering of those who believe in Jesus the Messiah and are baptized by one Spirit to form one body as a community of faith (1 Cor. 12:13). The church is under Jesus' authority for He is its Head (Col. 1:18). Second, believers of Jesus are citizens of God's Kingdom. This means that, although the actual establishment of the Kingdom awaits Jesus' return, believers belong to God's Kingdom in the present. Christians are those who have been moved from the power of darkness (Satan's kingdom) to the Kingdom of the Son of love, the Kingdom of God (Col. 1:13). Third, the saints of the church should display the righteousness that is worthy of God's Kingdom. This includes loving God, loving neighbors, and enjoying "righteousness, peace, and joy" in the Holy Spirit (Matt. 22:37-40; Rom. 14:17). Fourth, the church proclaims the Gospel of the Kingdom of heaven and presents the Way for people to enter God's Kingdom. The qualification for entering God's Kingdom is to be born again of water and the Holy Spirit (John 3:5). In this evil age, the church's mission to proclaim the Gospel of the Kingdom of heaven often faces persecutions from Satan and the world. Fifth, the church will receive rewards in God's Kingdom. If we saints endure, we will reign with the Lord (2 Tim. 2:12;

Rev. 20:6, 22:5). Looking forward to the rewards to come, the saints can endure and overcome the current persecutions with the help of the Holy Spirit (Phil. 3:14; Rom. 8:37).

Question 18 What does "Your Kingdom come" in the Lord's prayer mean?

Matt. 6:9-10   9 "This, then, is how you should pray: " 'Our Father in heaven, hallowed be your name, 10 your kingdom come, your will be done on earth as it is in heaven.

Jesus proclaimed, "The Kingdom of God is at hand" (Mark 1:14-15). He also proclaimed that the Kingdom of God has already come (Matt. 12:28). He explained God's Kingdom with various parables. He also taught how to enter the Kingdom and who enters the Kingdom. He proclaimed that, when the time comes, God's Kingdom will be fulfilled. The main and most important part of the prayer that Jesus taught is to ask for the Kingdom of God to come. With God's Kingdom already here, we should experience heaven in our spirits as well as in our families. Furthermore, we should experience heaven within the church as well. However, the most direct meaning of "Your Kingdom come" is when the kingdom of the world transforms into the Kingdom of Christ (Rev. 11:15).

Question 19 What is the church's main mission in this era?

Matt. 24:14   And this gospel of the kingdom will be preached in the whole world as a testimony to all nations, and then the end will come.

Matt. 28:19   Therefore go and make disciples of all nations, baptizing them in the name of the Father and of the Son and of the Holy Spirit,

The church's primary mission is to preach the Gospel of God's Kingdom and make disciples. The knowledge of God accompanies cultural and social responsibility. When Jesus returns, the saints will join Him in His reign over the nations, which will necessarily involve cultural and social issues (Rev. 2:26). However, the church's central mission in this generation is not cultural nor social reformation. Christians can still participate in all areas of culture for God's glory, where they endeavor to reveal and support the Christian worldview (1 Cor. 10:31). At the same time, Christians should be aware that true cultural or social reformation will not occur in these evil times. All of these are waiting for the Messianic Kingdom to come after Jesus' Second Advent.

The church, waiting for Jesus' return, should avoid both extremes of acting as if the church has nothing to do with any cultural or social areas and seeing only social reformation as the mission of the church before Jesus' return and His Kingdom.

Question 20 What does "already" and "not yet" mean in terms of God's Kingdom?

Luke 18:30   will fail to receive many times as much in this age and, in the age to come, eternal life."

Matt. 12:32   Anyone who speaks a word against the Son of Man will be forgiven, but anyone who speaks against the Holy Spirit will not be forgiven, either in this age or in the age to come.

Mark 10:30   will fail to receive a hundred times as much in this present age (homes, brothers, sisters, mothers, children and fields – and with them, persecutions) and in the age to come, eternal life.

Matt. 12:28   But if I drive out demons by the Spirit of God, then the kingdom of God has come upon you.

God's Kingdom has already been present since Jesus came to earth and began His ministry through His public life (Already). God's promises and plans are not always final or complete. In many cases, they can be incipient or partial. This is inaugurated eschatology, which refers to when the process of fulfilling promises and plans has begun. By casting out demons by the power of the Holy Spirit, Jesus began to conquer Satan's realm. When the time becomes full, Jesus will come again to complete God's Kingdom (Not yet).

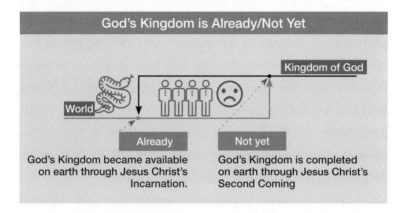

God's Kingdom is Already/Not Yet

Already — God's Kingdom became available on earth through Jesus Christ's Incarnation.

Not yet — God's Kingdom is completed on earth through Jesus Christ's Second Coming

Question 21 What is heaven in one's heart?

1 Cor. 6:19   Do you not know that your body is a temple of the Holy Spirit, who is in you, whom you have received from God? You are not your own;

1 Cor. 3:16   Don't you know that you yourselves are God's temple and that God's Spirit lives in you?

God's Kingdom means God's reign or control. God's Kingdom refers to the world ruled by Jesus Christ. Jesus said,

"My kingdom is not of this world" (John 18:36). His Kingdom is where the control, reign, and sovereignty of Christ are present and in force. Wherever Jesus goes, the Kingdom of heaven is realized there. Jesus Christ establishes His own kingship within the hearts of believers. If a person received Jesus as Lord and continuously submits to His reign, then God's Kingdom has come to that individual. Praying for God's Kingdom to come is an invitation for repentance in the lives and hearts of people who are rebelling against God's will (Matt. 5:3, 4:17). God's Kingdom is not in eating and drinking well but in bearing the fruits of righteousness, peace, and joy in the Holy Spirit (Rom. 14:17). Where God reigns, there is righteousness, peace, and unspeakable joy. God's Kingdom includes not only material satisfaction but also personal characteristics. God's Kingdom is the Kingdom of power that comes from living according to God's Word and from overcoming oneself and the world (1 Cor. 4:20).

Question 22 What institutions did God Himself create?

Gen. 2:22-24   22 Then the LORD God made a woman from the rib he had taken out of the man, and he brought her to the man. 23 The man said, "This is now bone of my bones and flesh of my flesh; she shall be called 'woman,' for she was taken out of man." 24 For this reason a man will leave his father and mother and be united to his wife, and they will become one flesh.

All institutions and structures of this world were made by men. There are two institutions that God Himself created with His own initiative: the family and the church. God created the family in the Garden of Eden and the church in John Mark's upper room (Acts 2).

We should all become the main characters of happy families. The family was created before the church. The children can meet with Jesus in their homes before they go to church. Therefore, we should make our homes God's Kingdom where He reigns.

Question 23 What is heaven at home?

When we obey God's law well, our homes become heavenly, and we can experience the utmost happiness.

Eph. 5:22   Wives, submit to your husbands as to the Lord.

Eph. 5:25   Husbands, love your wives, just as Christ loved the church and gave himself up for her

Eph. 6:1-4   1 Children, obey your parents in the Lord, for this is right. 2 "Honor your father and mother" – which is the first commandment with a promise – 3 "that it may go well with you and that you may enjoy long life on the earth." 4 Fathers, do not exasperate your children; instead, bring them up in the training and instruction of the Lord.

A happy family life is the most common hope of all mankind and the most important element of human life. Home is the place of human existence, the place of growth, and the cradle of personality. Home is a shelter, a nest, and the first economic unit. Home is the center of cultural creation, a museum of one's memories, the starting point of human relationships, and a place where mature relationships are cultivated. Home is where one's faith starts and becomes perfected. When God reigns over our precious families, heaven in our homes becomes realized.

People who are happy at home are also happy at church. Saints who have problems at home are more likely to cause problems at church. For this reason, the Bible teaches that people who are entrusted with positions in the church should be those who manage their homes well (1 Tim. 3:12). Those who have no problems in their marital life and take good care of their children can serve the church with stability. Home is a small church as well as a small heaven. Home is the foundation for spiritual ministry.

Family is God's prescription to solve the greatest human problem of solitude. Even if we fail in everything else, we need to succeed in our family lives. Make your home heavenly. Then you will become a happy person, and God's Kingdom will grow and expand.

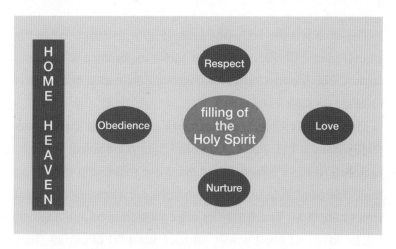

Question 24 What is heaven at church?

Eph. 1:23   which is his body, the fullness of him who fills everything in every way.

Eph. 2:19   Consequently, you are no longer foreigners and aliens, but fellow citizens with God's people and members of God's household,

Eph. 4:15-16   15 Instead, speaking the truth in love, we will in all things grow up into him who is the Head, that is, Christ. 16 From him the whole body, joined and held together by every supporting ligament, grows and builds itself up in love, as each part does its work.

The church is the body of Christ, Who is its Head. When the church obeys Christ's reign, we saints experience a heavenly church. The life of Christ flows through the whole body and is revealed through its members.

The heavenly church enjoys peace and joy, and experiences family (Rom. 14:17; Eph. 2:19; Mark 3:35). In a heavenly church, each believer is a minister, and there is a fellowship of sharing faith (Philem. 1:1-2, 1:6). It glorifies God by bearing abundant fruit (John 15:8). The believers are considerate of one another, stir up love and good works, and set beautiful examples (Heb. 10:24, John 13:15).

The heavenly church is a community called to heal the wounded who fell while walking on life's path. We should be able to look to each other and learn from one another to stand back up again. Therefore, we experience heaven by often gathering together and encouraging each other.

The heavenly church is a community overflowing with life in the abundant Presence of the Holy Spirit. The church overflowing with life is deeply committed to praying and demonstrating the works of the Word.

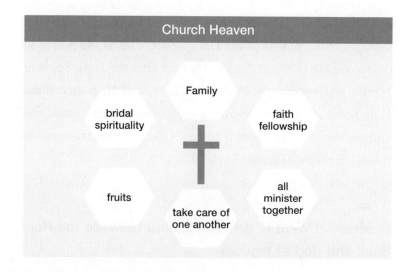

Question 25 **How does God's Kingdom expand?**

Matt. 24:14   And this gospel of the kingdom will be preached in the whole world as a testimony to all nations, and then the end will come.

Jesus showed examples of serving and loving others to expand God's Kingdom. And He sent the Holy Spirit. God's greatest gift to mankind was His only begotten Son and the Holy Spirit. While praying earnestly in Mark's upper room for 10 days, the disciples received the Holy Spirit on the day of Pentecost. From that moment, the disciples at last became Christ's witnesses. God's Kingdom expands through serving and loving one another (John 13:14, 13:34). God's Kingdom expands by the power of the Holy Spirit (Acts 1:8). A Christian's greatest strength is the power of the Holy Spirit. This is the power to overcome the Gates of Hades. By receiving the Holy Spirit in Mark's upper room, the church was born, and the power of the Holy Spirit enabled the church to exist in history as a victorious church overcoming all evil forces. God's Kingdom expands through Christ's witnesses (Acts 20:24).

Question 26 What is the relationship between the Holy Spirit and God's Kingdom?

Rom. 14:17   For the kingdom of God is not a matter of eating and drinking, but of righteousness, peace and joy in the Holy Spirit,

1 Cor. 4:20   For the kingdom of God is not a matter of talk but of power.

Matt. 12:28   But if I drive out demons by the Spirit of God, then the kingdom of God has come upon you.

The Holy Spirit enables us to experience God's Kingdom on this earth. The Holy Spirit transforms those who are perishing into the people of God's Kingdom (John 3:5). The Holy Spirit makes God's Kingdom dwell within us (1 Cor. 3:16). The Holy Spirit expands God's Kingdom (Acts 1:8).

Being full of the Holy Spirit should not stop at personal satisfaction. Being full of the Holy Spirit, we should pray for God's Kingdom to come not only in our souls but also in our homes, in our churches, in our societies, in our nations, and in all other areas of our lives by obeying Him.

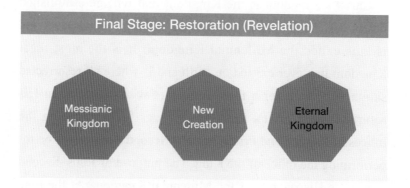

As all things are restored, Jesus will successfully fulfill God's Kingdom project on earth. God's Kingdom will be merged with the perfect and eternal Kingdom of Father God.

Question 27 What is Christ's Kingdom?

Rev. 11:15   The seventh angel sounded his trumpet, and there were loud voices in heaven, which said: "The kingdom of the world has become the kingdom of our Lord and of his Christ, and he will reign for ever and ever."

Rev. 20:6   Blessed and holy are those who have part in the first resurrection. The second death has no power over them, but they will be priests of God and of Christ and will reign with him for a thousand years.

Christ's Kingdom is the Kingdom that will be established on earth and ruled by Christ Himself for a thousand years and is thus called the Millennial Kingdom. It is the most ideal Kingdom that ever existed on earth and is where all resurrected saints will reign for a thousand years with Christ upon His return. Jesus Christ's First Advent was for performing the offices of Prophet and Priest, and His Second Advent will be for performing the office of the King. The purpose of Jesus' Second Advent is His reign over the Millennial Kingdom. At the time of Jesus' Second Advent, the resurrection of the saints who died, the transformation of the saints who are alive, the Great Tribulation on earth, and imprisonment of Satan in the Abyss will take place (Rev. 20:2-3). Then, the Millennial Kingdom will begin. Christ will be the King of kings, and the saints will rule together as the priests of God and Christ.

Question 28 When will justice and peace be realized?

Isa. 2:4   He will judge between the nations and will settle disputes for many peoples. They will beat their swords into plowshares and their spears into pruning hooks. Nation will not take up sword against nation, nor will they train for war anymore.

Only at the time of the Messianic Kingdom, there will be no wars, and justice will be realized. This is because the Almighty Lord Himself will rule over everything. Because Christ is the Prince of Peace, peace will abound on earth. All motives for war, such as hatred and strife, envy and jealousy, and anger and greed will disappear, and people will only be full of love, peace, delight, and joy.

Question 29 What does "full of the knowledge of the LORD" mean?

Isa. 11:9　　They will neither harm nor destroy on all my holy mountain, for the earth will be full of the knowledge of the LORD as the waters cover the sea.

On God's holy mountain, there will be no harm nor destruction anywhere. This is because the earth will be full of the knowledge of the LORD as the waters cover the sea. "The knowledge of the LORD" is not theoretical, objective knowledge about the LORD. The knowledge here is a vivid, experiential, and personal knowledge that is obtained only from living together. "The knowledge of the LORD," therefore, refers to knowing God experientially and personally through an intimate, gracious, truthful, and pure relationship with Him. The earth being filled with "the knowledge of the LORD" is compared here to the waters covering the sea. "As the waters cover the sea" reminds us of Noah's flood, when the waters came from 40 days of rain and from underground springs to cover the world even to the top of the highest mountain peak (Gen. 7:20). Remembering the waters of the LORD's judgment that covered the entire world long ago, blotted out all sinners, and gave birth to a completely new world, and reflecting upon the Messianic Kingdom to come where the knowledge of the LORD will cover the whole world to bring forth a completely new Kingdom of peace, the prophet Isaiah sang with his heart bursting with joy.

Question 30 Is the Millennial Kingdom a physical paradise?

Isa. 51:3   The LORD will surely comfort Zion and will look with compassion on all her ruins; he will make her deserts like Eden, her wastelands like the garden of the LORD. Joy and gladness will be found in her, thanksgiving and the sound of singing.

The Millennial Kingdom will be a physical paradise like the Garden of Eden. People will enjoy a paradise garden filled with beauty and joy. God desires to live with His people forever in a physical paradise. Diseases have brought great sorrow and unhappiness to mankind. Examples of incurable diseases include blindness, deafness, lameness, and muteness. However, on that Day, the eyes of the blind will be opened, the ears of the deaf will be unstopped, the lame will leap like a deer, and the mute tongue will shout for joy (Isa. 35:5-6). The characteristic of the Millennial Kingdom is, in a word, paradise. There will be no evil beasts there, and the wolf will live with the lamb, and the child will play with the cobra. All animals will be docile in nature. The air will be pure, and there will be adequate amounts of rain so there will be no shortage of water. At that time, there will be no more destruction nor harm in the world. This is because the world will be filled with the knowledge and fear of God (Isa. 11:6-9).

Question 31 What does creation wait for in eager expectation?

Rom. 8:19-21   19 The creation waits in eager expectation for the sons of God to be revealed. 20 For the creation was subjected to frustration, not by its own choice, but by the will of the one who subjected it, in hope 21 that the creation itself will be liberated from its bondage to decay and brought into the glorious freedom of the children of God.

"The creation waits in eager expectation for the sons of God to be revealed" (Rom. 8:19). It is waiting for "the sons of God," namely the saints, to be clothed in glorious, resurrected bodies and reign with the Lord in the Millennial Kingdom. When that Day comes, all creation will also enjoy glorious freedom like God's children. On that Day, there will be no harming nor destroying nor decaying in creation. The Millennial Kingdom will have the most suitable climate for living creatures as well as clean drinking water and pure air to breathe. The deserts will be transformed into fertile lands where plants grow abundantly, and forests become luxuriant. There will be no earthquakes, no volcanic explosions, no storms, no droughts, no floods, so there will be no famines. The food chain and the law of the jungle will vanish in the animal kingdom, and all animals will live peacefully together. Because there will be no environmental pressures nor obsessions, true peace and stability will be realized. The world where people will enjoy the blessing of longevity and the highest level of happiness will last for a thousand years.

Question 32 Where is the capital of the Millennial Kingdom?

Matt. 5:35   or by the earth, for it is his footstool; or by Jerusalem, for it is the city of the Great King.

Isa. 24:23   The moon will be abashed, the sun ashamed; for the LORD Almighty will reign on Mount Zion and in Jerusalem, and before its elders, gloriously.

Jesus will be the King of the Millennial Kingdom and reign from Jerusalem. He will establish shalom, prosperity, happiness, and perfect justice that mankind has always sought. In the Millennial Kingdom, the remnants of all the nations in the world will come to Jerusalem on the day of the Feast of Tabernacles every year to worship the King of kings, and thus, Jerusalem will become the center of worship (Zech. 14:16). The capital of the Millennial Kingdom, Jerusalem, is where Abraham offered Isaac and where Jesus died, resurrected, and ascended into heaven. Jesus will rule over the whole world with His Word from Jerusalem, and true peace will come to the whole world (Isa. 2:1-4; Mic. 4:1-3; Hab. 2:14).

Question 33 What is New Creation Eschatology?

Isa. 65:17   "Behold, I will create new heavens and a new earth. The former things will not be remembered, nor will they come to mind.

Rev. 21:1   Then I saw a new heaven and a new earth, for the first heaven and the first earth had passed away, and there was no longer any sea.

New Creation Eschatology is the belief that eternal life is not celestial, timeless, nor immaterial in nature but is living forever in the New Heaven and New Earth and the New Jerusalem. God's plan for His creation is not to destroy it and start all over from nothing but to redeem, purify, and renew it. God's creation includes both material and immaterial elements, and both are important (Col. 1:16). The Garden of Eden was originally a physical and spiritual place, and the coming Kingdom will be so as well. God does not forsake His own creation but restores it. New Creation Eschatology rejects the excessively spiritual Platonist tendency to view all material things in a negative light.[47] The Bible contains many material or physical promises. Not only spiritual promises but also physical promises will be fulfilled. Isaiah 65, 2 Peter 3, and Revelation 21-22 reveal that the present earth will be purified and restored to become the New Earth. The promise of the New Earth in the Book of Isaiah is connected to the promise of the restoration of Jerusalem which is a part of the Promised Land (Isa. 65:18-25). Therefore, the New Earth will still be this "earth" and will have geographical characteristics. God will perfect every aspect of His own creation according to His plan.

Question 34 What is God's eternal Kingdom?

Rev. 21:1-2   1 Then I saw a new heaven and a new earth, for the first heaven and the first earth had passed away, and there was no longer any sea. 2 I saw the Holy City, the new Jerusalem, coming down out of heaven from God, prepared as a bride beautifully dressed for her husband.

In the new world that is the New Heaven and New Earth, the New Jerusalem will come down out of heaven. This New Jerusalem is the eternal Kingdom of God, that is heaven and the eternal home of believers, that we saints have long looked forward to and yearned for. It is a perfect and eternal world governed by the laws of the eternal world that transcends the three-dimensional world and the current knowledge of physics. The New Jerusalem in the New Heaven and New Earth will itself be the Temple that is God's eternal dwelling place.

The New Jerusalem, where a truly perfect and eternal rest can be found (Rev. 21:4), is the perfect home for the saints to ultimately live eternally (Rev. 21:11, 21:21). The Holy City, New Jerusalem, will be the center of the new universe and new earth and will be the capital of the eternal Kingdom of God. The thrones of God and Christ the Lamb will be there, and God's glory will fill that world, and the river of living water and the tree of life there will provide eternal life to all who are to live forever.

Question 35 What will life be like in the new Jerusalem?

Rev. 21:6 He said to me: "It is done. I am the Alpha and the Omega, the Beginning and the End. To him who is thirsty I will give to drink without cost from the spring of the water of life.

The New Heaven and the New Earth is the perfected Kingdom of God, and the New Jerusalem is the eternal City of God. The saints will live forever by eating from the tree of life and drinking from the living water that will make believers never thirsty again. Eternal life has been the ideal life and life goal that all the saints have been yearning for. It is the life of utmost happiness in which all elements that make mankind unhappy have disappeared. The perfected life, eternal food, and eternal life are there.

Rev. 21:8 But the cowardly, the unbelieving, the vile, the murderers, the sexually immoral, those who practice magic arts, the idolaters and all liars – their place will be in the fiery lake of burning sulfur. This is the second death."

Because people of all kinds of uncleanness will have already been cast into the eternal lake of fire, the New Heaven and New Earth will be a world completely untainted by sin. It is a world where only the saints who became holy by being washed clean from their sins by the blood of Christ live together with God.

The resurrected body is a spiritual and holy body. Resurrection life is the most perfect and glorious life for mankind.

Rev. 21:26   The glory and honor of the nations will be brought into it.

When the saints enter God's Kingdom, each will have his or her own glory. The saints will live a truly happy and glorious life in resurrected bodies. The saints in the New Jerusalem will live in Divine Light, enjoying its transcendent beauty. It will be a glorious life, unaffected by the flow of time, with endless joy. Worshiping God fully, serving Him maturely with perfect knowledge, and being active and productive, the saints will experience deep satisfaction and glory in all aspects of their eternal lives. The saints will live a glorious life completely free from sinful nature and all evil circumstances.

Rev. 21:7   He who overcomes will inherit all this, and I will be his God and he will be my son.

The saints, who victoriously overcome sins, temptations, tribulation, and the Devil, will receive the blessing of inheritance as God's children. The most important thing that a saint can receive as God's child is God's Kingdom. Since God is the King of kings, the saints, who are God's heirs, will inherit kingship and reign as kings. In the New Jerusalem, the saints will enjoy eternal life, living water, and fruit from the tree of life.

Rev. 22:5 There will be no more night. They will not need the light of a lamp or the light of the sun, for the Lord God will give them light. And they will reign for ever and ever.

Rev. 22:4 They will see his face, and his name will be on their foreheads.

Although we saints believe in God and live diligently on this earth, life on earth is imperfect in every aspect. Even fellowship with God is bound to be imperfect due to human weaknesses and various limitations. When the human soul and body corrupted by sin, this broken image of God, is completely restored, fellowship with God will be made whole. Given the longing for even an imperfect fellowship with God on this earth, the perfect fellowship with God in the New Heaven and New Earth will be unspeakably more thrilling. In the New Jerusalem, the saints will walk with God under the tree of life planted alongside the river of living water, see God face-to-face, converse with Him, and dwell with Him forever. This is God's ultimate purpose for creating the universe, the earth, and mankind in the midst of it.

Conclusion

By believing in Jesus, we became citizens of God's Kingdom. On this earth, our mission is to enjoy and proclaim God's Kingdom. and at the same time, to preach it. Until the Lord returns to complete God's Kingdom and rule over it with us saints, let us enjoy God's Kingdom by being full of the Holy Spirit, pray for God's Kingdom to come, obey Him, and run forward with blessed hope.

Replacement Theology
and Restoration Theology

Introduction

Christian anti-Semitism originates from the flawed views of replacement theology. The church was established entirely by the Jews. However, in less than 100 years, the church turned its back on the Jewish nation. The bad fruit of anti-Semitism was born from the wayward roots of replacement theology. Both the Old and New Testaments support restoration theology rather than replacement theology. Before Israel's independence, Israel was missing from theology, but now theology must fully include the reality of Israel's presence. After Israel's independence, a few Christian denominations and mission organizations renounced replacement theology which teaches that Israel's election was transferred to the church. However, there are still some denominations that adhere to replacement theology.

Question 1 What is replacement theology or replacement theory?

Replacement theology or replacement theory teaches that God's covenant with the Jews was transferred to the church. According to this theory, in God's plan, the church replaces Israel. The Jews are no longer God's people. God does not have a specific plan for the nation of Israel. Instead, the church is God's people. After the Pentecost in the New Testament, "Israel" refers only to the church. The covenants originally given to Israel, and God's plan, purpose, and promises for Israel are now fulfilled in the church. In this view, many of God's promises to Israel must be interpreted only spiritually. Where it is written that Israel must be restored in the land, replacement theology interprets this to mean that the Christian church will be blessed.

Question 2 What is replacement theology's root?

Replacement theology's root is Satan who attempts to obstruct the First and Second Advents of Jesus. Satan ardently hates the Jewish people because Israel was chosen for the salvation of mankind. Esau hated Jacob with murderous intent (Gen. 27:41). Pharaoh persecuted the children of Israel and gave an order to kill all newborn Jewish boys (Exod. 1:16, 1:22). Haman attempted to kill not only Mordecai but also all his people, the entire Jewish nation (Esther 3:6). King Herod killed all Jewish boys under two years old within Bethlehem and its borders (Matt. 2:16). Satan tried to prevent the Messiah from coming in the first place, but, when Jesus came, Satan stirred up people to crucify Him. However, Satan was defeated by Jesus' resurrection (Col. 2:15). Satan, knowing his fate, tries to obstruct Israel's restoration to prevent the return of the Messiah. One of Satan's obstructions is replacement theology which wrongly argues that the church has replaced Israel in God's plan.

Question 3 Was Israel cursed and judged as a nation that crucified the Messiah and replaced by the church as God's people?

Matt. 27:23-25 23 "Why? What crime has he committed?" asked Pilate. But they shouted all the louder, "Crucify him!" 24 When Pilate saw that he was getting nowhere, but that instead an uproar was starting, he took water and washed his hands in front of the crowd. "I am innocent of this man's blood," he said. "It is your responsibility!" 25 All the people answered, "Let his blood be on us and on our children!"

Acts 4:27   Indeed Herod and Pontius Pilate met together with the Gentiles and the people of Israel in this city to conspire against your holy servant Jesus, whom you anointed.

Who crucified Jesus? They were the rulers of Rome, the Gentiles, and the Jews. Since Jesus died for all mankind, His death was on account of not only the sins of the Jewish nation but also our sins. If Israel was forsaken by God due to their sins and disobedience and was replaced by the church, the church too will be forsaken because the church has disobeyed God and committed sins no less than Israel. If God revoked the eternal covenant He made with Israel because of their sins, He will revoke the promise with the church too because of believers' sins. However, God has never forsaken Israel. At present, about 6.8 million Jews are living in the Promised Land. And the number of believers among the Jewish people is exponentially growing.

Question 4 Is the New Testament superior to the Old Testament?

Advocates for replacement theology argue that, since the New Testament is a more developed and more complete revelation than the Old Testament, the prophecies about Israel in the Old Testament must be understood through the lens of the New Testament and at times be redefined.

However, progressive revelation never changes the meaning of any prior revelations. New revelations can bring to light those portions that were not understood earlier. However, the contents of the revelation already given cannot be changed. The New Testament reaffirms the eschatology of the Old Testament. 2 Thessalonians 2:1-4 mentions the LORD's Day and God's Temple. By quoting Isaiah 59:20-21, the New Testament confirms that Israel's salvation is connected to the New Covenant (Rom. 11:26-27). Above all, Jesus Himself acknowledges Israel's restoration (Acts 1:6-7). If God changes the meaning of an Old Testament passage, it cannot be a revelation to those who first received it. Acts 2 and 15 indicate that some of the Old Testament prophecies were being fulfilled at that time. However, there is no assertion that the Old Testament prophecies were "spiritually" completed in the church.

Question 5 Is Israel a model to reveal Christ and the church?

Replacement theologians view Israel as a type to reveal the larger and more important Christ and the church. As such, they claim that Christ and the church are the true Israel.

In that view, what relates to Israel is applied to the church, but the use of the name "Israel" is exactingly avoided. Although many aspects of God's covenants for Israel are typical in terms of looking forward to their final fulfillment, Israel itself has never been described strictly as a type to be replaced by an antitype.

By the very nature of God's covenants and promises for Israel, Israel cannot be a type. Jeremiah 31:35-37 prophesies that, unless the sun, moon, and stars cease to exist, the nation of Israel will persist, and Isaiah 66:8 prophecies that Israel will be reborn in an instant. In opposition, some replacement theologians argue that Israel's Independence in 1948 and Jerusalem's restoration in 1967 are not revealed in the Old and New Testaments. However, they are wrong. The New Testament tells the future of Israel (Matt. 19:28, 23:39; Luke 21:24; Acts 1:6; Rom. 11:26; Rev. 7:4-8). Because the New Testament predicts Israel's future, the state of Israel cannot fit into the criterion for being a type.

Question 6 Has Israel been permanently rejected?

Matt. 21:43   "Therefore I tell you that the kingdom of God will be taken away from you and given to a people who will produce its fruit.

Matt. 21:45   When the chief priests and the Pharisees heard Jesus' parables, they knew he was talking about them.

Matt. 23:39   For I tell you, you will not see me again until you say, 'Blessed is he who comes in the name of the Lord.' "

Replacement theologians think that God's Kingdom was taken from Israel and given to the church. In that view, God's people are now the church, not Israel. However, even the chief priests and Pharisees understood that Jesus' parable was referring to them (Matt. 21:45). Replacement theology believes that Israel was abandoned by God because the Jews rejected the Messiah, but there were Jews who followed Jesus even to the site of His crucifixion and visited His empty tomb. The numerous people, who received the fullness of the Holy Spirit in Mark's upper room and became witnesses of the gospel, were Jews, and most of the 500 brothers who witnessed Jesus' ascension were Jews. The early church experienced great revival, and, despite persecution at the hands of Rome, saints along with Stephen kept their faith and risked martyrdom. Furthermore, most of the authors of the Bible were the Jews, and the first missionaries to bring the gospel to the Gentiles were Jews. Matthew 23:39 predicts that Israel will cry out for salvation, and welcome and worship the Messiah. Israel's rejection is temporary, not permanent.

Question 7 Is the church the true Israel?

Gal. 6:16   Peace and mercy to all who follow this rule, even to the Israel of God.

As written by Paul in Galatians 6:16, "all who follow this rule" refers to Gentile Christians, and "the Israel of God," refers to Jewish Christians. "The Israel of God" are all Jews who believe in Christ and are Abraham's descendants both physically and spiritually. In the Bible, there is no instance where Israel, modified by the definite article "the," refers to a nation other than Israel. Paul rebuked the Judaists who were insisting that circumcision is necessary for salvation and praised those Jews in Galatia who did not agree with them. These Jewish Christians, who did not follow the Judaists, are "the Israel of God."

Replacement theologians claim that Galatian 6:16 indicates that the church, which became God's people by believing the gospel of Jesus Christ, is the true Israel. However, the New Testament never states that the church is Israel. The word "Israel" appears in the New Testament 73 times, always referring to the Jews. In nearly all cases, "Israel" refers to the nation and people of Israel. In only a few cases, "Israel" refers to believing Jews of a Hebrew background. In the New Testament, even after the church is born, the nation of Israel is still called "Israel" (Acts 3:12, 4:10, 5:21, 5:31, 5:35, 21:28).

In the Book of Acts, the word "Israel" is used 20 times, and the word "ekklesia" (the church) is used 19 times. While Israel and the church coexist, there is always a clear distinction between Israel and the church.

Question 8 Is the church the spiritual Israel?

Rom. 9:6   It is not as though God's word had failed. For not all who are descended from Israel are Israel.

Believing Jews are the spiritual Israel. In Romans, the Anchor Bible explains that all Jews are Israel in a national sense, but, in a limited sense, "Israel" refers to believing Jews. The second "Israel" in Romans 9:6 refers to Jewish Christians, who are the people of Israel who believe in Christ.

Question 9 Does Israel's identity and role disappear because believing Jews and believing Gentiles have become one?

Eph. 2:16   and in this one body to reconcile both of them to God through the cross, by which he put to death their hostility.

Eph. 2:18   For through him we both have access to the Father by one Spirit.

Replacement theologians argue that, since Jewish believers and Gentile believers have become one, there can be no specific status or role for the nation of Israel. However, the spiritual unity of believing Jews and believing Gentiles will take place with Israel's future restoration. There are replacement theologians who claim that, according to the Bible, the status of Jews and Gentiles have been completely abolished in Christ. However, Gentile believers cannot be part of Israel. Apostle Paul teaches that they become a part of a new structure, called "the one new man."

Ephesians 2:11-22 teaches that the Gentiles who were far off from God were brought close to Him through Jesus Christ. Therefore, the salvation status of believing Gentiles changed. Gentile believers become partakers of God's covenants and promises to Israel, but Gentile believers have not become Israel. Paul emphasized unity, but he did not mean that Gentiles and Jews are the same. In Christ, Jews cannot become Gentiles, and Gentiles cannot become Jewish Christians.

Question 10 Are the Gentiles participants or acquirers of Israel's covenant?

Rom. 11:17   If some of the branches have been broken off, and you, though a wild olive shoot, have been grafted in among the others and now share in the nourishing sap from the olive root,

Rom. 11:23-24 23 And if they do not persist in unbelief, they will be grafted in, for God is able to graft them in again. 24 After all, if you were cut out of an olive tree that is wild by nature, and contrary to nature were grafted into a cultivated olive tree, how much more readily will these, the natural branches, be grafted into their own olive tree!

The Book of Romans emphasizes that the Gentiles are now connected to God's promises. Jewish believers and Gentile believers have unity in salvation. However, this does not mean that the church is now the true Israel. There is a difference between saying that Gentile believers participate in God's covenants with Israel and saying that Gentile believers have become Israel. The Gentile believers are partakers of the covenant, not takers. This passage does not exclude the future role of the state of Israel and does not indicate that the church is Israel today.

For both Jews and Gentiles, the only Way to salvation is by faith in Jesus Christ. However, the New Testament teaches that the Jews still have a special position in God's historical work of salvation for mankind in Christ.

Question 11 Is the church the new Israel because it enjoys the fulfillment of the New Covenant?

2 Cor. 3:6   He has made us competent as ministers of a new covenant – not of the letter but of the Spirit; for the letter kills, but the Spirit gives life.

Replacement theologians argue that, although the New Covenant was made with Israel, the church is enjoying its fulfillment, so the church is the new Israel.

The Old Testament does not teach that the New Covenant is only for the nation of Israel. The New Covenant is fulfilled with both Israel and the church (Heb. 8:8-13; Jer. 31:31-33). To show that the nation of Israel will be saved (Rom. 11:26), Paul quotes the verse about the New Covenant in Romans 11:27. He teaches that Israel is still connected to the New Covenant even after the church is born. Hebrews 8 is about the superiority of the New Covenant over the Mosaic Covenant. It is not about whether the church is the true Israel or not. As the church participates in the spiritual blessing of the New Covenant, the complete eschatological fulfillment of the New Covenant will be realized with Israel in the Millennial Kingdom.

Question 12 Does the Old Testament teach Israel's restoration?

Jer. 31:35-37   35 This is what the LORD says, he who appoints the sun to shine by day, who decrees the moon and stars to shine by night, who stirs up the sea so that its waves roar – the LORD Almighty is his name: 36 "Only if these decrees vanish from my sight," declares the LORD, "will the descendants of Israel ever cease to be a nation before me." 37 This is what the LORD says: "Only if the heavens above can be measured and the foundations of the earth below be searched out will I reject all the descendants of Israel because of all they have done," declares the LORD.

As long as we see the sun, moon, and stars, we know that Israel is still in God's plan. The Old Testament clearly teaches Israel's restoration. God intends the nation of Israel to be His channel for blessing all people in the world (Gen. 12:2-3). After Jesus' Second Advent, all nations will gather in Jerusalem to worship God and keep the Feast of Tabernacles (Isa. 2:2; Zech. 14:16). The nations will play an important role on the New Earth (Rev. 21:24, 21:26; Rev. 22:2).

Deuteronomy 30:1-6 predicts that the nation of Israel will be scattered due to their disobedience but will one day be saved as a nation and will experience the restoration of their land. Jeremiah 30, 32, and 33 promise Israel's restoration, including both spiritual and physical blessings. Ezekiel 36 promises that the nation of Israel will return to their own land in the future and will be physically and spiritually restored. Thus, the Old Testament clearly teaches Israel's restoration.

Since the Abrahamic Covenant (Gen. 12:1-3,15:18-21) and the New Covenant (Jer. 31) are everlasting and unconditional, we expect that God will ensure their fulfillment for the people of Israel with whom He originally made these covenants.

Question 13 Do the Synoptic Gospels teach Israel's restoration?

Luke 22:30   so that you may eat and drink at my table in my kingdom and sit on thrones, judging the twelve tribes of Israel.

Matt. 23:39   For I tell you, you will not see me again until you say, 'Blessed is he who comes in the name of the Lord.' "

Luke 21:24   They will fall by the sword and will be taken as prisoners to all the nations. Jerusalem will be trampled on by the Gentiles until the times of the Gentiles are fulfilled.

Some replacement theologians point out that imagining that there are words in the Old Testament that have not been fulfilled by the ministry of Christ is itself a problem. However, the New Testament reaffirms the expectation for Israel's restoration and salvation taught in the Old Testament. In the New Testament, Jesus teaches that the apostles will rule over the twelve tribes of Israel. When Jesus states that there will be rewards when God's Kingdom is established, He is presupposing Israel's restoration. The New Testament teaches that Israel's relationship with God is not over, and one day Jerusalem will accept the Messiah with praises (Matt. 23:39). Luke 21:24 teaches that the destruction of Jerusalem will last for a limited time, and that, in God's plan, there will be a period when the Gentiles occupy Jerusalem.

However, the day will come when Jerusalem will not be trodden down by the Gentiles, which means the Jews will dwell in their land again. This Word was fulfilled by the recapturing of Jerusalem during the Six-Day War in 1967.

Question 14 Did Jesus and the apostles believe in Israel's restoration?

Acts 1:6-7   6 So when they met together, they asked him, "Lord, are you at this time going to restore the kingdom to Israel?" 7 He said to them: "It is not for you to know the times or dates the Father has set by his own authority.

After Jesus taught the work of God's Kingdom for 40 days, the apostles believed in Israel's restoration. The apostles still believed that the Messianic Kingdom will soon be established on earth. They also knew that Ezekiel 36 and Joel 2 connect the outpouring of the Holy Spirit promised by Jesus with the arrival of His Kingdom. Acts 1:6-7 demonstrates that the apostles' expectations of a literal, earthly kingdom reflected what Jesus taught and the Old Testament prophecies. Otherwise, Jesus would have corrected their thoughts regarding this essential aspect of His teachings. Through a sermon, Peter declared the restoration of all things to come (Acts 3:19-21).

Question 15 In Romans 11, about Israel's restoration, who is "all Israel?"

Rom. 11:26-27 26 And so all Israel will be saved, as it is written: "The deliverer will come from Zion; he will turn godlessness away from Jacob. 27 And this is my covenant with them when I take away their sins."

Romans 9-11 firmly support Israel's restoration, so that no one can claim that the church replaced the Jewish people. The salvation of "all Israel" will be accomplished according to the promises of the New Covenant given to Israel in the Old Testament. Like the word "Israel" mentioned 10 times in Romans 9-11, the word "Israel" mentioned in Romans 11:26 refers to the nation of Israel. "All Israel" is not Jewish believers in the Messiah Jesus throughout the Church Age who are already saved but rather all the Jews who will live during the tribulation in the Last Days who will be saved. It is correct to understand "all Israel" literally. However, it is not necessary to conclude that every single Israelite will be saved. Israel has always been treated as a whole (nationally). Therefore, the interpretation is that Israel will be saved as a whole.

Question 16 If Gentile believers have become Abraham's descendants by faith, aren't they the same as Israel?

1 Pet. 2:9-10   9 But you are a chosen people, a royal priesthood, a holy nation, a people belonging to God, that you may declare the praises of him who called you out of darkness into his wonderful light. 10 Once you were not a people, but now you are the people of God; once you had not received mercy, but now you have received mercy.

Exod. 19:6   you will be for me a kingdom of priests and a holy nation.' These are the words you are to speak to the Israelites."

Galatians calls Gentile believers "children of Abraham." However, the designation as "children of Abraham" given to Gentile believers does not imply that Gentile believers are spiritual Jews or part of Israel. It indicates that Gentile believers have become "children of Abraham" by faith and God's channel of blessing through obedience.

Question 17 Is 1 Peter 2:9 evidence that Israel's identity has been transferred to the church?

1 Pet. 2:9-10   9 But you are a chosen people, a royal priesthood, a holy nation, a people belonging to God, that you may declare the praises of him who called you out of darkness into his wonderful light.

10 Once you were not a people, but now you are the people of God; once you had not received mercy, but now you have received mercy.

Exod. 19:6   you will be for me a kingdom of priests and a holy nation.' These are the words you are to speak to the Israelites."

The saints are kings, because the saints rule the world by serving others and will eventually reign over all nations with Christ, the King (2 Tim. 2:12; Rev. 5:10, 20:6, 22:5). The saints are priests, because, through the merits of Jesus Christ, the saints come directly before God to serve and worship Him, and the saints lead many to God, intercede for them, and bless them. This spiritual status of the saints is truly noble and is due to God's great grace transcending the legal framework of the Old Testament law which restricted by nationality, lineage, age, and gender. However, just as the designation as "children of Abraham" for Gentile believers does not indicate that Gentile believers have become part of Israel, the terms used for Israel in the Old Testament that are used for Gentile believers in the New Testament do not indicate that the church has become identical with Israel.

Question 18 Can Israel's election and calling be changed depending on their actions?

Rom. 9:4-5   4 the people of Israel. Theirs is the adoption as sons; theirs the divine glory, the covenants, the receiving of the law, the temple worship and the promises. 5 Theirs are the patriarchs, and from them is traced the human ancestry of Christ, who is God over all, forever praised! Amen.

Rom. 11:29   for God's gifts and his call are irrevocable.

Even as Israel currently continues in unbelief, the New Testament clearly states that the adoption as sons, the Divine glory, the covenants, the receiving of the law, the temple worship, and the promises still belong to Israel as privileges. The New Testament states that God's faithfulness toward Israel is due to the promises He gave to Israel's patriarchs. The New Testament reveals that the election and calling of Israel is immutable.

Question 19 What is the relationship between Israel and the Gentiles in regard to God's blessings as described in Romans 11?

Rom. 11:11-12   11 Again I ask: Did they stumble so as to fall beyond recovery? Not at all! Rather, because of their transgression, salvation has come to the Gentiles to make Israel envious. 12 But if their transgression means riches for the world, and their loss means riches for the Gentiles, how much greater riches will their fullness bring!

Rom. 11:15   For if their rejection is the reconciliation of the world, what will their acceptance be but life from the dead?

Douglas J. Moo, professor of New Testament at Trinity Theological Seminary and Wheaton College, summarizes Romans 11 as God's blessing leaping back and forth between Israel and the Gentiles.

(vv. 11-12) Israel's fall → salvation reaches the Gentiles → fullness of the Gentiles

(vv. 15) rejecting Israel → reconciliation of the world → accepting Israel → resurrection

(vv. 17-23) cultivated olive tree branches break → wild olive tree branches are grafted in → broken cultivated olive tree branches are regrafted in

(vv. 25-26) Israel's hardening in part → fullness of the Gentiles → all Israel is saved

Relations between Israel & the Gentiles (Rom. 11)		
Israel		**Gentiles**
Fall (verse 11)		
Loss (verse 12)		riches
Broken off (verse 17)		
Revival! Revival! Revival!	Acceptance (verse 15)	Resurrection of the dead (Second Coming)

Question 20 Why can't God forsake Israel?

Rom. 11:1   I ask then: Did God reject his people? By no means! I am an Israelite myself, a descendant of Abraham, from the tribe of Benjamin.

Ps. 119:89-90   89 Your word, O LORD, is eternal; it stands firm in the heavens. 90 Your faithfulness continues through all generations; you established the earth, and it endures.

1 Sam. 15:29   He who is the Glory of Israel does not lie or change his mind; for he is not a man, that he should change his mind."

Ezek. 39:25   "Therefore this is what the Sovereign LORD says: I will now bring Jacob back from captivity and will have compassion on all the people of Israel, and I will be zealous for my holy name.

God's sovereign election of Israel is just as unconditional and unchangeable as His election of each believer. This is because God's decision is rooted in His unchanging character and is expressed in His unilateral and eternal Abrahamic Covenant. For His holy Name, God never forsakes Israel and restores them. The more we believe in God's sovereignty in terms of His election, the more we should believe the truth that He will save and restore Israel on His election of His own people.

Question 21 What is the difference between Israel and the church?

Gal. 6:16   Peace and mercy to all who follow this rule, even to the Israel of God.

1 Cor. 12:13   For we were all baptized by one Spirit into one body – whether Jews or Greeks, slave or free – and we were all given the one Spirit to drink.

Acts 15:15-18   15 The words of the prophets are in agreement with this, as it is written: 16 " 'After this I will return and rebuild David's fallen tent. Its ruins I will rebuild, and I will restore it, 17 that the remnant of men may seek the Lord, and all the Gentiles who bear my name, says the Lord, who does these things' 18 that have been known for ages.

The root of Israel begins with God's calling of Abraham in Genesis 12. Israel refers to the descendants of Abraham, Isaac, and Jacob. Israel is a nation with promises and covenants made by God. They are individual and national Israelites. Some Jews believed in Jesus, and some did not. In this age, Israelites who believe in Jesus are called the remnant and the Israel of God.

The church begins in Acts 2. The church is the community of the New Covenant consisting of believing Jews and believing Gentiles in this age between Jesus' First and Second Advents. The church consists of those who believe in Jesus the Messiah and were baptized by the Holy Spirit into the body of Christ. Both Israel and the church are important in God's plan and are necessary for understanding the Bible's story line.

Question 22 How is God's plan to save the world related to the nation of Israel?

Gen. 12:2-3   2 "I will make you into a great nation and I will bless you; I will make your name great, and you will be a blessing. 3 I will bless those who bless you, and whoever curses you I will curse; and all peoples on earth will be blessed through you."

Gen. 22:18   and through your offspring all nations on earth will be
blessed, because you have obeyed me."

The list of 70 clans (nations) of Noah's descendants in
Genesis 10 reveals God's care for the nations on the earth.
Noah's descendants were scattered and now form 260 nations
and 24,000 tribes. To bless the tribes and nations living on the
earth, God called Abraham and Israel and appointed them as a
kingdom of priests (Exod. 19:6). Israel, a priestly nation, made
atonement for the Israelites' sins on the Day of Atonement, but,
on the Feast of Tabernacles, Israel made atonement for the sins
of all the nations of the world. At that time, Israel offered 70
bulls (Num. 29:13-34), which represented all nations on this earth
given the 70 clans (nations) in Genesis 10, and Israel prayed for
all the nations in the world and blessed them.

Question 23 What are two ways Israel blesses the world?

First, Israel became the channel and means through which the
Messiah came.

Rom. 9:5   Theirs are the patriarchs, and from them is traced the
human ancestry of Christ, who is God over all, forever praised! Amen.

Second, the Offspring of David, the Messiah, will rule and serve the nations.

Isa. 2:2-4   2 In the last days the mountain of the LORD's temple will be established as chief among the mountains; it will be raised above the hills, and all nations will stream to it. 3 Many peoples will come and say, "Come, let us go up to the mountain of the LORD, to the house of the God of Jacob. He will teach us his ways, so that we may walk in his paths." The law will go out from Zion, the word of the LORD from Jerusalem. 4 He will judge between the nations and will settle disputes for many peoples. They will beat their swords into plowshares and their spears into pruning hooks. Nation will not take up sword against nation, nor will they train for war anymore.

Jerusalem will be at the center of the Messianic Kingdom. The nations will gather in Jerusalem to worship God and learn His ways. There will be true peace among the nations. This shows that there will be harmony between Israel and the nations. For the first time in history, the Lord, the Ruler, will pass perfect judgments. The nations will no longer prepare for wars and will instead use their resources for peace. This is more than the spiritual salvation of the church today. These things have not yet occurred in human history but will happen when the Messianic Kingdom comes.

Question 24 Does the Bible say that Israel will be scattered due to their failures and God's judgment and then return to the Promised Land?

Deut. 30:4-5   4 Even if you have been banished to the most distant land under the heavens, from there the LORD your God will gather you and bring you back. 5 He will bring you to the land that belonged to your fathers, and you will take possession of it. He will make you more prosperous and numerous than your fathers.

Ps. 147:2   The LORD builds up Jerusalem; he gathers the exiles of Israel.

Amos 9:15   I will plant Israel in their own land, never again to be uprooted from the land I have given them," says the LORD your God.

As God already said in Deuteronomy, He allowed the Israelites to be taken into Babylonian captivity due to their disobedience. When the Israelites repented there, He brought them back to their homeland. In 70 A.D., the Jerusalem Temple was destroyed, and the Israelites were scattered all over the world. However, in accordance with God's promises, they returned, declared independence in 1948, and continue to return from all over the world.

Replacement theologians think that Amos 9:15 is related to spiritual Israel, not physical Israel. They think that, in the

Messianic age to come, all God's people, whether believing Jews or believing Gentiles, are "spiritual Israel," the Lord's church which will be firmly established on the rock of salvation without ever being shaken. However, Israeli Prime Minister Benjamin Netanyahu quoted the last portion of Amos 9 in his keynote speech at the 68th U.N. General Assembly in 2013 and ended his speech by saying, "Ladies and gentlemen, the people of Israel have come home never to be uprooted again." [48]

Question 25 Due to Israel's unbelief in this age, did God replace Israel with the church to proclaim His message of salvation to the world?

Matt. 28:19-20 19 Therefore go and make disciples of all nations, baptizing them in the name of the Father and of the Son and of the Holy Spirit, 20 and teaching them to obey everything I have commanded you. And surely I am with you always, to the very end of the age."

Acts 1:8   But you will receive power when the Holy Spirit comes on you; and you will be my witnesses in Jerusalem, and in all Judea and Samaria, and to the ends of the earth."

The church does not replace Israel, but the church is used by God to share the message of Jesus the Messiah to a world that is lost in this age.

Question 26 Despite Israel's unbelief, there are blessings that come in this age. What are the blessings that come when Israel is full?

Rom. 9:4-5   4 the people of Israel. Theirs is the adoption as sons; theirs the divine glory, the covenants, the receiving of the law, the temple worship and the promises. 5 Theirs are the patriarchs, and from them is traced the human ancestry of Christ, who is God over all, forever praised! Amen.

Rom. 11:12   But if their transgression means riches for the world, and their loss means riches for the Gentiles, how much greater riches will their fullness bring!

Rom. 11:15   For if their rejection is the reconciliation of the world, what will their acceptance be but life from the dead?

The people of Israel have eight privileges: the adoption as sons, the Divine glory, the covenants, the receiving of the law, the temple worship, the promises, the patriarchs, and Christ being born from them. God revealed Himself to us Gentiles through them and gave us salvation by His grace. If the identity of Israel has disappeared, as claimed by replacement theologians, then the blessings coming from Israel's salvation would be meaningless. The fall of the Jews, which was their rejection of the Gospel, became the trigger for the Gospel of salvation to be preached to the Gentiles. However, the fullness of Israel, which will be their acceptance of the Gospel, will bring a greater blessing to the world than their fall. This is because, when Israel returns to Christ through national repentance, Christ will return, and, at that time, the resurrection of the dead will occur, and the Kingdom of God will be completed.

Question 27 Who are the sealed servants of God from the 12 tribes of Israel that appear in the Book of Revelation?

Rev. 7:3-8   3 "Do not harm the land or the sea or the trees until we put a seal on the foreheads of the servants of our God." 4 Then I heard the number of those who were sealed: 144,000 from all the tribes of Israel. 5 From the tribe of Judah 12,000 were sealed, from the tribe of Reuben 12,000, from the tribe of Gad 12,000, 6 from the tribe of Asher 12,000, from the tribe of Naphtali 12,000, from the tribe of Manasseh 12,000, 7 from the tribe of Simeon 12,000, from the tribe of Levi 12,000, from the tribe of Issachar 12,000, 8 from the tribe of Zebulun 12,000, from the tribe of Joseph 12,000, from the tribe of Benjamin 12,000.

Replacement theology claims that the church is Israel and argues that 144,000 is a symbolic number that refers to all saints including believing Jews and believing Gentiles. If so, it is difficult to explain the following in verse 9: "After this I looked and there before me was a great multitude that no one could count, from every nation, tribe, people and language." It is also difficult to explain the meaning of each tribe's name. The words "those who were sealed...from all the tribes of Israel" speaks of a very simple and practical fact. Any other explanation here will inevitably result in a misinterpretation. Many heresies have appeared from the wrong interpretation of this text. It is God Who classifies each tribe and fills the 144,000 in total, taking 12,000 from each tribe. We must not commit the error of limiting or ignoring what Almighty God will do.

Question 28 Can the church be perfected when the full number of Gentile believers is filled?

Rom. 11:24   After all, if you were cut out of an olive tree that is wild by nature, and contrary to nature were grafted into a cultivated olive tree, how much more readily will these, the natural branches, be grafted into their own olive tree!

Eph. 2:18   For through him we both have access to the Father by one Spirit.

Eph. 2:22   And in him you too are being built together to become a dwelling in which God lives by his Spirit.

Replacement theology does not acknowledge a national, historical, or lineal Israel. However, God's promised plan cannot be fulfilled only by Gentile believers. A remnant of the Jews must return and be regrafted into the cultivated olive tree where the branches broke. Thus, the church will become complete only when the believing Gentiles and believing Jews are united to become one new man in the Holy Spirit and become a dwelling place for God.

Question 29 In what form will Israel exist in the New Jerusalem, the eternal city that is the completion of God's history of salvation?

Rev. 21:1-2   1 Then I saw a new heaven and a new earth, for the first heaven and the first earth had passed away, and there was no longer any sea. 2 I saw the Holy City, the new Jerusalem, coming down out of heaven from God, prepared as a bride beautifully dressed for her husband.

Rev. 21:12   It had a great, high wall with twelve gates, and with twelve angels at the gates. On the gates were written the names of the twelve tribes of Israel.

If God had forsaken Israel and replaced them with the church, then Jerusalem would not be called the eternally glorious capital of God's everlasting Kingdom. And there would be no reason to have the names of the twelve tribes of Israel engraved on the twelve gates of the great, high walls of the wonderful, important, and everlasting New Jerusalem. The existence of the names of the twelve tribes means that the twelve tribes exist and occupy important positions.

Question 30 While saying that Jesus' First Advent is a literal fulfillment of God's promises, can we say that God's promises about Israel are symbols?

Luke 24:44   He said to them, "This is what I told you while I was still with you: Everything must be fulfilled that is written about me in the Law of Moses, the Prophets and the Psalms."

Because Jesus came to fulfill the writings of Moses and the prophets, He came as prophesied to the prophesied place and carried out His prophesied life and ministry. Jesus' birth as a Jew, His growth, His ministry, His death, and His resurrection were accurately predicted in the Old Testament. To fulfill that Word, the Lord became Incarnated. The stage for His ministry was also prophesied and was the land of Israel. If we believe in the literal fulfillment of the prophecies in the Old Testament regarding Jesus' First Advent, we must also believe the prophecies about Israel literally as well. It is a contradiction to view the prophecies about the Messiah literally while viewing the prophecies about Israel symbolically. Therefore, the assumption that Israel has been replaced by the church is wrong. This is because Christ's remaining ministry will be fulfilled only when the Old Testament prophecies related to Israel are fulfilled.

Question 31 While believing that Jesus's Second Advent will occur to fulfill God's Word, is it possible to think that Israel has been replaced by the church?

Acts 1:10-11   10 They were looking intently up into the sky as he was going, when suddenly two men dressed in white stood beside them. 11 "Men of Galilee," they said, "why do you stand here looking into the sky? This same Jesus, who has been taken from you into heaven, will come back in the same way you have seen him go into heaven."

Zech. 14:4   On that day his feet will stand on the Mount of Olives, east of Jerusalem, and the Mount of Olives will be split in two from east to west, forming a great valley, with half of the mountain moving north and half moving south.

In the Bible, there are far more prophecies about the

Messiah's Second Advent than for His First Advent, and His First Advent is ultimately for the sake of His Second Advent. The Bible states Jesus' Second Advent will occur in the land of Israel as well. Jesus will return in the same way the disciples saw Him ascend into heaven. Just as the Messiah's First Advent was fulfilled literally, His Second Advent will be fulfilled literally. God will carry out all His plans for Israel so that He can bring His Son, Jesus Christ, back to earth as a Jewish man. At the time of Jesus' Second Advent, the geographical and historical Israel will welcome the coming Messiah. If Israel was forsaken forever due to their sin of not accepting the Messiah at His First Advent, then all these prophecies would not be fulfilled. And all the prophecies would become purposeless. And we would have an empty future and become the most pitiful people. This is why we cannot ever accept the theology that Israel has been replaced by the church.

Question 32 What are the key points of the Balfour Declaration (November 2, 1917)?

"His Majesty's Government view with favour the establishment in Palestine of a national home for the Jewish people, and will use their best endeavours to facilitate the achievement of this object, it being clearly understood that nothing shall be done which may prejudice the civil and religious rights of existing non-Jewish communities in Palestine, or the rights and political status enjoyed by Jews in any other country."[49]

Question 33 What role did the Balfour Declaration play in the re-establishment of Israel?

The Balfour Declaration was crucial in gathering Jews back to their ancient land. Although many of those involved were not pro-Jewish and helped for their own self-interests, God used governments and individuals to fulfill His purposes for His chosen people, as always. Shamefully, Britain failed to keep their promise despite declaring that they would "use their best endeavors" to achieve the establishment of the Jewish state. However, God's timing is always accurate, and, when the time came, God used the United Nations to bring about the establishment of the Jewish state in a single day.

Question 34 Who were the people who influenced the existence of the Balfour Declaration?

1) English theologian and reformer John Wycliffe (1320-1384) and Bible man William Tyndale's (1494-1536) translation of the Bible into English and the publication of the King

James Bible in 1611 served as catalysts for great change.[50] The newly translated English Bible opened the eyes of many new readers to Biblical truths, causing them to rediscover many Biblical prophecies about the importance of the Jewish people to God and their return to their ancient land.[51] In addition, by reading the Bible directly, Protestant Reformers came to reject Catholicism as the corrupt church depicted in the New Testament.[52] Originally, these Protestants were called evangelicals. Later, this name was given to participants of the revival movements that swept through England and America in the 18th century. That is, this name was first derived from the Puritans. Many Puritans often prayed for the return of the Jews to their ancient land.[53]

2) Protestant Reformer John Calvin (1509-1564) acknowledged the Jewish people's special position in the future. In his commentary on Isaiah, Calvin expressed his belief that, even if one may conclude that the Jews were forsaken due to their hardness, the Jews still have hope because God's gifts and calling for them are irrevocable. Calvin believed that, if the Jews whose ancestors were chosen by God and given His covenants are not included, then Christ cannot be the Redeemer of the world.

In his commentary on Romans, Calvin wrote, "When the Gentiles shall come in, the Jews also shall return from their defection to the obedience of faith; and thus shall be completed the salvation of the whole Israel of God, which must be gathered from both; and yet in such a way that the Jews shall obtain the first place, being as it were the first-born in God's family."[54]

After Calvin, there were some changes in Biblical interpretation. More people began to examine the Bible's context and to interpret the Bible in a natural, direct way. In particular, Puritan interpreters began to publish books and articles about the positive future of the nation of Israel as God's chosen people.

3) Oliver Cromwell (1599-1658), an English statesman and soldier, and his government agreed in 1656 to permit the re-entry of Jews into England.[55] Devout Protestants including Cromwell viewed the conversion of Jews to Christianity as essential before Christ's return to rule over the world and so regarded reaccepting the Jews as the first step toward this goal.[56] In addition to these religious reasons, there was also a practical reason for international trade. They believed that Jewish settlement in London would greatly benefit their trade.[57]

4) Samuel Rutherford (1600-1661), a Scottish pastor and principal of St. Mary's College at St. Andrews University, also penned powerful defenses for the Jewish nation.

"O to see the sight, next to Christ's coming in the clouds the most joyful! Our elder brethren the Jews and Christ fall upon each other's necks and kiss each other! They have long been asunder, they will be kind to one another when they meet. O day! O longed-for and lovely day-dawn!"[58]

5) John Owen (1616-1683), an English theologian and Dean

of Christ Church at Oxford University, wrote, "Moreover, it is granted that there shall be a time and season, during the continuance of the kingdom of the Messiah in this world, wherein the generality of the nation of the Jews, all the world over, shall be called and effectually brought unto the knowledge of the Messiah, our Lord Jesus Christ; with which mercy they shall also receive deliverance from their captivity, restoration unto their own land, with a blessed, flourishing, and happy condition therein."[59]

6) Jonathan Edwards (1703-1758) was the most influential spiritual leader in 18th century America who sparked the Great Awakening, served as the Dean of Princeton University, and was a Calvinist. He foresaw Israel's future accurately.

Jonathan Edwards stated that the land of Canaan will be the center of Christ's Millennial Kingdom.[60] He believed that the return of the Jews to their ancient land is indispensable for the promise of the land to be fulfilled.[61] According to Edwards, God made the Jews a visible monument to show His grace and power.[62] Edwards believed that Israel will once again become a special nation in the future.[63] At that time, all Israel will be saved. The Jews scattered all over the world will cast off their unbelief, change their hearts marvelously, and loathe their past unbelief and stubbornness. Then, they will come to the glorious Christ together, humbly repenting and joyfully accepting Christ as their glorious King and Savior, and will proclaim the praise of Christ to other nations with one heart, in one mind, and in one voice.

7) Anglican Bishop John Charles Ryle (1816-1900) taught about the future of Israel. "I believe that the Jews shall ultimately be gathered again as a separate nation, restored to their own land, and converted to the faith of Christ, after going through great tribulation (Jeremiah 30:10-11, 31:10; Romans 11:25-26; Daniel 12:1; Zechariah 13:8-9)." [64]

8) Charles Haddon Spurgeon (1834-1892), a great English evangelist and preacher in the 19th century, stated as follows. "It is certain that the Jews, as a people, will yet own Jesus of Nazareth, the Son of David as their King, and that they will return to their own land, and they shall build the old wastes, they shall raise up the former desolations, and they shall repair the old cities, the desolations of many generations." [65]

Spurgeon's key teaching points about Israel's national restoration to their ancient land were:

- The nation of Israel will come to faith in Christ.
- Israel will have a national and geo-political identity.
- The political system will be a monarchy, for the King shall reign.
- Israel will dwell in the Promised Land.
- The borders will conform to the promises given to Abraham and David.
- Israel will have a special position among the nations in the Millennial Kingdom.
- However, Israel will remain spiritually part of the church.

- There will be national prosperity that is admired by the whole world.
- The Old Testament prophecies should not be treated as symbols.[66]

9) Theodor Herzl (1860-1904) presents a conclusive vision in his book *The Jewish State*.

"Therefore I believe that a wondrous generation of Jews will spring into existence. The Maccabeans will rise again. Let me repeat once more my opening words: The Jews who wish for a State will have it. We shall live at last as free men on our own soil, and die peacefully in our own homes. The world will be freed by our liberty, enriched by our wealth, magnified by our greatness. And whatever we attempt there to accomplish for our own welfare, will react powerfully and beneficially for the good of humanity."[67]

10) William Hechler (1845-1931), the chaplain to the British Embassy in Vienna, introduced Theodor Herzl to many leaders in Europe and helped him. In 1884, Hechler wrote a treatise entitled *The Restoration of the Jews to Palestine* in which he viewed the return of the Jews to their ancient land as a precondition for Jesus' return. He wrote, "It is the duty of every Christian to love the Jews."[68]

11) Scientist Chaim Weizmann (1874-1952) discovered a method for the mass production of synthetic acetone and thus played an important role in the British war industry during World War I.[69] Weizmann became a lecturer at Manchester

University in 1904 and soon became a leader among British Zionists. Arthur Balfour was a conservative Member of Parliament for Manchester East at the time, and Weizmann met him during Balfour's election campaign.[70] Balfour was in favor of establishing the Jewish state but believed that the proposal of the British Uganda Programme would receive more approval from politicians. Mainstream Zionists at the time refused this proposal, and Weizmann later persuaded Balfour, the Foreign Secretary at the time, to help establish the Jewish state in Palestine as the Zionists had hoped from the beginning. Weizmann became the first president of Israel after their independence.[71]

12) Christian Zionism preceded Jewish Zionism among secular and religious Jews. The expectation for the Jews' national return to their ancient land, generally referred to as Restorationism, was widely embraced among many denominations.[72] These included the Puritans, early Methodists, Congregationalists, Baptists such as C. H. Spurgeon, Presbyterians such as Samuel Rutherford, Horatius and Andrew Bonar, and Robert Murray M'Chyene.[73] Many Anglicans, such as J. C. Ryle and Charles Simeon also had similar views.[74]

Question 35 How did 20th century theologians address Israel's restoration in their eschatology?

1) Louis Berkhof (1873-1957), a Dutch-American Reformed theologian and professor at Calvin Theological Seminary, stated that the following must occur before Jesus' Second Advent: (1) God's calling for the Gentiles, (2) the national repentance of Israel before God, (3) great apostasy and the Great Tribulation, and (4) the antichrist's appearance.[75] Regarding the timing of Jesus' Second Advent, Louis Berkhof said that the Bible teaches that these "events must precede the coming of the Lord" and urged believers "to be awake, to be alert, to be prepared."[76]

2) Hyung-Ryeong Park (1897-1978), a representative conservative Reformed Presbyterian theologian in Korea, listed the events that will occur before Jesus' Second Advent as follows:

(1) The worldwide spread of the Gospel

(2) The national repentance of Israel before God

(3) Great apostasy and the Great Tribulation

(4) The appearance of the antichrist.[77]

3) Martyn Lloyd-Johns (1899-1981), an English physician and evangelical preacher, said that, at some point in the future, there will be a massive conversion of the entire nation of Israel (Rom. 11:25-26).[78]

4) Herman Ridderbos (1909-2007), a Reformed theologian and professor of New Testament in Kampen, Netherlands,

observed that there is no conflict nor ambiguity between the New Testament church as God's people and Israel as the object of God's irrevocable grace and gift of calling. Israel is still fulfilling their role in God's redemption plan.

5) George E. Ladd (1911-1982), a professor at Fuller Theological Seminary, believed that the New Testament confirms the literal salvation of Israel and thought as follows.[79] Israel is the vehicle that God has chosen to save the whole world.[80] This was the core of the promise given to Abraham (Gen. 12:1-3, 17:6).[81] Israel's hardening and their consequent departure from the ranks of God's people is only a partial and temporary dispensation. This will last only until the full number of Gentiles is filled. God will restore the Jews once again as the cultivated olive tree, and then the veil will be taken away from their eyes (2 Cor. 3:16) so they will believe and be part of God's people. In this way, all Israel will be saved (Rom. 11:26). Ladd also believed that, through Israel's salvation, greater riches will be poured out for the Gentiles.[82]

6) Anthony A. Hoekema (1913-1988), a disciple of Louis Berkhof, discussed the following signs in *The Bible and the Future*:

> (1) Signs testifying to God's grace: the worldwide spread of the Gospel, the full number of Jewish believers
>
> (2) Signs of rebellion against God: tribulation, apostasy, antichrist
>
> (3) Signs of God's judgment: wars, earthquakes, famines.[83]

7) Walter C. Kaiser, Jr. (1933-), the president emeritus of Gordon-Conwell Theological Seminary and former president of the Evangelical Theological Society (ETS), states that some Christian theologians make the erroneous claim that God's covenants with Israel were revoked due to their unbelief and that the church is qualified to receive those covenants.[84]

The Biblical prophets teach in the Pentateuch and the Prophets that God has not forsaken Israel, and Paul does as well in Romans 9-11. Genesis 15 emphasizes that the covenant between Jehovah and Abraham is a unilateral, everlasting covenant. The national, historical Israel and the future eschatological Israel must not be separated nor divided. Kaiser explains that "the salvation of the Gentiles is closely related to the salvation of Israel, two arms of the one and same divine purpose and plan of God." [85]

8) James Dunn (1939-2020), an English Biblical scholar and Scottish pastor who wrote a commentary on Romans, acknowledges Israel's identity and calling more strongly than anyone else.[86] Dunn believed that Israel still retains their former status in God's dispensation.[87] Dunn observed that the phrase, "all Israel," utilized by Paul in Romans, is not a new concept but rather a general idiom referring to Israel as a whole.[88] Dunn stated that historical Israel is still Israel and that even now the Jewish people are Israelites.[89] He noted that, if God excludes Israel, the olive tree planted a long time ago by God Himself, then Christianity would not be able to understand itself as its

branch.[90] Dunn emphasized that this can be understood in light of God's calling and choice.[91]

10) Wayne Grudem (1948-), an American evangelical theologian, foresaw God's special future calling for the Jews in His plan. He was certain that Romans 9-11 teaches the mass conversion of the Jewish people in the future.

Question 36 How have viewpoints on replacement theology and restoration theology changed historically?

Michael J. Vlach, a professor at The Master's Seminary, concludes that overviews of church history from replacement and restoration perspectives reveal mixed and conflicting views toward Israel and their land.[92] Jesus and the apostles taught about Israel's salvation and restoration. The early church in the patristic era sometimes took a mixed position on this issue, promoting both the importance of Israel's future and the replacement viewpoint that the church has taken Israel's place. In the Middle Ages, the replacement viewpoint was dominant. At the beginning of the Protestant Reformation, the replacement viewpoint was accepted, but the next generation opened the door widely for faith in the nation of Israel's importance. The 19th and 20th centuries witnessed the widespread belief in Israel's future restoration. At the end of the 20th century, several denominations and Christian organizations renounced the traditional viewpoint that Israel's election had been transferred to the church.

Unfortunately, the replacement viewpoint still exists and poses a challenge to restoration theology's perspective. However, many today affirm that God never forsook His people Israel, and that Israel will experience salvation and restoration, including the restoration of their land. Currently and into the near future, the replacement viewpoint is unlikely to become prevalent again, and restoration theology will prevail.

Conclusion

Israel continues to be important for God's purpose. The church does not replace Israel and does not make the nation of Israel inadequate. The church is God's instrument to proclaim, in this age, the Messiah Jesus and His Kingdom, while Israel is remaining in unbelief. In the future, when the nation of Israel becomes saved, Israel will serve other nations in Jesus' Kingdom. Understanding the Bible's storyline accurately means understanding the roles of both Israel and the church.

Archbold, Norma Parrish, and Marita Brokenshaw. *Mountains of Israel: The Bible & the West Bank* [이스라엘의 산들]. Translated by Oh Sook-hee. Anyang, South Korea: The Message of Love, 2006.

Balfour, Arthur James. "Balfour Declaration 1917." *The Avalon Project at the Yale Law School: Documents in Law, History and Diplomacy*. Accessed August 31, 2023. https://avalon.law.yale.edu/20th_century/balfour.asp.

Bavinck, Herman. *Reformed Dogmatics: God and Creation.* Translated and edited by John Vriend, vol. 2. Grand Rapids, MI: Baker Academic, 2004.

Berkhof, Louis. *Systematic Theology*. Grand Rapids, MI: Wm. B. Eerdmans Publishing Co., 1941.

Blaising, Craig A., and Darrell L. Bock. *Progressive Dispensationalism* [하나님 나라와 언약]. Translated by Kwak Chul-ho. Seoul, South Korea: Christian Literature Center, 2005.

Blomberg, Craig L. Case for Historic Premillennialism: An Alternative to *"Left Behind" Eschatology* [역사적 전천년설]. Translated by Seong-wook Jung and Hyeong-wook

Cho. Seoul, South Korea: Christian Literature Center, 2014.

Bock, Darrell L., and Mitch Glaser, ed., *The People, the Land, and the Future of Israel Israel and the Jewish People in the Plan of God* [이스라엘 민족, 영토 그리고 미래]. Translated by Jinseop Kim and Hyukseung Kwon. Seoul, South Korea: East Wind Korea, Inc., 2014.

Bray, Gerald. "The Seeds None Could Afford: How Martyrs Built the Early Church." June 16, 2023. https://www.desiringgod.org/articles/the-seeds-none-could-afford.

Blumenthal, Ariel L. One New Man: Reconciling Jew & Gentile in One Body of Christ [한 새 사람: 이스라엘과 열방 모두를 위한 복음]. Translated by Revive Israel. Seoul, South Korea: Revive Israel, 2018.

Brown, Michael L. *Our Hands Are Stained with Blood: The Tragic Story of the Church and the Jewish People* [유대민족의 비극적 역사와 교회]. Translated by Youngwoo Kim. Seoul, South Korea: Hansalang, 2008.

Bum, Lee Mun. "역사적으로 보는 성경, 창세기 1" ["The Bible through Historical Geography, Genesis 1"]. Lecture at 예수교 장로회 합동측 전서노회 세미나 [Presbyterian Church in Korea (HapDong), South Jeolla Presbytery seminar], July 17, 2018. https://www.youtube.com/watch?v=7Bmv5ZUAUKQ.

Calvin, John. *Commentaries on the Epistle of Paul the Apostle to the Romans*. Translated and edited by John Owen.

Grand Rapids, MI: Wm.. B. Eerdmans Publishing Co., 1947.

Center for the Study of Global Christianity at Gordon-Conwell Theological Seminary. *Christianity in its Global Context, 1970-2020: Society, Religion, and Mission.* South Hamilton, MA: Center for the Study of Global Christianity at Gordon-Conwell Theological Seminary, 2013. https://www.gordonconwell.edu/wp-content/uploads/sites/13/2019/04/2ChristianityinitsGlobalConte xt.pdf.

------. "Global Pentecostalism." Accessed September 3, 2023. https://www.gordonconwell.edu/center-for-global-christianity/research/global-pentecostalism/.

------. "Status of Global Christianity, 2023, in the Context of 1900-2050." Accessed September 4, 2023. https://www.gordonconwell.edu/wp-content/uploads/sites/13/2023/01/Status-of-Global-Christianity-2023.pdf.

Chang, Young Ihl. 구약신학의 역사적 기초 [*The Historical Basis of Old Testament Theology*]. Seoul, South Korea: Presbyterian University and Theological Seminary Press, 2001.

Cho, Cheol-hwan. 하나님은 이스라엘을 버리셨는가? [*Has God Cast Away Israel?*]. Seoul, South Korea: Elijah, 2016.

Dunn, James D.G. World Biblical *Commentary: Romans 9-16* [WBC 성경주석: 로마서(하)]. Volume 38B. Translated by Chul Kim and Chun-Suk Chae. Seoul, South Korea:

Solomon Press, 2005

Eckert, Harald. *Israel, the Nations and the Valley of Decisions* [이스라엘, 나라들, 그리고 심판의 골짜기]. Translated by Bethany Ministry Headquarters. Seoul, South Korea: Haneul-yangsig, 2015.

Glashouwer, Willem J. J. *Why Israel?* [Why 이스라엘?]. Translated by Jung Won-il. Seoul, South Korea: Haneul-yangsig, 2014.

------. Why Jerusalem? Christians For Israel International, 2015.

Gowan, Donald E. *Eschatology in the Old Testament* [구약성경의 종말론]. Translated by Chan-hyuk Hong. Seoul, South Korea: Christian Literature Center, 1999.

Han, Jeong-geon. 종말론 강해 [*Exposition of Eschatology: Commentary on the Book of Revelation of Daniel*]. Seoul, South Korea: Christian Literature Center, 1992.

------. 종말론 입문 [*Introduction to Eschatology*]. Seoul, South Korea: Christian Literature Center, 1994.

Heidler, Robert D. *Messianic Church Arising* [메시아닉 교회]. Translated by Hyun-woo Jin. Gua-Chun, South Korea: WLI Korea, 2008.

Hoekema, Anthony A. *The Bible and the Future* [개혁주의 종말론]. Translated by Yong-jung Lee. Seoul, South Korea: Revival and Reformation, 2012.

Im, Sarah. 기적의 이스라엘 [*Miracle Israel*]. Seoul, South Korea: KIBI, 2003.

Intrater, Asher. *Alignment*. Frederick, MD: Revive Israel Media,

2017.

Jewish Virtual Library. "Demographics of Israel: Jewish Population of Israel Relative to World Jewish Population (1882 - Present)." December 29, 2022. Accessed September 3, 2023, https://www.jewishvirtuallibrary.org/jewish-population-of-israel-relative-to-world-jewish-population.

Jewish Virtual Library. "Vital Statistics: Latest Population Statistics for Israel." April 25, 2023. Accessed August 30, 2023, https://www.jewishvirtuallibrary.org/latest-population-statistics-for-israel.

Johnson, Gaines R. "The Lost Rivers of the Garden of Eden – Found." In *The Bible, Genesis & Geology*. Copyright 1997-2021. Accessed March 15, 2018. https://www.kjvbible.org/rivers_of_the_garden_of_eden.html.

Juster, Daniel, and Keith Intrater. *Israel, the Church and the Last Days* [마지막 때의 교회와 이스라엘]. Translated by Ju-sung Kim. Seoul, South Korea: Israel Ministry Publisher, 2013.

Kaiser, Walter C. *Back toward the Future* [성경과 하나님의 예언]. Translated by Young-chul Kim. Seoul, South Korea: Yeosulun, 1991.

------. *Uses of the Old Testament in the New* [신약의 구약사용]. Translated by Ki-moon Sung. Go-Yang, South Korea: CH Books, 1997.

------. "Jewish Evangelism in the New Millenium in Light of

Israel's Future (Romans 9-11)." *In To the Jews First: The Case for Jewish Evangelism in Scripture and History*, edited by Darrell L. Bock and Mitch Glaser, 40-52. Grand Rapids, MI: Kregel Publications, 2008a.

------. *The Messiah in the Old Testament* [구약에 나타난 메시아]. Translated by Geun-sang Rtu. Seoul, South Korea: Christian, 2008b.

------. *The Promise-Plan of God: A Biblical Theology of the Old and New Testaments*. Grand Rapids, MI: Zondervan, 2008c.

------. *Mission in the Old Testament : Israel as a Light to the Nations* [구약성경과 선교]. Translated by Peter Im. Seoul, South Korea: Christian Literature Center, 2013.

Kim, John. 이스라엘과 대체신학 [*Israel and Replacement Theology*]. Seoul, South Korea: Yeyoung Communication, 2014.

Kim, Myung Hyun. 에덴동산과 4개의 강 위치 [Location of the Garden of Eden and the 4 Rivers]. Lecture at Institute of Bible Science, August 19, 2021. https://www.youtube.com/watch?v=vojJEA68ldI&t=19s.

Kim, Paul In-Sik. 하나님의 마스터플랜 [*God's Master Plan*]. Seoul, South Korea: Church Growth Institute, 2017.

------. 이스라엘의 회복과 종말 [*Israel's Restoration and the End Times*]. Seoul, South Korea: Christian Literature Center, 2020.

Ladd, George Eldon. "Historic Premillennialism." in *The*

Meaning of the Millennium: Four Views, edited by Robert G. Clouse, 17-40. Downers Grove, IL: InterVarsity Press, 1977.

Lewis, Gordon R., and Bruce A. Demarest. *Integrative Theology* [통합신학]. Translated by Gwi-tak Kim. Seoul, South Korea: Revival and Reformation, 2009.

Lloyd-Johns, Martyn. "Future of the Jews: A Sermon on Romans 11:28-32." Accessed September 3, 2023. https://www.mljtrust.org/sermons/book-of-romans/future-of-the-jews/.

McDonald, Tristan, and Elizabeth Oxbury. *Balfour 100*. Telford, United Kingdom: Prayer for Israel, 2017.

Netanyahu, Benjamin. "Full Text of Netanyahu's 2013 Speech to the U.N. General Assembly." *The Times of Israel*, October 1, 2013. https://www.timesofisrael.com/full-text-netanyahus-2013-speech-to-the-un-general-assembly/.

Oh, Hwa-pyeong. 이스라엘 고난과 회복 [*Israel's Suffering and Restoration*]. Seoul, South Korea: Bedeulo-seowon, 2009.

------. 로마서 9장–11장과 이스라엘 [*Romans 9-11 and Israel*]. Seoul, South Korea: Han-saesalam, 2017.

Pache, René. *The Return of Jesus Christ* [그리스도의 재림]. Translated into Korean by Jeon Jun-Sik. Seoul, South Korea: Maranatha, 1988.

Park, Hyung-Ryeong. 조직 신학 [*Systematic Theology*]. Vol. 7. Seoul, South Korea: Reformist Publisher, 2017.

Park, Yong-mee. "2020년 세계 기독교 인구는 33.3%" ["The

World Christian Population in 2020 as 33.3%"]. 기독신문 [*Christianity Daily*], January 2, 2014. https://www.kidok. com/news/articleView.html?idxno=83958.

Payne, J. Barton. *Encyclopedia of Biblical Prophecy: The Complete Guide to Scriptural Predictions and Their Fulfillment. New York*, NY: Harper & Row, 2009.

Pew Research Center. "Jewish Americans in 2020." May 11, 2021. Accessed September 3, 2023, https://www. pewresearch.org/religion/2021/05/11/the-size-of-the-u-s-jewish-population/.

Piper, John Stephen. "Missions Exists Because Worship Doesn't: A Bethlehem Legacy, Inherited and Bequeathed." October 27, 2012. https://www.desiringgod. org/messages/missions-exists-because-worship-doesnt-a-bethlehem-legacy-inherited-and-bequeathed.

Price, Randall. *Fast Facts on the Middle East Conflict* [중동문제 진실은 무엇인가]. Translated by Sohee Oh. Anyang, South Korea: The Message of Love, 2010.

Prince, Derek. *The Last Word on the Middle East* [하나님께서 결코 잊지 않으신 이스라엘]. Translated by In-pyeong No. Seoul, South Korea: Eun-seog, 1991.

------. *Destiny of Israel and the Church* [이스라엘과 교회의 운명]. Translated by Jun Eun-young. Seoul, South Korea Elijah, 2016.

Richter, Sandra L. *Epic of Eden : A Christian Entry into the Old Testament* [에덴에서 새 에덴까지]. Translated by Seog-in Yun. Seoul, South Korea: Revival and Reformation, 2013.

Simons, Jan Jozef. *The Geographical and Topographical Texts of the Old Testament*. Leiden, Netherlands: Brill, 1959.

Slomovitz, Philip. "Purely Commentary." *The Detroit Jewish News*, June 22, 1979. https://digital.bentley.umich.edu/djnews/djn.1979.06.22.001/2.

Stager, Lawrence E. "Jerusalem as Eden." *Biblical Archaeology Review* 26, no. 3 (May/June 2000): 36-66.

Twain, Mark. *The Innocents Abroad*. 1869 1st edition. Project Gutenberg. Produced by David Widger, last updated October 11, 2022. https://www.gutenberg.org/files/3176/3176-h/3176-h.htm.

U.S. Center for World Mission. "The Amazing Countdown Facts." *Mission Frontiers* (September-October 2009): 30-33.

------. "The Amazing Countdown Facts." November 2014. Accessed September 4, 2023. https://eote.org/wp-content/uploads/2014/11/Countdown-Facts.pdf.

Vlach, Michael J. *Has the Church Replaced Israel? A Theological Evaluation*. Nashville, TN: B&H Publishing Group, 2010.

------. *Premillennialism: Why There Must Be a Future Earthly Kingdom of Jesus*. Los Angeles, CA: Theological Studies Press, 2015.

------. *Dispensationalism*. Los Angeles, CA: Theological Studies

-Press, 2016.

------. *He Will Reign Forever: A Biblical Theology of the Kingdom of God*. Silverton, OR: Lampion Press, LLC, 2017.

Weissmandl, Michael Dov. *Min ha-Meẓẓar*. New York, NY: Emunah Press, 1960.

Winter, Ralph D., and Bruce A. Koch. "Finishing the Task: The Unreached Peoples Challenge." *International Journal of Frontier Missions* 16, no. 2 (Summer, 1999): 67-76.

Worldometer. "Regions in the world by population (2023)." Accessed September 4, 2023. https://www.worldometers.info/world-population/population-by-region/.

Wycliffe Global Alliance. "Vision 2025." Accessed September 3, 2023. https://www.wycliffe.net/more-about-what-we-do/philosophy-and-principle-papers/vision-2025/.

Yoo, Se-jin. "유럽 전역서 반유대범죄 확산…佛 74% · 獨 60%이상 증가" ["Anti-Semitic Crimes Spread across Europe… 74% in France, more than 60% in Germany"]. *Newsis*, February 15, 2019. https://mobile.newsis.com/view.html?ar_id=NISX20190215_0000560081.

Endnotes

1. J. Barton Payne. *Encyclopedia of Biblical Prophecy: The Complete Guide to Scriptural Predictions and Their Fulfillment* (New York, NY: Harper & Row, 2009), 631-682.
2. Herman Bavinck, *Reformed Dogmatics: God and Creation*, trans. and ed. John Vriend, vol. 2 (Grand Rapids, MI: Baker Academic, 2004), 553–554.
3. John Stephen Piper, "Missions Exists Because Worship Doesn't: A Bethlehem Legacy, Inherited and Bequeathed," October 27, 2012, https://www.desiringgod.org/messages/missions-exists-because-worship-doesnt-a-bethlehem-legacy-inherited-and-bequeathed.
4. Jan Jozef Simons, *The Geographical and Topographical Texts of the Old Testament* (Leiden, Netherlands: Brill, 1959), 40-41.
5. Gaines R. Johnson, "The Lost Rivers of the Garden of Eden – Found," in *The Bible, Genesis & Geology*, copyright 1997-2021, accessed March 15, 2018, https://www.kjvbible.org/rivers_of_the_garden_of_eden.html.
6. Lawrence E. Stager, "Jerusalem as Eden," *Biblical Archaeology Review* 26, no. 3 (May/June 2000).
7. Johnson, "The Lost Rivers of the Garden of Eden – Found."
8. Myung Hyun Kim, 에덴동산과 4개의 강 위치 [Location of the Garden of Eden and the 4 Rivers], August 19, 2021, https://www.youtube.com/watch?v=vojJEA68ldI&t=19s.
9. Lee Mun Bum, "역사적으로 보 는 성경, 창세기 1" ["The Bible through Historical Geography, Genesis 1"], lecture at 예수교 장로회 합동측 전서 노회 세미나 [Presbyterian Church in Korea (HapDong), South Jeolla
10. Ibid.
11. Young Ihl Chang, 구약신학의 역사적 기초 [*The Historical Basis of Old Testament Theology*] (Seoul, South Korea: Presbyterian University and

Theological Seminary Press, 2001), 32.

12. Ibid.

13. Ibid.

14. René Pache, *The Return of Jesus Christ* [그리스도의 재림], trans. into Korean by 전준식 [Jun-Sik Chun] (Seoul, South Korea: Maranatha, 1988), 8-9. The original quote in French is: "Comme on l'a dit, la prophétie marche sur les cimes de l'Histoire. Elle ne projette sa lumière que sur les sommets. La seule explication totale de la prophétie nous sera donnée par son accomplissement."

15. Jewish Virtual Library, "Vital Statistics: Latest Population Statistics for Israel," April 25, 2023, accessed August 30, 2023, https://www.jewishvirtuallibrary.org/latest-population-statistics-for-israel.

16. Se-jin Yoo, "유럽 전역서 반유대범죄 확산…佛 74%·獨 60%이상 증가" ["Anti-Semitic Crimes Spread across Europe… 74% in France, more than 60% in Germany"], *Newsis*, February 15, 2019, https://mobile.newsis.com/view.html?ar_id=NISX20190215_0000560081.

17. Jewish Virtual Library, "Demographics of Israel: Jewish Population of Israel Relative to World Jewish Population (1882 - Present);" Jewish Virtual Library, "Vital Statistics: Latest Population Statistics for Israel."

18. Philip Slomovitz, "Purely Commentary," *The Detroit Jewish News*, June 22, 1979, https://digital.bentley.umich.edu/djnews/djn.1979.06.22.001/2.

19. Ariel L. Blumenthal, One New Man: Reconciling Jew & Gentile in One Body of Christ [한 새 사람: 이스라엘과 열방 모두를 위한 복음], trans. Revive Israel (Seoul, South Korea: Revive Israel, 2018), 119.

20. Ibid.

21. Wycliffe Global Alliance, "Vision 2025," accessed September 3, 2023, https://www.wycliffe.net/more-about-what-we-do/philosophy-and-principle-papers/vision-2025/.

22. Ralph D. Winter and Bruce A. Koch, "Finishing the Task: The Unreached Peoples Challenge," *International Journal of Frontier Missions* 16, no. 2 (Summer, 1999): 67. See also the graph on page 68 and the pie chart on page 74 in the article.

23. Ibid., 67.

24. U.S. Center for World Mission, "The Amazing Countdown Facts," *Mission Frontiers* (September-October 2009): 32.

25. Ibid.; U.S. Center for World Missions, "The Amazing Countdown Facts," November 2014, accessed September 4, 2023, https://eote. org/wp-content/uploads/2014/11/Countdown-Facts.pdf.

26. Center for the Study of Global Christianity at Gordon-Conwell Theological Seminary, "Global Pentecostalism," accessed September 3, 2023, https://www.gordonconwell.edu/center-for-global-christianity/ research/global-pentecostalism/.

27. Center for the Study of Global Christianity at Gordon-Conwell Theological Seminary, "Status of Global Christianity, 2023, in the Context of 1900-2050," accessed September 4, 2023, https://www. gordonconwell.edu/wp-content/uploads/sites/13/2023/01/Status-of-Global-Christianity-2023.pdf. Data from the Center for the Study of Global Christianity was utilized to calculate these percentages.

28. Ibid.

29. Ibid.

30. Ibid.

31. Center for the Study of Global Christianity at Gordon-Conwell Theological Seminary, *Christianity in its Global Context*, 1970-2020: Society, Religion, and Mission (South Hamilton, MA: Center for the Study of Global Christianity at Gordon-Conwell Theological Seminary, 2013), 7.

32. Ibid., 15.

33. Ibid.

34. Ibid.

35. Ibid.

36. Kim Jin Sup, "유대인과 이방인의 '원뉴맨'" ["The Jews and Gentiles' 'One New Man'"], in 2017 이스라엘 목회자 세미나 강의안 [*2017 Korean Pastors' Israel Seminar Booklet*], ed. Paul In-Sik Kim, (Seoul, South Korea: ICG Books, 2017), 128.

37. Hwa-pyeong Oh, 이스라엘 고난과 회복 [*Israel's Suffering and Restoration*] (Seoul, South Korea: Bedeulo-seowon, 2009), 77-87.

38. Ibid.

39. Ibid.

40. Michael Dov Weissmandl, *Min ha-Meẓẓar* (New York, NY: Emunah Press, 1960).

41. Gerald Bray, "The Seeds None Could Afford: How Martyrs Built the Early Church," June 16, 2023, https://www.desiringgod.org/articles/the-seeds-none-could-afford.

42. Mark Twain, *The Innocents Abroad*, 1869 1st edition, Project Gutenberg, produced by David Widger, last updated October 11, 2022, https://www.gutenberg.org/files/3176/3176-h/3176-h.htm.

43. Michael J. Vlach, *He Will Reign Forever: A Biblical Theology of the Kingdom of God* (Silverton, OR: Lampion Press, LLC, 2017), 535.

44. Ibid.

45. Ibid., 537

46. Ibid.

47. Michael J. Vlach, *He Will Reign Forever: A Biblical Theology of the Kingdom of God*, 14.

48. Benjamin Netanyahu, "Full Text of Netanyahu's 2013 Speech to the U.N. General Assembly," *The Times of Israel*, October 1, 2013, https://www.timesofisrael.com/full-text-netanyahus-2013-speech-to-the-un-general-assembly/.

49. Arthur James Balfour, "Balfour Declaration 1917," *The Avalon Project at the Yale Law School: Documents in Law, History and Diplomacy*, accessed August 31, 2023, https://avalon.law.yale.edu/20th_century/balfour.asp.

50. Tristan McDonald and Elizabeth Oxbury, *Balfour 100* (Telford, United Kingdom: Prayer for Israel, 2017), 6-7.

51. Ibid., 7.

52. Ibid.

53. Ibid.

54. John Calvin, *Commentaries on the Epistle of Paul the Apostle to the Romans*, trans. and ed. John Owen (Grand Rapids: Wm.. B. Eerdmans Publishing Co., 1947), 437.

55. Tristan McDonald and Elizabeth Oxbury, *Balfour 100*, p. 7.

56. Ibid.

57. Ibid.

58. Ibid., 8.

59. Ibid.

60. John Kim, 이스라엘과 대체신학 [*Israel and Replacement Theology*] (Seoul, South Korea: Yeyoung Communication, 2014), 88-89.

61. Ibid., 89.

62. Ibid.

63. Ibid.

64. Tristan McDonald and Elizabeth Oxbury, *Balfour 100*, 12.

65. Ibid.

66. Ibid.

67. Ibid., 14.

68. Ibid., 16.

69. Ibid., 17.

70. Ibid.

71. Ibid.

72. Ibid., 9.

73. Ibid.

74. Ibid.

75. Louis Berkhof, *Systematic Theology* (Grand Rapids, MI: Wm. B. Eerdmans Publishing Co., 1941), 697-701.

76. Ibid., 697.

77. Hyung-Ryeong Park, 조직 신학 [*Systematic Theology*], Vol. 7 (Seoul, South Korea: Reformist Publisher, 2017).

78. Martyn Lloyd-Johns, "Future of the Jews: A Sermon on Romans 11:28-32," accessed September 3, 2023, https://www.mljtrust.org/sermons/book-of-romans/future-of-the-jews/.

79. John Kim, 이스라엘과 대체신학 [Israel and Replacement Theology], 90.

80. Ibid.

81. Ibid.

82. Ibid.

83. Anthony A. Hoekema, *The Bible and the Future* [개혁주의 종말론], trans.

Yong-jung Lee (Seoul, South Korea: Revival and Reformation, 2012).

84. Walter C. Kaiser, "Jewish Evangelism in the New Millenium in Light of Israel's Future (Romans 9-11)," in *To the Jews First: The Case for Jewish Evangelism in Scripture and History*, ed. Darrell L. Bock and Mitch Glaser (Grand Rapids, MI: Kregel Publications, 2008), 40-41. For Korean readers, this text has been translated by Jinseop Kim and published by East Wind Korea, Inc. in Seoul, South Korea, as 첫째는 유대인에게.

85. Ibid., 44-45.

86. James D.G. Dunn, *World Biblical Commentary: Romans 9-16* [WBC 성경주석: 로마서(하)], trans. by Chul Kim and Chun-Suk Chae (Seoul, South Korea: Solomon Press, 2005), 38B:293.

87. Ibid., 240.

88. Ibid., 307.

89. Ibid., 259.

90. Ibid., 284.

91. Ibid., 282, 300.

92. Michael J. Vlach, *Has the Church Replaced Israel? A Theological Evaluation* (Nashville, TN: B&H Publishing Group, 2010).